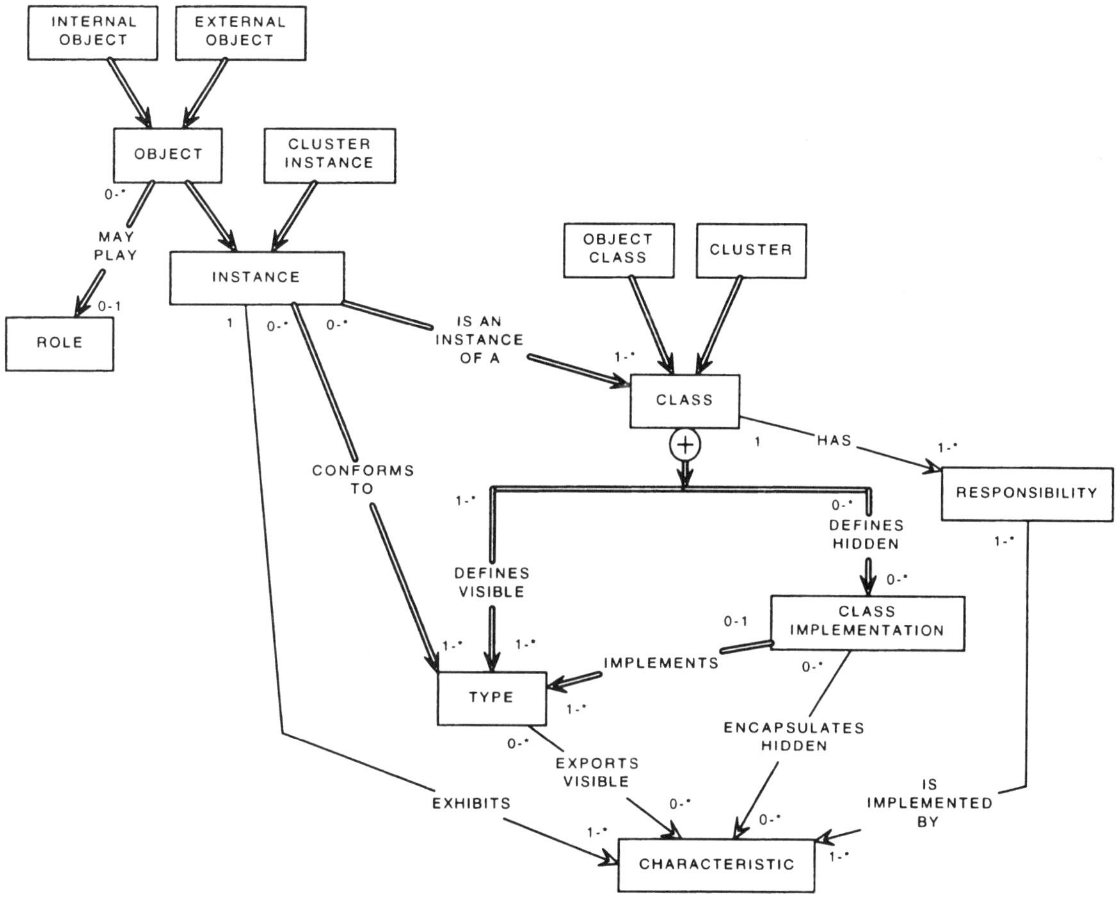

Partial Metamodel for Key Concepts

SIGS REFERENCE LIBRARY

Donald G. Firesmith
Editor-in-Chief

1. Directory of Object Technology, *edited by Dale J. Gaumer*

2. Dictionary of Object Technology: The Definitive Desk Reference,
Donald G. Firesmith and Edward M. Eykholt

3. Next Generation Computing: Distributed Objects for Business,
edited by Peter Fingar, Dennis Read, and Jim Stikeleather

4. C++ Gems, *edited by Stanley B. Lippman*

5. OMT Insights: Perspectives on Modeling from the Journal of Object-
Oriented Programming, *James Rumbaugh*

6. Best of Booch: Designing Strategies for Object Technology,
Grady Booch (Edited by Ed Eykholt)

7. Wisdom of the Gurus: A Vision for Object Technology,
selected and edited by Charles F. Bowman

8. Open Modeling Language (OML) Reference Manual,
Donald Firesmith, Brian Henderson-Sellers, and Ian Graham

9. Java™ Gems: Jewels from *Java™ Report*,
collected and introduced by Dwight Deugo, Ph.D.

10. The Netscape Programmer's Guide: Using OLE to Build
Componentware Apps, *Richard B. Lam*

11. Advanced Object-Oriented Analysis and Design Using UML,
James J. Odell

Additional Volumes in Preparation

OPEN Modeling Language (OML) Reference Manual

Donald Firesmith
Brian Henderson-Sellers
Ian Graham

Foreword by
Meilir Page-Jones

PUBLISHED BY THE PRESS SYNDICATE OF THE UNIVERSITY OF CAMBRIDGE
The Pitt Building, Trumpington Street, Cambridge CB2 1RP, United Kingdom

CAMBRIDGE UNIVERSITY PRESS
The Edinburgh Building, Cambridge CB2 2RU, UK	http://www.cup.cam.ac.uk
40 West 20th Street, New York, NY 10011-4211, USA	http://www.cup.org
10 Stamford Road, Oakleigh, Melbourne 3166, Australia

Published in association with SIGS Books & Multimedia

© 1998 Cambridge University Press

First published in 1998

Composition by Doric Lay Publishers

Printed in the United States of America

A catalog record for this book is available from the British Library

Library of Congress Cataloging-in-Publication Data is available.

ISBN 0-521-64823-8 paperback

Contents

Foreword

OPEN, which stands for Object-Oriented Process, Environment and Notation, is the name of a consortium founded by about two dozen eminent methodologists in the object-oriented field. OML is the OPEN Modeling Language, which is a notation for depicting object-oriented systems and which is backed by the semantics of a robust metamodel. OML was developed by Don Firesmith and his colleagues, Brian Henderson-Sellers and Ian Graham, with considerable input from other members of the OPEN consortium.

Designing a notation to express graphically the full suite of object-oriented constructs, together with the interactions among these components, is a curiously difficult undertaking. The reason for the difficulties lies in the number and variety of object-oriented constructs that an effective notation must capture.

It goes without saying that a serious object-oriented notation must support both static constructs (such as inheritance, aggregation and association) as well as dynamic ones (such as object communication and state transition). In addition, both instances and classes—and, while we're at it, types—must be represented. And, as if that were not enough, different levels of encapsulation, from the humble stand-alone procedure to the sophisticated cluster, all demand their places in the symbolic panoply. Finally, a complete notation must be able to show the interactions between an object-oriented software system and the agents and events that surround the system.

Facing such a wide array of targets for object-oriented adornment, a development team could be forgiven for running amuck in their iconography—or, as the notation-development community might more properly say—allowing non-orthogonality to creep into the resulting symbol set. I commend Don Firesmith and his team for having built their notation instead on a firm foundation of orthogonal concepts (laid out and defined in the OPEN metamodel), expressed by a tractable alphabet of suitable symbols. Much of this sense of orthogonality further extends to the diagrams supported by OML.

The designers of a new notation have an important responsibility to the whole software world for the notation that they produce, because style of language has a decided influence on style of thought. (At least, that is my observation, despite linguists continuing ambivalence on the subject.) This particular design team have nailed their colors to the linguistic mast in no uncertain way in declaring OMLs direction. OML is designed to promote, *inter alia*: purity in object-oriented thinking and a consequent break with the traditional procedure/data diarchy; consideration of requirements gathering as well as system design; high levels of abstraction; easy separation of issues (such as analysis and design issues) via traits; scalability to substantial system structures; and support for multiple object-oriented programming languages. In these goals, I believe that the OML team has largely succeeded.

It would be disingenuous for me to end this foreword without mentioning the notation wars, as some people term the current discourse among object-oriented methodologists. I do not hold the view that there must be A Single Lawful Notation, as sanctioned by some August Body of Official Folks. Science has ever resisted the theocratic edict—and long may that remain so. We need innovation from more than one source, for, lacking the proof of physical experiment, we can only pit software ideas against one another in order to determine their fitness and utility.

I hope that the marketplace will also resist any unilateral decree and make its choices based on merit (although, admittedly, the marketplace has seldom shown itself to be a paragon of reflective scientific thought). But, whatever the marketplace judgment on object-oriented notations may finally be, I trust that software developers and tool vendors will give the notation, concepts and underlying metamodel of OML their full attention, because OML has several valuable approaches (such as traits) that are scarcely to be found elsewhere.

Meilir Page-Jones
Bellevue, Washington
January 1997

OPEN Modeling Language (OML)
Reference Manual

1 Overview

T HIS first section provides an overview of the OPEN Modeling Language (OML) Reference Manual. It documents the purpose of the reference manual, summarizes its structure, explains its copyright, lists the internationally-recognized methodologists that have formally adopted OML at the time of its writing, provides a point of contact for comments concerning the specification, and acknowledges the primary sources of the information that it contains.

1.1 Purpose

OPEN (Object-oriented Process, Environment, and Notation) is an international *de facto* standard object-oriented development method developed and maintained by the OPEN Consortium.[1] OPEN consists of the OPEN Modeling Language (OML) as well as process, metrics, etc.

The purpose of this document is to specify OML, a small but vital component of the complete OPEN method. As illustrated in Figure 1.1, OML consists of two interrelated parts: (1) a metamodel that specifies the syntax and semantics of underlying concepts of object-oriented modeling and (2) the Common Object Modeling Notation (COMN[2]) that is used to document the models produced by using OPEN.

To the extent practical, this specification documents the syntax, semantics, and rationale behind OML. Our purpose here is to document the current version of OML so that object-oriented modelers may learn and use it, upperCASE vendors may support it, and both can provide us with feedback for future versions. This

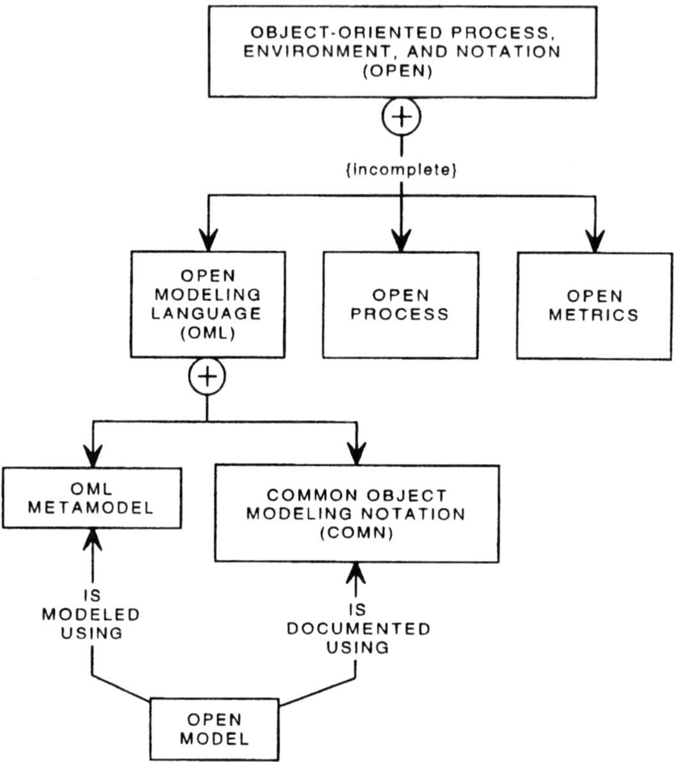

Figure 1.1. Partial metamodel[3] for OPEN.

document should be read in conjunction with the associated Process Specification document. The three documents making up the OPEN documentation include:

- COMN Summary
- OML Reference Manual
- Process Specification

---

[1]As of this writing, the OPEN Consortium consists of 26 internationally recognized OO methodologists, researchers, who endorse, develop, and teach the OPEN approach to OO development.

[2]Pronounced like the word "common."

[3]This specification uses rectangles for nodes on metamodels and uses all capital letters for labels. This notation for metamodeling is an informal extension to COMN and not an official part of the notation.

The scope of this specification is the totality of OML. Although the current version of OML can be used to model a wide variety of applications, this specification may be extended in the future with annexes providing additional notation to meet the needs of specific organizations and application (e.g., C++ physical design, embedded real-time).

1.2   Document Structure

Following a statement of the Goals and Philosophy of OML (Section II), the Common Notation section (III) documents those common nodes and arcs that are used in multiple diagram types. The Diagrams section (IV) documents the different kinds of diagrams used in OML. Section V covers Class Responsibility Collaborator (CRC) cards, and is followed by a number of Appendices that:

- link icons to diagram types,
- delineate COMN "light"[4] from the complete COMN,
- contrast COMN with Rational's UML, and
- provide a glossary of terms.

1.3   Copyright

OML is intended to be an open standard; it is not a proprietary language of the OPEN Consortium or of any of its methodologists. As such, the OML may be used freely by anyone, anywhere. We actively encourage the growing number of developers, CASEtool vendors, training firms, consulting firms, and authors who are adopting and using OML so that there is a wide-spread infrastructure supporting OPEN. It is in the industry's best interests for there to be consistent support for and use of the OML. We have only attached a copyright notice on this and other OPEN documents to prevent commercial for-profit reproduc-

---

[4]COMN light is the core subset of critical, foundational, language-independent OML notations that have widespread use, are suitable for beginners, and excludes those notations used by only advanced modelers for atypical situations.

tion and to support the configuration management of these documents to prevent multiple unauthorized versions of them. Anyone can use the concepts and techniques of this document to model object-oriented systems; we only request its source be acknowledged.

1.4 Point of Contact

Comments on any aspect of the OML or this document should be sent (preferably by e-mail) directly to its primary author and point of contact:

> Donald G. Firesmith
> e-mail: Donald_Firesmith@Stortek.com
> voice: (303) 661-5943
> Storage Technology Corporation
> 2270 South 88th Street
> Mailstop 5210
> Louisville, CO 80028 USA

There is also an OPEN user group mailing list covering all aspects of OPEN to which anyone can subscribe by sending an email to listserv@csse.swin.edu.au with the text message SUBSCRIBE OPEN "your name."

1.5 Adopting Methodologists

As defined by the following sections, OML (including COMN) has been reviewed and adopted by the following methodologists who are members of the OPEN Consortium:

- **Donald G. Firesmith**

  Storage Technology Corporation, Louisville, Colorado, USA, Donald_Firesmith@Stortek.com

- **Ian Graham**

  Swiss Bank Corporation (SBC), Warburg, London, England, 101710.3061@compuserve.com

- **Brian Henderson-Sellers**

  Centre for Object Technology Applications and Research (COTAR) at Swinburne University of Technology, Hawthorn, Victoria, Australia, brian@csse.swin.edu.au

- **Meilir Page-Jones**

  Wayland Systems, Bellevue, Washington, USA, 76334.1247@compuserve.com

1.6   Acknowledgments

As a truly open standard, OML is a group effort that has drawn on the inputs of numerous methodologists, researchers, vendors, and users. In addition to its many reviewers, we would like to specifically acknowledge the contributions of the following people, programming languages, and notations (listed in alphabetical order):

- Grady Booch — mechanisms and bi-directional aggregation.
- Ed Colbert — the original use of the term "interaction diagram."
- Larry Constantine — emphasis on the importance of the semiotics[5] of the notation.
- Desmond D'Souza — emphasis on roles as modeling elements.
- Eiffel — assertions and the inheritance annotation stereotypes.
- Embley, Kurtz, and Woodfield — state modeling.
- Donald Firesmith — drop-down boxes, the notation for types and class implementations; using attachment and nesting to differentiate visible and hidden characteristics respectively; the use of internal collaboration diagrams; the notation for interface and implementation inheritance; cluster inheritance; the "precedes" relationship between use cases; and layer diagrams.
- Erich Gamma et al. — the note icon that can be used to annotate any other icon with arbitrary information.

---

[5]Semiotics is the study of the meaning and understandability of icons.

- Yossi Gil — traits.
- Ian Graham — process, task scripts, and early user testing at European Conferences.
- Brian Henderson-Sellers — double-line arrow notation for inheritance; layering and aggregation concepts; for emphasizing the importance of the semiotics of the notation; and early user-testing at American and Australian conferences.
- Ari Jaaksi at Nokia — logic boxes on sequence diagrams.
- Ivar Jacobson — use cases.
- Scott Krutsch — the documentation of responsibilities on referential relationships.
- Bertrand Meyer — emphasis on assertions.
- Meilir Page-Jones — emphasis of the distinction between type and class, the use of his tablet notation for objects and classes.
- MOSES — using the same icon for objects and classes; uni-directional associations; using CRC cards at the cluster level; layering techniques; selective visibility.
- Jean Pierre Paillet at Footprint Software — the aggregation symbol.
- Trygve Reenskaug — emphasis on roles.
- Bran Selic — emphasis on semantics and the use of English labels on system-level sequence diagrams.
- UML — the term "sequence diagram."
- Rebecca Wirfs-Brock — the concept of stereotypes, her emphasis on responsibilities, and the term "collaboration diagram."

Every document is to some extent only as good as its reviewers. Although the number of these reviewers is too large to acknowledge all of them individually, special mention must be made of the especially thorough work of Scott Krutsch of Knowledge Systems Corporation, Hadar Ziv of the University of California at Irvine, and Rob Allen of Swinburne University of Technology.

The diagrams in this document were drawn with version 4.0 of ObjectMaker from Mark V Systems Ltd. using beta version support for OML COMN.

2   OML Philosophy and Goals

THE purpose of any modeling notation is to faithfully capture and communicate the model, and this communication is primarily with people rather than with CASE tools. OML was designed according to the following philosophy in order to achieve the following goals:

- *Like an OOPL.* A graphical modeling language such as OML is to object-oriented analysis and design what an object-oriented programming language (OOPL) is to object-oriented programming. It must define both a syntax and its semantics, and that requires a detailed language reference manual to do so completely.

- *Language Influences Thought.* The language one uses can profoundly influence the way one thinks. For example, the choice of OOPL influences the likely physical design of the software programmed in that language. Similarly, the modeling language used can also influence the kind of requirements and design models produced. For example, some modeling notations emphasize a data-driven design whereas other modeling languages such as OML emphasize a more responsibility-driven design.

- *Object Paradigm.* OML is an *object-oriented* modeling language. Therefore, it must be consistent with the object paradigm and support the modeling of all major object-oriented concepts. OPEN is responsibility driven rather than data (i.e., attribute) driven.

  Specifically, OML is based on the fundamental concepts of object-orientation (e.g., objects, classes, types) and how they relate to one another. OML is driven more by concepts supported by pure OOPLs such as Smalltalk, Java, and Eiffel than by hybrid OOPLs such as C++ and Ada95.

OML COMN is not merely a traditional functional modeling (data flows) or data modeling notation, minimally extended to make it partially work for objects. Indeed, notation for non-object-oriented concepts is optional and not a part of the core notation.

Three typical examples of this OML emphasis on pure object-orientation are:

1. OML emphasizes objects, types, classes, and their responsibilities rather than the early identification of properties as do some notations strongly based on entity relationship attribute (ERA) relational database modeling techniques (e.g., OMT, UML, Shlaer/Mellor, Coad, Fusion).

2. OML emphasizes unidirectional relationships over bi-directional relationships because unidirectional relationships are the default in the object paradigm (i.e., objects use internal properties to reference other objects). Bi-directional relationships are derived from two unidirectional relationships that are semi-strong inverses of one another and require all of the additional operations to ensure referential integrity.

3. COMN draws aggregation arcs from the aggregate to the part (because that is how aggregate objects are defined and reference their parts in the object-oriented world) rather than from the part to the aggregate (which is how relational database tables are joined via foreign keys).

- *Object-Oriented Development Cycle.* OML must be usable during the entire iterative, incremental development cycle from initial requirements elicitation through maintenance and enhancement. It should also support and facilitate as seamless of a process as is practical.

  OML supports all development activities from requirements elicitation, analysis, and specification through logical and physical design to code generation. However, physical design and code generation which are language specific are not a part of COMN Light[1].

  As the modeler's knowledge increases over time, the notation must be able to capture the model at the current correct level of abstraction, which evolves as the model is elaborated. The notation should not force

---

[1]COMN Light is the beginner subset of COMN, containing the most useful parts of the complete COMN and leaving out COMN's advanced and language-specific features.

the modeler to document implementation details during initial requirements elicitation.

For example, COMN uses drop-down boxes to display the appropriate information (e.g., description, responsibilities) at the appropriate time (e.g., analysis) rather than forcing the modeler to concentrate on design details (e.g., attributes, operations) during initial analysis.

- *Ease of Learning and Use.* OML will be used to communicate with domain experts, business analysts, customers, and users as well as professional modelers and programmers. Thus, it must be easy to learn and use.

  1. *Intuitiveness.* Because OML is intended to communicate object-oriented models to humans including non-software professionals, it must be unambiguous, consistent, and comply with our best understanding of iconic design principles. Because object-oriented modeling will continue to be new to most modelers for the next few years, it is critical that the notation be intuitive and imply what it means. In other words, it should not give incorrect cognitive/visual signals.

     To the extent practical, OML COMN avoids representing concepts by arbitrary icons and symbols that must be remembered by rote. For example, COMN annotates interface (blackbox) inheritance and implementation (whitebox) inheritance arcs with a whitebox and blackbox respectively, and COMN does not use arbitrary symbols (e.g., $ to represent class vs. instance-level characteristics).

     To the extent practical, COMN must imply what is intended. For example, COMN draws the aggregation arc from the aggregate to its parts and uses a plus sign to represent that "the whole is (more than) the sum of its parts." Similarly, COMN uses arrowheads on all arcs to represent the direction of dependency and visibility.

  2. *State of the Art.* Based on over a decade of experience, we have learned a great deal about how to make a notation easy to understand, learn, and use. More than 90% of those who will be doing OO modeling in the future have yet to learn any OO modeling technique[2], and they will not be primarily software professionals who are used to arcane graphical jargons. Therefore, it is critical that methodologists be willing to abandon their obsolete, non-intu-

---

[2]In fact, most object-oriented developers do not currently use any modeling technique at all and will benefit from a state-of-the-art notation.

itive notations which largely had to be learned by rote and replace them with the currently best available notation based on established human-computer interaction (HCI) principles. Due to the current emphasis on method convergence, now may represent the industry's last best chance for significantly improving the notation before it is forever chiseled in granite.

Thus, the members of the OPEN Consortium have largely taken a revolutionary rather than evolutionary approach to notation in which no previous, traditional notation has dominated COMN.

3. *Ease of Drawing.* COMN is easy to draw by hand and easy for upperCASE tool vendors to implement. Indeed, regardless of upperCASE tool availability, most initial modeling will continue to be done on whiteboards. To the extent practical, COMN has avoided mandating conventions (e.g., italics, color) that are hard to do by hand, while allowing individual CASE tool vendors to create competitive advantage by using such conventions (e.g., drawing exceptions objects and classes in red). COMN also uses the same notation when drawn by hand and by CASEtool.[3]

4. *Simplicity.* COMN light concentrates on documenting the key modeling constructs. It relegates language-specific concepts to extensions of the core notation. Too many details can clutter up a diagram, making it hard to understand, and should best be relegated to either drop-down boxes or pop-up screens that can present a relatively-unlimited amount of information. The primary purpose of a diagram is **not** to provide enough information to generate code but rather to communicate with human beings. At the same time, a CASE tool should store all information in such a way as to permit the forward engineering of code from models and the reverse engineering of models from code.

   For example, COMN light does not attempt to display the visibility (e.g., public, protected, private) of C++ characteristics (e.g., data members, member functions).

5. *Scalability.* COMN is usable on smaller informal projects and larger, more complex projects. COMN currently comes in two forms:

---

[3]Although drop-down boxes are primarily designed as a way of dynamically providing flexibility when using an upperCASE tool, they can and have been drawn statically on whiteboards and paper.

COMN Light (a subset for beginners and small, simple applications) and the complete Standard COMN for experienced users. Large projects are supported by OML's inclusion of powerful clustering constructs and COMN's inclusion of diagrams (e.g., Configuration Diagrams, Layer Diagrams, Deployment Diagrams) that allow the developer to attack large applications. The OPEN Consortium intends to eventually augment Standard COMN with extensions for particular situations and for use in specific subdomains to meet the needs of advanced users on complex projects.

6. *Consistency with Previous Notation.* COMN does not include new icons, just to be new, but rather reuses traditional icons wherever practical. COMN only introduces new notations when traditional notations violate other goals of the OML or if a sufficiently better notation exists. Since most of the industry has yet to transition to object orientation, we feel that the goals of ease of learning and simplicity far outweigh any advantages of using a less effective, yet more traditional notation.

- *Multiple Views.* Because COMN is used to model business domains and applications with a great deal of inherent complexity, no single view or diagram type is adequate to capture all important aspects of the resulting model. COMN therefore offers a set diagram types that provide relatively orthogonal[4] views of the single underlying model. Some diagrams document static architecture, whereas others document dynamic behavior. Some diagrams view the model at a very high, blackbox level of abstraction, whereas others open up the blackbox to display encapsulated details. The OML metamodel provides a way to capture the single underlying model and check for consistency.

---

[4]These views are relatively orthogonal in that each diagram provides a view of the underlying model that can be understood and studied separately. However, these diagrams are related to each other in interesting and useful ways because they provide views of a single underlying model, and this allows CASE tool vendors to provide coherent cross-referencing and consistency checking.

3   Common Notation

UNLIKE traditional approaches, an object-oriented method typically uses the same concepts, terminology, and notation throughout all activities of the development cycle. As a result, the same notation can and should be used in many different kinds of diagrams. This section documents the common nodes and arcs shared by different kinds of COMN diagrams.

Each subsection covering a set of related common nodes or arcs has the following format:

1. *Definitions* of the different kinds of metamodeling elements covered

2. *Partial OML Metamodel* that documents these metamodeling elements that are pertinent to the subsection

3. *COMN Notation* defining the icons for these metamodeling elements

4. *Stereotypes* of the icons

5. *Applicable Diagrams* on which the icons can occur

6. *Rules* capturing the syntax of the icons

7. *Guidelines* for using the icons

8. *Examples* using the icons

3.1   Common Nodes

The following nodes are used in multiple diagrams:

1. Objects and their Classes and Types

2. Clusters and their Classes and Types

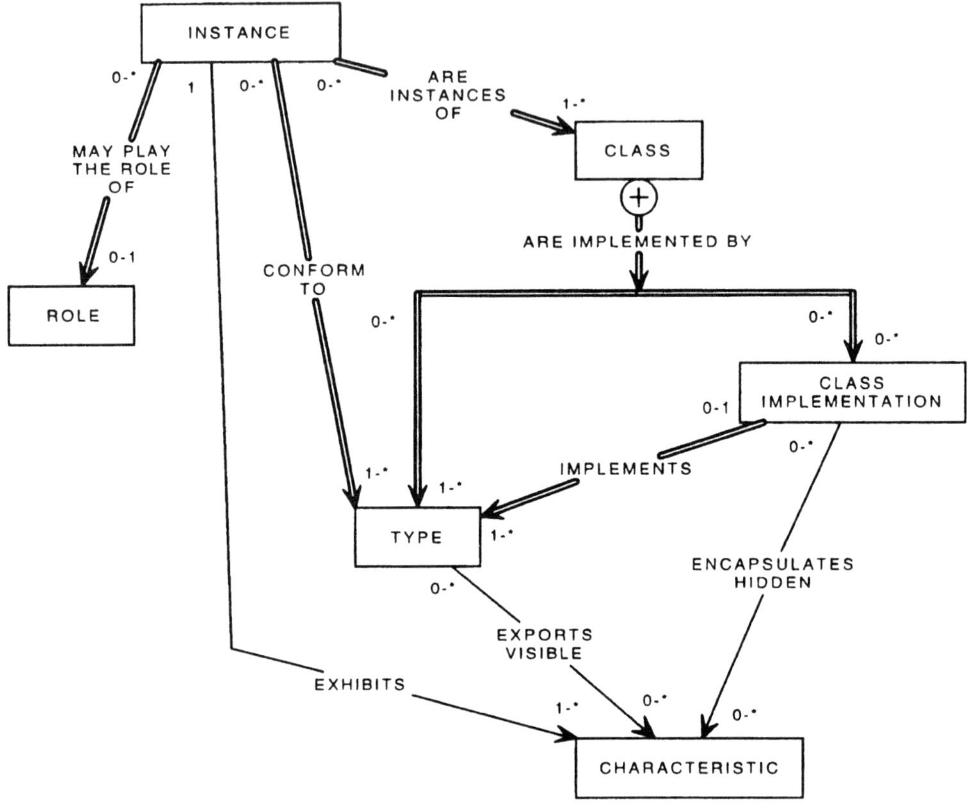

Figure 3.1. Partial metamodel for instances, classes, types, and class implementations.

3. Scenarios and their Classes and Types

4. Drop-Down Boxes

5. Non-OO Modeling Elements

Definitions

The following definitions define the fundamental concepts underlying both objects and clusters. These definitions provide semantics to the nodes on the partial metamodel illustrated by Figure 3.1:

instance *n.* any uniquely-identified abstraction that uses characteristics to model a single thing that is important in the current application.

class *n.* any uniquely defined abstraction that models a kind of thing and that defines individual instances of that kind. A class has a visible interface consisting of one or more types and a hidden implementation consisting of one or more class implementations that together implement the types.[1]

type *n.* any declaration of visible characteristics that form all or part of the interface of a single kind of instance. An instance conforms to a type if and only if its interface is consistent with the type (i.e., the set of characteristics in the interface of the instance is a superset of the set of characteristics declared by the type). A type defines a protocol on which clients can rely and which implementations must satisfy.

class implementation *n.* any declaration of hidden characteristics that form all or part of the implementation of a single kind of instance.

role *n.* any partial declaration of a kind of instance, the declared characteristics of which are required to fulfill a cohesive set of responsibilities. Such an instance is said to play the role.

characteristic *n.* any property, behavior, or assertion documenting a node on a model.

The following definitions provide semantics to the relationship arcs on the partial metamodel illustrated by Figure 3.1:

instance of *n.* the classification relationship from an instance to one of its classes whereby the instance is consistent with the complete definition provided by the class. An instance is an instance of a class if and only if its interface conforms to each of the types of the class and its implementation is defined by the class implementations of the class.

conforms to *n.* the classification relationship from an instance to one of its types whereby the interface of the instance is consistent with the type. An instance conforms to an type if and only if its interface is consistent with the type (i.e., the set of characteristics in the interface of the instance is a superset of the set of characteristics declared by the type).

---

[1]Note that the terms type and class are not synonymous. A type defines an interface but does not provide an implementation. A class provides both an interface and an implementation.

implements *n.* the implementation relationship from a class implementation to one of the types of the corresponding class whereby the instances of the class conform to the type.

is implemented by *n.* the implementation relationship from a class to one of its class implementations whereby the class implementation implements one or more of the types of the class.

is implementation of *n.* the implementation relationship from a class to one of its types whereby the class provides a class implementation that implements the type.

Figure 3.1 is a partial OML metamodel that documents some of the key concepts providing a foundation to both objects and clusters. This metamodel captures the following information:

- Each instance is an instance of one or more classes.
- Each instance conforms to one or more types.
- Each class is an implementation of one or more types.
- Each class is implemented by one or more class implementations.
- Each class implementation implements one or more associated types.
- Each type declares zero or more visible characteristics.
- Each class implementation declared zero or more hidden characteristics.
- Each instance exhibits one or more characteristics declared by the type(s) and class implementation(s) of its classes.

3.1.1 Objects and their Classes and Types

Definitions

The following definitions provide semantics to the partial metamodels documented in Figures 3.2 through 3.4:

object *n.* any uniquely-identified abstraction that uses its *characteristics* to model a single thing that is important to model. In order to be a complete abstraction, an object captures all of the essential characteristics (i.e., *properties, behavior,* and *rules*) of the thing being modeled while ignoring the thing's non-essential, diversionary details.

Objects can be partitioned into either internal objects or external objects as follows:

- **internal object** *n.* any object that is within the scope of the current context (e.g., business, system, application).
- **external object** *n.* any object that is outside the scope of the current context (e.g., business, system, application) but is nevertheless important to document during modeling (e.g., because it interacts with the application or implies the existence of a corresponding internal object).

External objects can be partitioned by kind as follows:

— **actor** *n.* any external that models a role played by a human.

— **hardware external** *n.* any external that models a hardware device, either with or without significant processing power.
— **other external** *n.* any external that is not an actor, hardware external, persistent memory external, or software external.
— **persistent memory external** *n.* any external that models some persistent memory (e.g., a file, a database, a relational database table, a tape, a disk).
— **software external** *n.* any external that models some software (e.g., a legacy application).

External objects can be partitioned by the degree that they are out of context as follows:

— **direct external** *n.* any external that interacts directly with the current application.
— **indirect external** *n.* any external that interacts indirectly with the current application via other externals.

External objects can be partitioned by dependency as follows:

— **client external** *n.* any external that depends on the current application.
— **peer external** *n.* any external that is both a client external and a server external.
— **server external** *n.* any external on which the current application depends.

Objects can be partitioned into either concurrent objects or sequential objects as follows:

- **concurrent object**[2] *n.* any object that is *inherently* capable of running concurrently (i.e., simultaneously) with other objects because it contains, either directly or indirectly, one or more of its own threads of execution. An object may be concurrent because:
  - — it directly has its own thread of execution (e.g., an object in the Actor language),
  - — one or more of its properties are concurrent, or
  - — one or more of its operations are directly concurrent (i.e. have their own inherent thread of execution).

- **sequential object** *n.* any object that is not *inherently* capable of running concurrently (i.e., simultaneously) with other objects because it does not contain, either directly or indirectly, one or more of its *own* threads of execution.

multiobject *n.* any homogeneous collection of objects that are instances of the same class or type.

[object] class[3] *n.* any class that is also an object that defines (and optionally can be used to instantiate) objects (its *instances*) that have the same or similar characteristics. Contrast with cluster class (a.k.a., cluster).

[object class] type[4] *n.* any type declaring the visible characteristics that form all or part of the interface of a single kind of object.

[object] metaclass *n.* any class, the instances of which are all of the object classes.

[object] class implementation *n.* any declaration of hidden characteristics that form all or part of the implementation of a single kind of object.

object interface *n.* the externally visible characteristics of an object.

---

[2]OML does not use the terms active and passive as synonyms for concurrent and sequential because concurrent objects (e.g., some objects containing tasks in Ada95) can be passive, only using their thread to protect themselves from corruption due to simultaneous access.

[3]Because "classes of objects" are more common than "classes of cluster instances," object classes are usually just called "classes" and classes of cluster instances are usually just called "clusters" even though the term class by itself is actually ambiguous.

[4]Although the term "type" when used by itself is also technically ambiguous, it typically means object class type.

object protocol *n.* any cohesive set of visible exported characteristics of an object that conforms to an object class type.

object implementation *n.* the encapsulated hidden characteristics of an object defined by the corresponding object class implementation.

object characteristic *n.* any resource or feature (e.g., property, operation, or assertion[5]) that makes up an object.

- **class-level characteristic** *n.* any characteristic of a class as a whole rather than its instances. For example, constructor operations (e.g., new in Smalltalk) are class-level operations.

- **instance-level characteristic** *n.* any characteristic of an instance of a class rather than the class as a whole. For example, initialization operations that set the values of the properties of an instantiated object are instance-level operations.

[object] operation *n.* any functional abstraction that models a discrete activity, action, or behavior that is performed by an object, typically in response to a message. An operation consists of a *signature* (i.e., interface) and a *method* (i.e., implementation).

[object] property *n.* any kind of characteristic capturing a static aspect of its encapsulating object or class.

All properties are either logical or physical. Logical properties are used during requirements analysis and logical design, whereas physical properties are used during physical design, forward engineering to code, and reverse engineering from code. A property is assumed to be logical unless explicitly annotated as physical.

- **logical property** *n.* any property that implements a responsibility for knowing by representing a query that can be made of its object or class.

  A logical property it typically implemented by an operation that returns a copy or reference to an object that results from either referencing one or more physical properties, calculating the returned value, or sending messages to servers.

- **physical property** *n.* any property consisting of a named reference[6] to an object.

---

[5]Assertions are captured either in drop-down boxes or in the signatures of related operations.

OML also recognizes the following partition of properties:

- **attribute** *n.* any descriptive property. An attribute is usually hidden, but may be visible. An attribute provides the only reference to an internal hidden object, the life span of which matches that of the object of which it is an attribute. An attribute may reference only a single object.

- **part** *n.* any property of an aggregate that references a component of the aggregate. A part is usually hidden, but may be visible. An object is typically a part of only one aggregate at a time. The life span of a part is usually that of its aggregate, but need not be. At least some of the parts of an aggregate reference each other, thus creating a structure (e.g., a car engine) that depends on the correct interaction of its parts. The aggregate can thus be considered to have emergent properties, compared to the sum of the parts.

- **entry** *n.* any property of a container that references an object contained by the container. An entry is usually hidden, but may be visible. An object is typically an entry of only one container at a time. The life span of an entry is usually not that of its container, but could be. The entries of a container do not reference each other and any organization is provided by the container (e.g., a car trunk).

- **link** *n.* any property that references an external object. Although the link is usually hidden, the object it references is not. Multiple links in multiple objects may reference the same object. The life span of the object referenced by a link is independent of the object encapsulating the link.

- **exception** *n.* any object modeling an exceptional or error condition that is raised by an operation in order to notify a client that the condition (e.g., an assertion has been violated) has occurred.

assertion *n.* any business rule that is a constraint on the property values of an object.

- **invariant** *n.* any assertion that must hold both before and after the execution of all operations.

- **precondition** *n.* any assertion that must hold before the execution of the associated operation(s).

---

[6]A property is different from the object it references. A property that does not reference an object is called a dangling property and represents either an error in the model or a reference that is temporarily uninitialized.

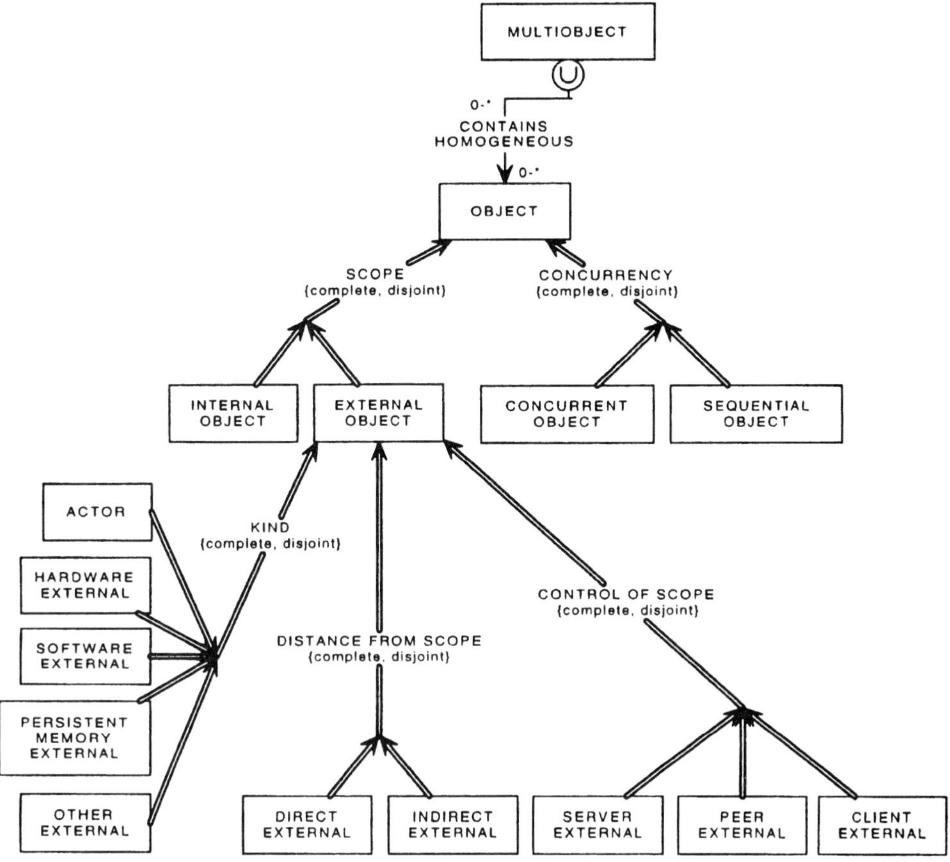

Figure 3.2. Partial metamodel documenting the kinds of objects.

- **postcondition** *n.* any assertion that must hold after the execution of the associated operation(s).

stereotype *n.* any character string of enumeration type that is used to conceptually classify a modeling element independently from inheritance or provide some other important information about the modeling element. Stereotypes provide a facility for metaclassification.

OML Metamodel

Figure 3.2 is a partial OML metamodel that documents some of the important kinds of objects. This partial metamodel captures the following information:

- Each object is either an internal object or an external object with regard to a given scope.
- With regard to a given scope, each external object is either:

  — a direct external or an indirect external.
  — a client external, a peer external, or a server external.

- Each external object is either an actor, a hardware external, a software external, a persistent memory external, or an other external.
- Each multiobject is a collection that contains zero or more homogeneous objects.

Figure 3.3 is a partial OML metamodel that documents the semantically important relationships between objects and their classes and types. This partial metamodel captures the following information:

- Each object is an instance of one or more object classes, but not all classes[7] need to have instances.
- Each object class is a kind of object that may know how to instantiate objects as its instances using its type(s) and class implementation(s) which together define its instances.[8]
- Each class may be defined in terms of zero or more other classes via inheritance.
- Each class is an instance of a single metaclass, which is a kind of class with other classes as its instances. Therefore, a metaclass is also a kind of object because it is a class and a class is a kind of object.
- Each metaclass is defined in terms of one other metaclass (class Metaclass) via inheritance. The use of this metaclass prevents an infinite recursion of classes.
- Each class consists of one or more object class types implemented by one or more object class implementations.
- Each object consists of two main parts: one or more object protocols and an object implementation.

---

[7]Unless explicitly stated, the term class by itself will mean object class rather than cluster class or external class.

[8]A concrete class provides a complete definition of its instances and can therefore be instantiated. An abstract class, however, only provides a partial definition and cannot therefore be instantiated to produce a semantically meaningful object.

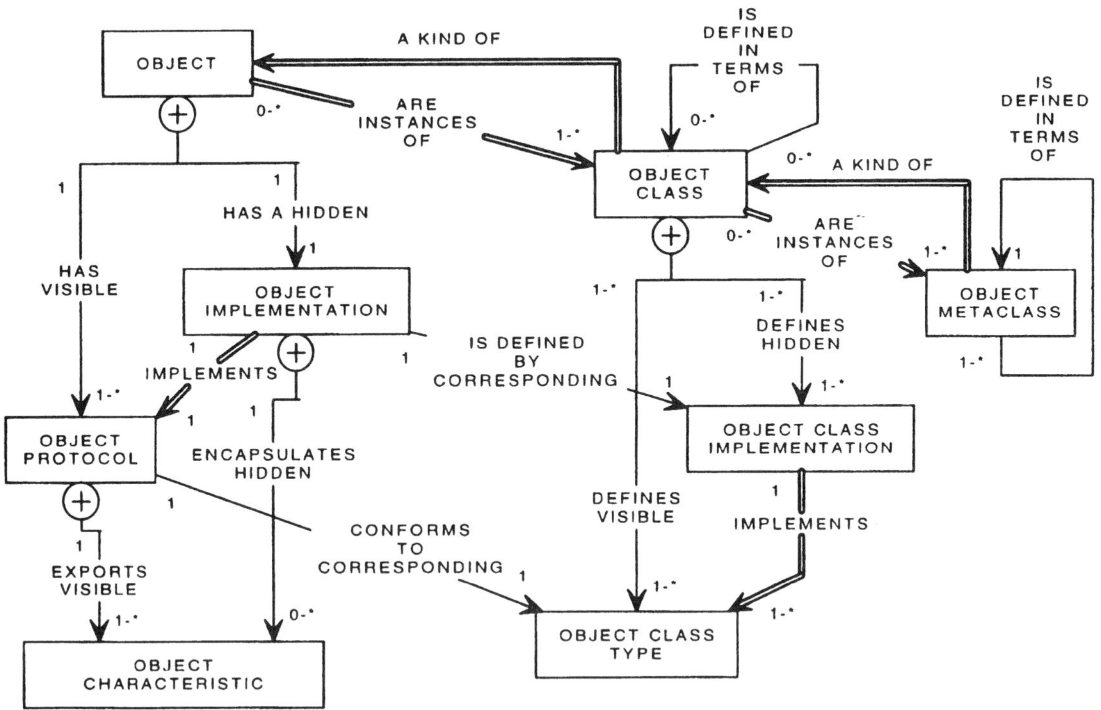

Figure 3.3. Partial metamodel documenting objects and their classes and types.

- Each object protocol consists of one or more visible exported characteristics (and the implicit behavioral dependencies among them) that conform to the corresponding type of the class.
- Each object implementation encapsulates zero or more hidden characteristics that are defined by the corresponding class implementation.

Figure 3.4 is a partial OML metamodel that documents the different kinds of object characteristics. This partial metamodel captures the following information:

- Object characteristics come in the following three kinds: operations, properties, and assertions.
- Each object operation consists of a signature implemented by a method.
- Object operations operate on properties and my not violate assertions defined on these properties.

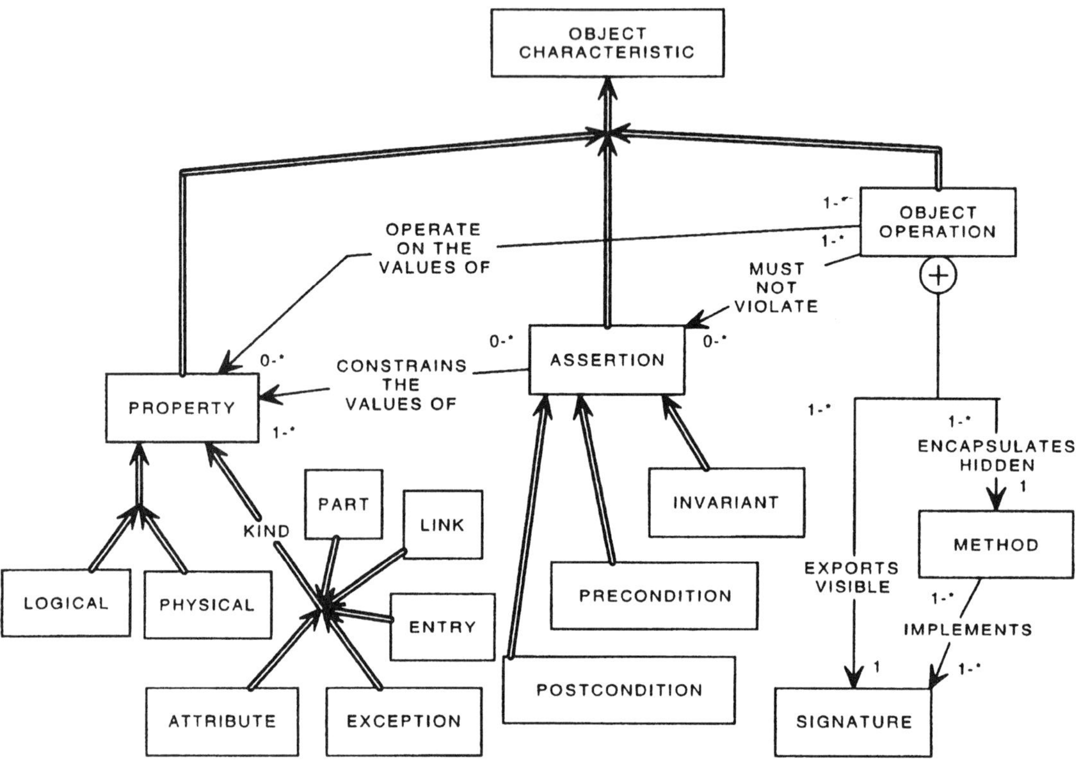

Figure 3.4. Partial metamodel documenting object characteristics.

- Properties can be completely and disjointedly partitioned by kind into attributes, parts, entries, links, and exceptions.

- Properties can be completely and disjointedly partitioned into physical and logical properties.

- Assertions can be completely and disjointedly partitioned into invariants, preconditions, and postconditions.

- Assertions constrain property values and operations depend on property values.

- Because each class is itself an object, it also has its own class-level interface and implementation as well as defining the interface and implementation of its instances.

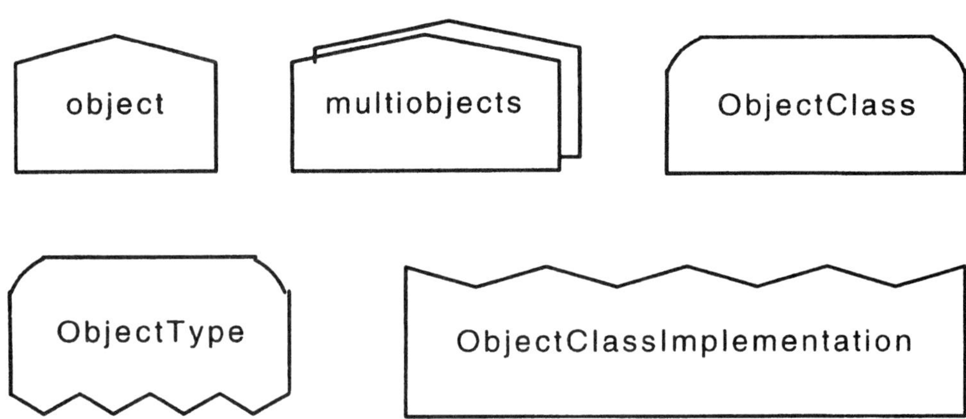

Figure 3.5. Basic object-level icons.

COMN Notation

The following paragraphs document the COMN notation for the concepts documented in the preceding metamodel.

Figures 3.5 and 3.6 document the basic icons for objects, object classes, object types, and object class implementations. Figures 3.7 and 3.8 document the labeling conventions for these icons.

object. A single object is represented by a house shape (i.e., a solid pentagon, the sides of which are vertical). The label of an object icon is a character string consisting of either:

- the name of the object, a space, a colon, a space, and the name of its class or type (e.g., 'aTriangle : Triangle'),
- the name of the corresponding object (e.g., 'aTriangle') if the class or type is either unimportant or understood, or
- a colon followed by a space followed by the name of the object's class or type (e.g., ': Triangle') if the name of the object is unimportant.

actor. One or more human actors is represented by a traditional stick figure. The label of an actor external icon is a character string placed either above, below, or as near as is practical to the stick figure so as to avoid arcs to or from the icon. The name of a class of actor externals is preceded by a capital C.

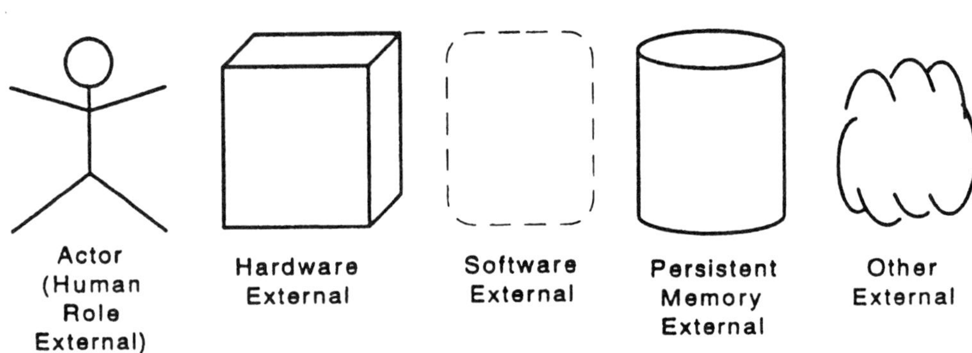

Figure 3.6. Icons for externals.

hardware external. One or more hardware externals is represented by a three-dimensional box. The label of a hardware external icon is a character string placed inside the corresponding icon. The name of a class of hardware externals is preceded by a capital C.

software external. One or more software externals is represented by a rounded rectangle with dashed boundaries. The label of a software external icon is a character string placed inside the corresponding icon. The name of a class of software externals is preceded by a capital C.

persistent memory. One or more persistent memory externals is represented by a three-dimensional cylinder. The label of a persistent memory icon is a character string on the front side of the cylinder. The name of a class of persistent memory externals is preceded by a capital C.

other external. One or more other externals of the same kind is represented by a cloud. The label of an other external icon is a character string placed inside the corresponding cloud. The name of a class of other externals is preceded by a capital C.

multiobject. Multiple objects of the same class or type are represented by a stack of two object icons, the front icon placed below and to the left of the back icon. The label of a multiobject icon is a character string consisting of either:

- the name of the corresponding collection object, an optional space, a colon, a space, the name of the collection class or type, and the name class or type of the entries (e.g., 'triangles : List [Triangle]'),

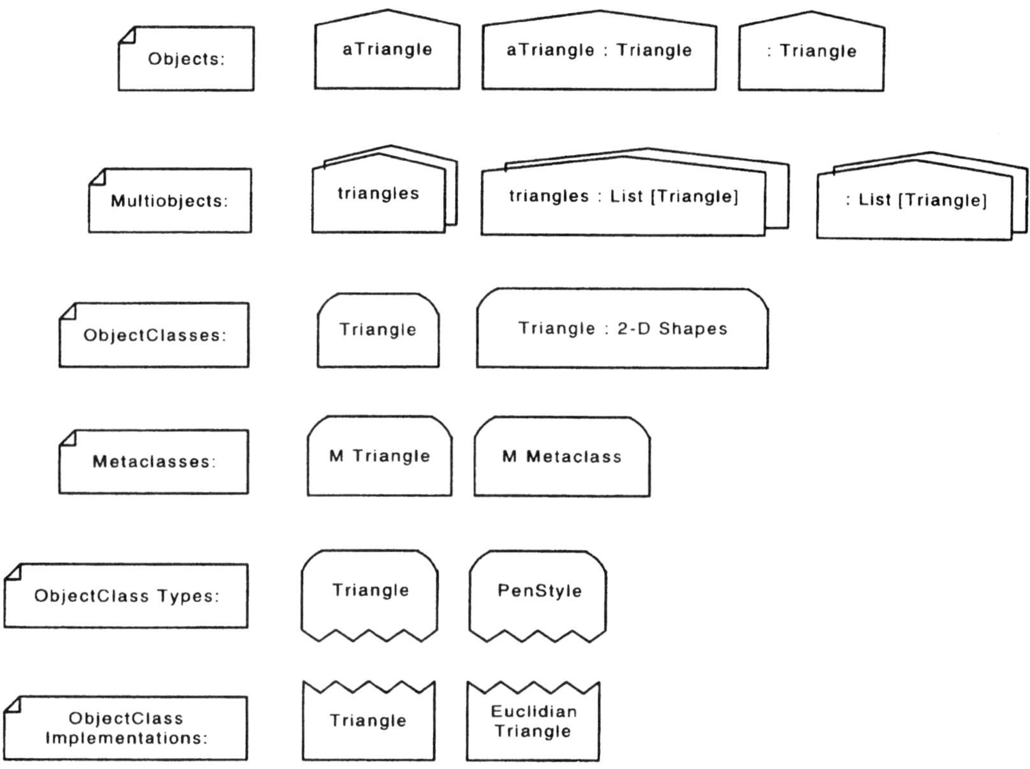

Figure 3.7. Labeling of object-level icons.

- the name of the corresponding collection of objects (e.g., 'triangles') if the class or type is either unimportant or understood, or
- a colon, a space, the name of the collection class or type, and the name of the class or type of the entries (e.g., ': List [Triangle]') if the name of the collection is unimportant.

object class. An object class is represented by the tablet icon (i.e., a solid rectangle, the top two corners of which are rounded). The label of an object class icon is a character string consisting of the name of the class, optionally a colon followed by the cluster of the class (e.g., 'Triangle', 'Triangle : 2D Shapes'). The label of a class can be printed in a larger font size or in boldface if the class node contains other nodes so that its label could be lost in the details.

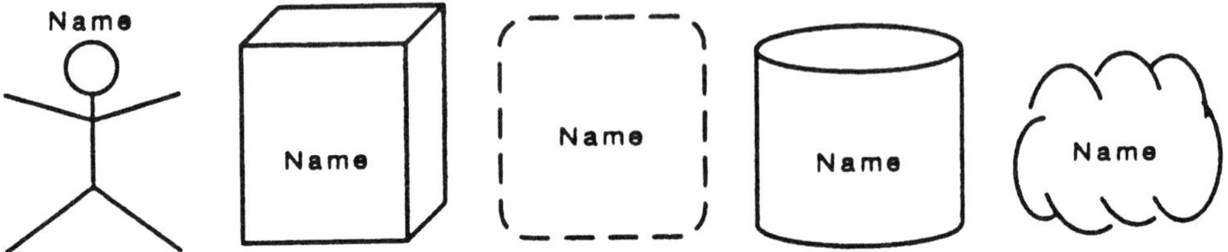

Figure 3.8. Labeling externals.

object metaclass. Since an object metaclass is itself a kind of class, it is also represented by a tablet (i.e., solid rectangle, the top two corners of which are rounded). The label of an object metaclass icon is a character string consisting of the name of the class. Metaclasses are annotated with the stereotype "metaclass."

object class type. An object type is represented by a solid rectangle, the top two corners of which are rounded, and the bottom of which is jagged. The label of an object type icon is a character string consisting of the name of the type. Thus, the icon for an object type is the top half of the icon for an object class, horizontally ripped in two.

object class implementation. An object class implementation is represented by a solid rectangle, the top of which is jagged. The label of an object class implementation icon is a character string consisting of the name of the class implementation. Thus, the icon for an object class implementation is the bottom half of the icon for an object class, horizontally ripped in two.

concurrency. As illustrated on Figure 3.10, a concurrent object or class is indicated by preceding the label of the object or class with two slashes "//", whereby the parallel lines signify parallel processing.

multiplicity. The corresponding multiplicity of a multiobject or class can by indicated by optionally placing the multiplicity (e.g., 5, 1-*) above the icon's label. Because of its importance, a singleton class is indicated by placing the multiplicity between two hyphens (i.e., '-1-').

visibility and encapsulation. Throughout COMN, the technique illustrated in Figure 3.9 is used to distinguish externally visible nodes from hidden ones:

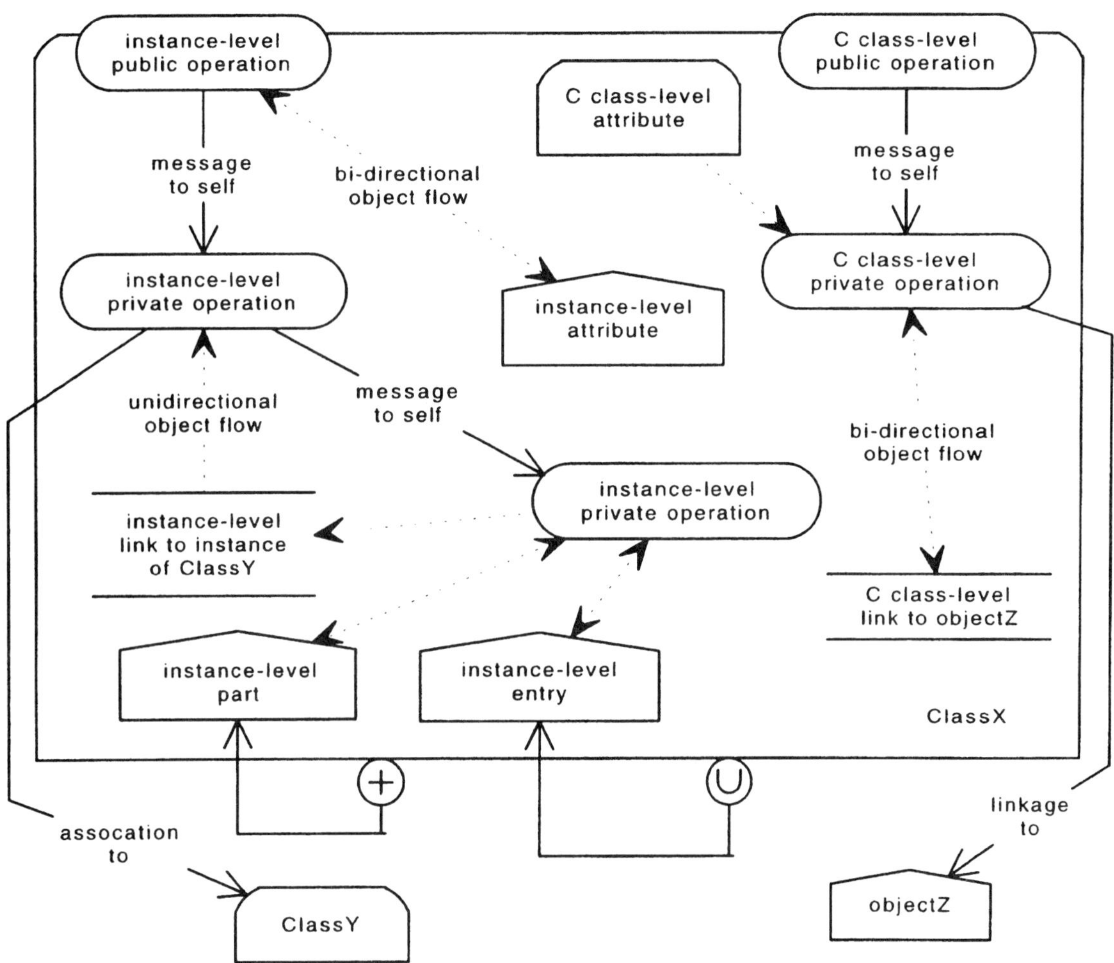

Figure 3.9. Internal collaboration diagram documenting the icons for object characteristics.[9]

- any icon drawn straddling to the boundary of an object or object class represents a characteristic that is part of the public (i.e., externally visible) interface of the object or object class.

---

[9]There is no semantic meaning in the differing shape of the arrowheads on this or other CONM diagrams. Either style is acceptable. However, we recommend that CASE tool vendors select a single, consistent style. See Chapter 4 on collaboration diagrams for the description of object flow.

- any icon drawn within the boundary of an object or object class represents a characteristic that is part of the hidden implementation of the object or object class.

  Objects and classes form namespaces. The names of object and class characteristics must only be unique within the object or class in which they are encapsulated.

operation. As illustrated on Figure 3.9, an operation (both signature and method) is represented by an oval labeled with either the name or the entire signature of the operation. Visible operations straddle the boundary of an object or class, whereas hidden operations are nested inside the boundary of the encapsulating object or class. The arcs on this diagram are defined later and can be safely ignored for purposes of the current discussion.

property.
- Properties referencing encapsulated objects (i.e., attributes, parts, entries, and exceptions) are represented by an object icon, either straddling the boundary of the icon of its object or class (if the property is visible) or nested within the boundary of the icon of its object or class (if the property is hidden). The labels of physical properties are followed by the stereotype {physical}.
- Properties referencing external objects (i.e., links) are represented by the traditional datastore icon (i.e., two parallel horizontal line segments), labeled between the horizontal line segments with the name of the object referenced.

stereotypes. Stereotypes are documented as character strings that are either placed below the label of the node and enclosed in curly braces or else listed in the appropriate drop-down box after the label "stereotypes."

Default Stereotypes

Object stereotypes include:

- Controller vs. Coordinator vs. Information Holder vs. Interfacer vs. Notifier vs. Service Provider vs. Structurer
- GUI Layer vs. Application Layer vs. Domain Layer vs. Infrastructure Layer

- Concurrent vs. Sequential
- Persistent vs. Temporary
- Exception
- Location
- Distribution Unit
- Presentation vs. View vs. Coordinator vs. Model vs. Wrapper
- Internal vs. External

External object stereotypes include:

- Direct vs. Indirect
- Client vs. Peer vs. Server

Class stereotypes include:

- Controller vs. Coordinator vs. Information Holder vs. Interfacer vs. Notifier vs. Service Provider vs. Structurer
- Concrete vs. Abstract vs. Deferred
- Parameterized
- Metaclass
- View vs. Domain vs. Foundation
- Concurrent vs. Sequential
- Singleton
- Exception
- Location
- Distribution Unit
- Presentation vs. View vs. Coordinator vs. Model vs. Wrapper
- Internal vs. External

Type stereotypes include:

- Controller vs. Coordinator vs. Information Holder vs. Interfacer vs. Notifier vs. Service Provider vs. Structurer
- Parameterized
- Metaclass
- View vs. Domain vs. Foundation

- Location
- Distribution

Role stereotypes include:

- Controller vs. Coordinator vs. Information Holder vs. Interfacer vs. Notifier vs. Service Provider vs. Structurer

Characteristic stereotypes include:

- Public vs. Protected vs. Private

Applicable Diagrams

Icons can occur on the following kinds of diagrams:[10]

- Object icons:
  - Cluster Diagrams
  - Collaboration Diagrams
  - Whitebox Sequence Diagrams

- External object icons:
  - Context Diagrams
  - Cluster Diagrams
  - Deployment Diagrams
  - Use Case Diagrams
  - Software Collaboration Diagrams
  - Blackbox Sequence Diagrams

- Object class icons:
  - Cluster Diagrams
  - Inheritance Diagrams
  - Collaboration Diagrams
  - Whitebox Sequence Diagrams

---

[10]Diagram types are discussed in detail in Chapter 4.

- Object class type icons:
  - Cluster Diagrams
  - Inheritance Diagrams
  - Collaboration Diagrams
  - Whitebox Sequence Diagrams

- Object characteristic icons:
  - Internal Collaboration Diagrams

Node Parenting Rules

The following node parenting rules document the permitted straddling and nesting of visible and hidden subnodes.

Objects may:

- export operation signatures and properties.[11]
- hide operations and properties.

Hardware externals may:

- export hardware externals and software externals.
- hide hardware externals and software externals.

Persistent memory externals may:

- export persistent memory externals.[12]

Software externals may:

- export software externals.
- hide software externals.

---

[11] In order to maximize maintainability and information hiding, properties should usually not be exported. If a property is logically part of the interface of its object (e.g., the switch on a motor, the color of an object), then a better solution is usually to provide a public read accessor to the property, even if this would violate the Law of Demeter by allowing a client to send messages directly to a property after obtaining a reference to it.

[12] For example, a relational database may export tables.

Object classes may:

- export operation signatures.
- hide operations and properties.

Object types may:

- export operation signatures.

Object class implementations may:

- hide operations and properties.

Usage Guidelines

1. Emphasize types over classes during requirements analysis and logical design because classes involve design (e.g., implementation) decisions.
2. Use the object icon to represent an individual object. Consider using object icons rather than type or class icons if:
   - Only a single object is required (e.g., Singleton pattern)
   - Objects are more important than classes (e.g., in embedded applications rather than MIS applications)
   - Different objects of the same class occur in different places in the architecture.
3. Consider using type or class icons rather than object icons if:
   - Classes are more important than objects (e.g., on Inheritance Diagrams, on MIS applications)
   - When all instances of a class are treated the same way in the application.
4. Use the multiobject icon to represent a collection of objects of the same [possibly abstract] class.
5. Where practical:
   - Place client externals above the current application node.
   - Place server externals below the current application node.
   - Place peer externals even with the current application node.
6. List stereotypes in a drop-down box if there are so many that they would clutter up the icon.

Rationale

The house icon for normal objects was chosen for several reasons. It is space efficient and easy to draw. It is similar to the class icon while still being clearly distinguishable from classes, which are special objects that are used to define other objects. The class icon can contain the object icon inside it, implying that it is more than just a class and has extra contents (which define the instance). One can cut one's self with a knife, but not with a knife class. The object icon is sharp and the class icon is smooth.

Although classes are a kind of object, they are important enough to justify their own icon. The basic tablet shape for the icon for classes and metaclasses is taken from the notation of Meilir Page-Jones and Brian Henderson-Sellers. This distinctive shape was chosen in order to:

- Avoid ambiguity because the traditional shape (rectangle) is heavily overloaded.
- Clearly differentiate COMN as a pure OO modeling language from other notations (e.g., OMT, UML, Coad, Shlaer/Mellor) which are more data driven due to their strong roots in traditional data modeling and entity relationship (ER) attribute diagrams.
- Be similar to the object icon because classes are a kind of object.

The same icon is used for object classes and object metaclasses because both are classes.

In order to avoid confusion, it is important to differentiate (1) the externals external to the application from (2) the objects and classes inside the application that either model or interface with these externals. Because they represent different things having different responsibilities, they should be modeled differently. This is especially important because we often use the same name (label) for both the external and its corresponding object and class.

Only human actors tend to play multiple roles.

Different kinds of externals require different icons:

- Whereas a stick figure is intuitive when used to represent a human actor, it does not make sense to use a stick figure to represent a hardware device.
- A three-dimensional box intuitively represents a hardware box.
- It is traditional to use a cylinder to represent a database.

- A cloud intuitively represents a non-tangible concept.
- OML uses the dashed rounded rectangle to represent any collection of software larger than a single class. This icon is therefore used to represent software externals as well as clusters, layers, and subdomains.

Because a class is essentially the union of its types and implementations, the icons will be more intuitive if the union of the icons for types and class implementation results in the icon for classes. Conversely, if a class is torn apart (decomposed into its component parts), it results in one or more types and one or more implementations "with torn edges."

Properties are *not* objects, even in pure languages such as Smalltalk. Instead, properties are merely data (e.g., a memory address in C++) that are used as references or pointers to objects. Nevertheless, it is still intuitive to use the icon for the object referenced to represent a property referencing an *encapsulated* object because (1) the distinction between the reference and the object referenced is not important except for pedagogical reasons and (2) this greatly minimizes the clutter of internal collaboration diagrams. However, a datastore icon was chosen to represent the reference to an *external* object because (1) the distinction between the internal reference and the external referenced object is important in this case and (2) the datastore icon is the traditional icon for representing data.

The difference between logical and physical properties is critical. *Logical* properties are required for a responsibility driven approach to implement responsibilities for knowing and to support the formal specification of the public protocol in terms of assertions on public operations. However, if *physical* properties are addressed too early, physical design decisions will creep into the requirements and produce a data-driven design. Logical properties were chosen over physical properties as the default in order to emphasize logical modeling over physical modeling and to support responsibility driven modeling over data-driven modeling.

The use of parallel lines "//" to represent parallel processing is intuitive and easy to remember.

COMN always uses the single object icon to represent a single object and the multiple object icon to represent collections of multiple objects.

Stereotypes are placed below the label of the node they describe because the label of the node is mandatory, is more important than the stereotype(s), and should not be lost in the clutter that multiple stereotypes may produce.

Assertions in OML are strongly influenced by the work of Bertrand Meyer and the Eiffel programming language.

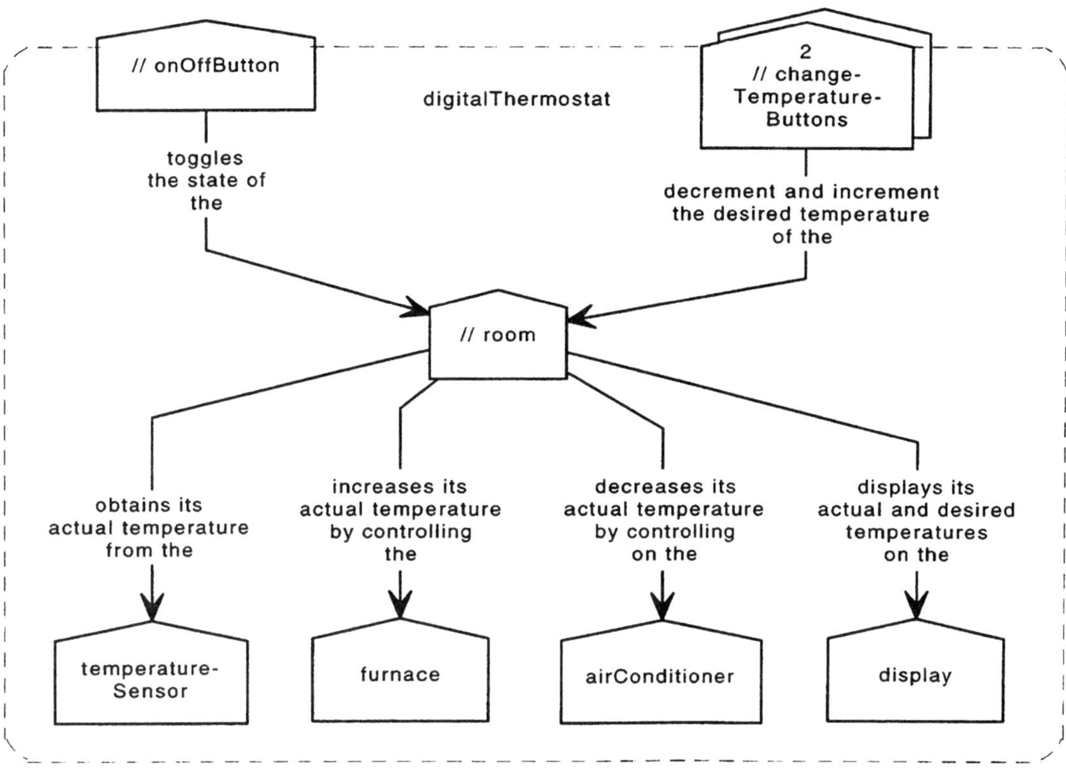

Figure 3.10. Object Icons on a cluster diagram for a digital thermostat.

Examples

Figure 3.10 illustrates the use of object and multiobject icons in a cluster diagram of a cluster[13] that captures the software domain objects that execute in a digital thermostat application. Note that only components that are part of the cluster's inbound interface are drawn on the boundary of the cluster. The buttons objects were made concurrent in order to handle hardware interrupts and the room object was made concurrent in order to be able to handle simultaneous messages from multiple buttons.

Figure 3.11 illustrates the use of external object icons on a software context dia-

---

[13]Clusters will be discussed in the next section.

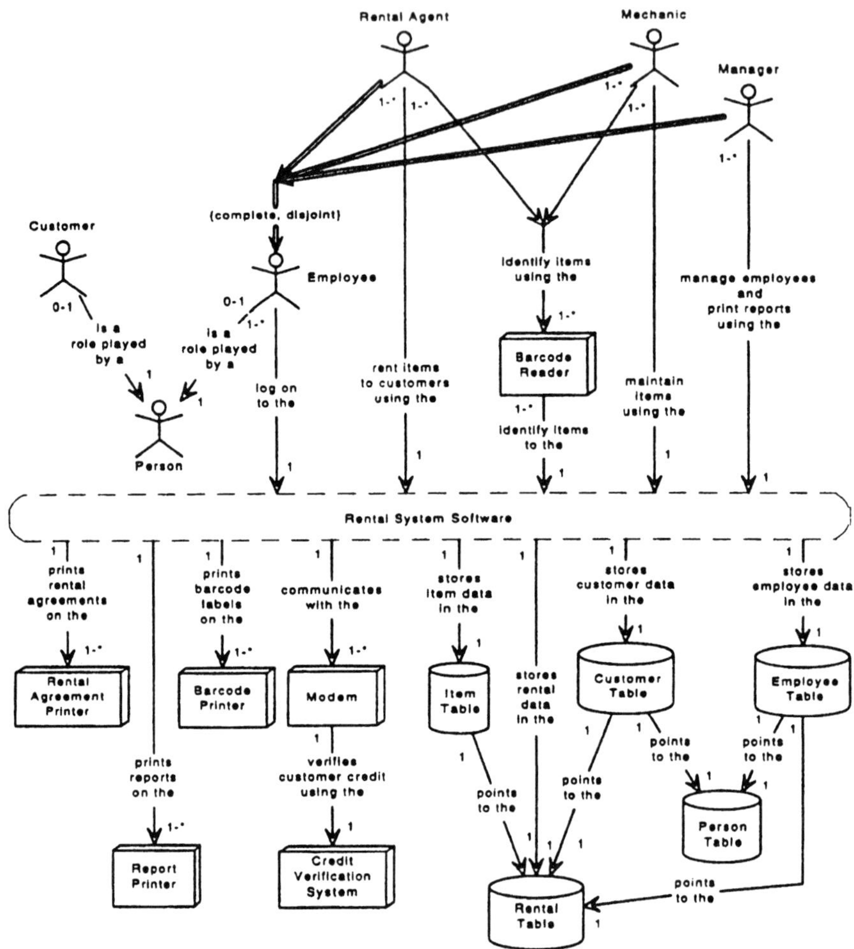

Figure 3.11. External icons on a software context diagram for a rental system.

gram for a rental system. The rental system itself is a single cluster which interacts with a number of employee actors (Rental Agent, Mechanic, and Manager) and with a number of hardware and database externals that request and supply services.

Figure 3.12 documents the class inheritance hierarchy for the Money class as used in a vending machine application. Abstract classes are documented with the optional dotted outline. Although all COMN relationships (including the specialization relationships in this diagram) are binary, they can be conceptually

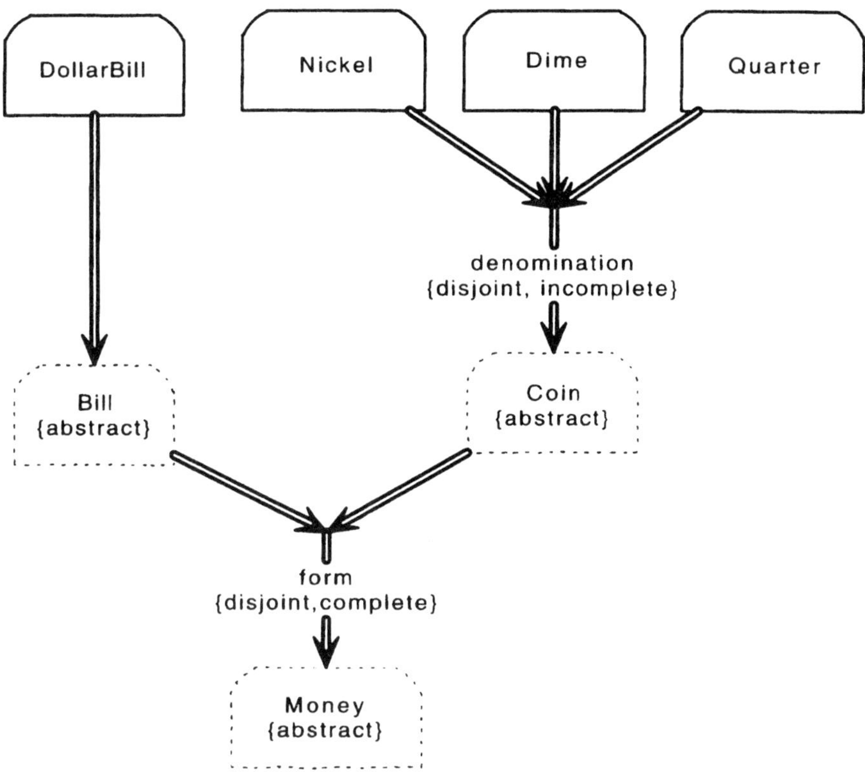

Figure 3.12. Inheritance diagram for a money hierarchy showing class icons.

joined to show partitions or to minimize the clutter of the would result from numerous equivalent relationships pointing to the same node.

Figure 3.13 documents the inheritance hierarchy for a typical Java class showing the separate inheritance of its types (also known as interfaces in Java) and class implementations. The class illustrated has two separate types (Type 1 and Type 2) providing separate views of the class and a single implementation (Class Implementation 1) which supports these two types. The type inheritance structures include both specialization and interface (blackbox) inheritance. These types are implemented by appropriate class implementations, which are themselves derived via implementation (whitebox) inheritance. Thus, OML supports separate inheritance hierarchies for types and implementations, and these hierarchies may have different properties. For example, Java supports multiple inher-

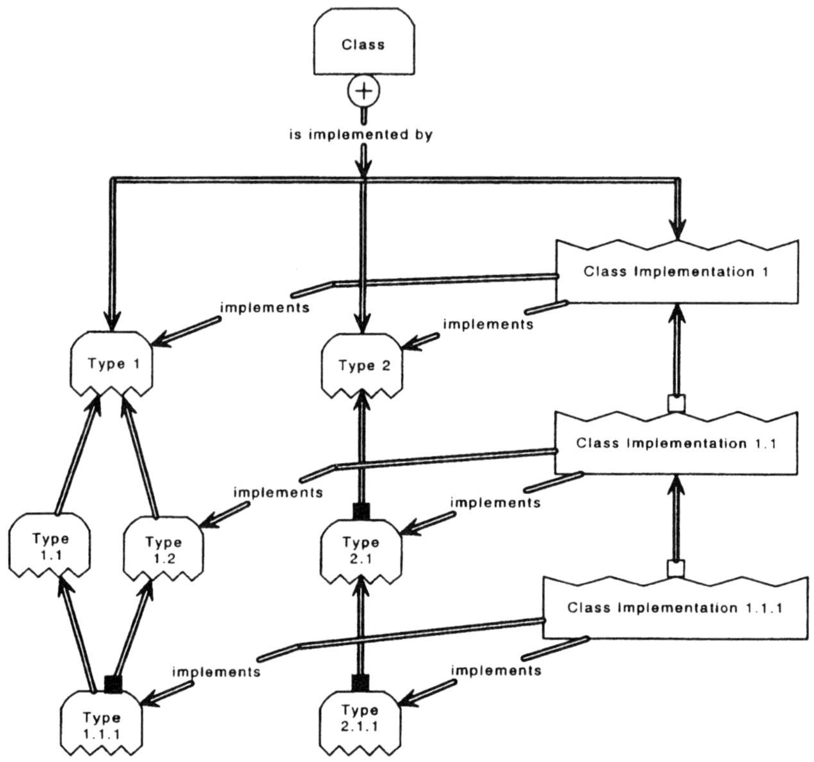

Figure 3.13. Inheritance diagram showing the separate inheritance of types and class implementations (for example, in Java).

itance between types, but only single inheritance between class implementations.

Figure 3.14 illustrates the use of class icons in a cluster diagram for a rental application. The Domain Cluster exports some visible classes (Item, Rental, Customer, and Employee) and hides some (Person). The Customer and Employee delegate common responsibilities (e.g., know name, address, phone number) to the Person class, thereby allowing the same person object to be both a customer and an employee. Also internal to the Domain Cluster is the encapsulated cluster, Credit Verification Cluster. This cluster diagram also illustrates a bi-directional association (between Rental and Customer) including both associated unidirectional association labels (as specified later in this document). These two labels can be read as "Rental is made to a Customer" and "Customer rents items via a Rental."

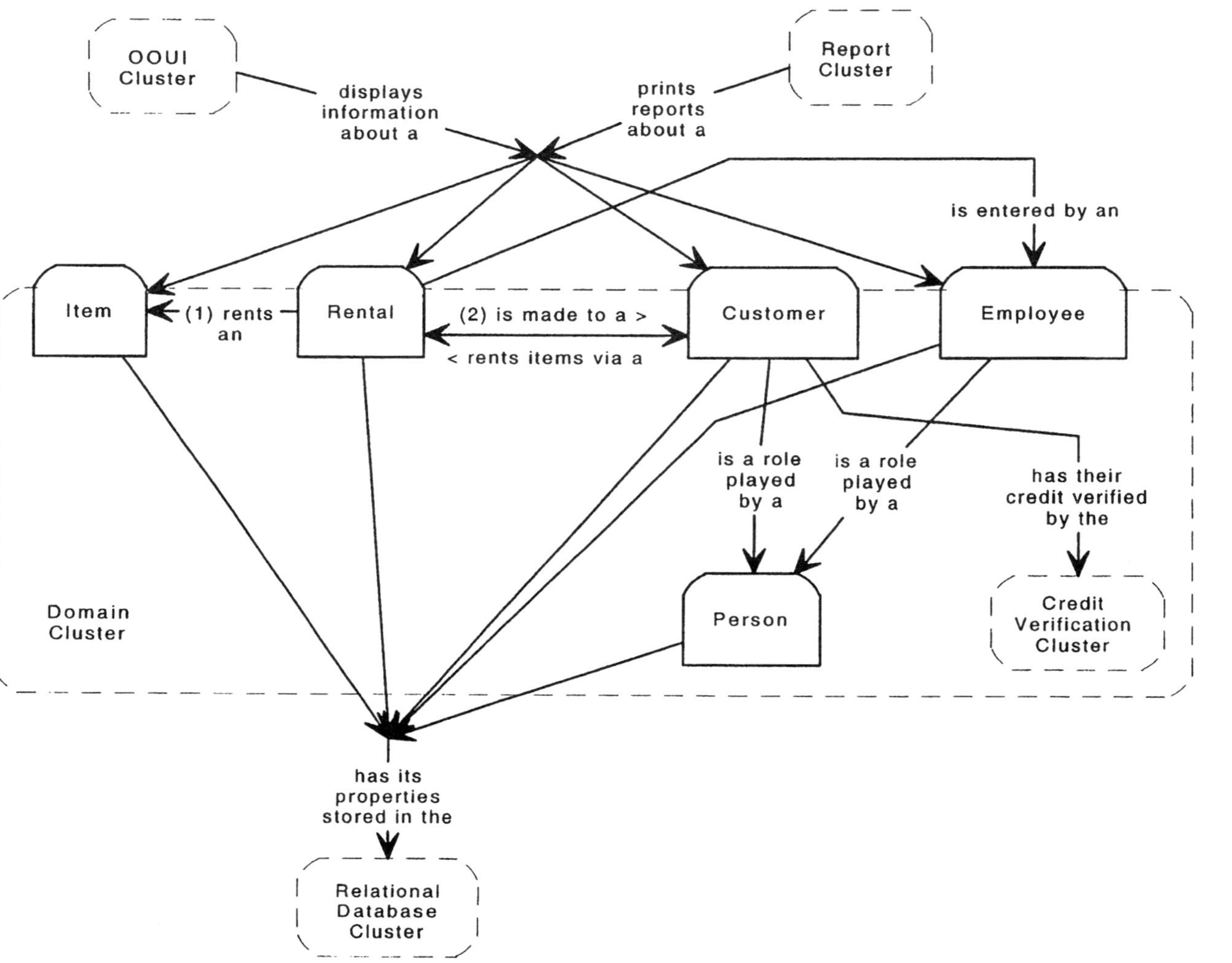

Figure 3.14. Class icons on a cluster diagram for a rental application.

Figure 3.15 illustrates the use of class icons in an internal collaboration diagram of a Customer class from a vending machine application. This diagram documents the Customer class, its internal characteristics, the internal collaborations between its characteristics, and its external collaborations with its clients and servers. The ovals represent visible and hidden operations, and the object icons represent encapsulated parts. The order of message passing and the associated operation execution is labeled on the arcs. The figure uses the Smalltalk naming convention for the names of the classes and operations. This includes the use of colons to separate keywords (add) from their parameters (aMoney).

3.1.2 Clusters and their Classes and Types

Definitions

The following definitions provide semantics to the associated partial metamodel:

cluster instance *n.* any uniquely-identified instance of a cluster class that is a cohesive collection of collaborating objects, classes, cluster instances, and optionally non–object-oriented software such as common global data and common global operations. Clustering is also used to control size and complexity by providing a unit of modularity larger than a class. A cluster is usually used to encapsulate the software that is typically developed as a unit by a small team, but it is also used to capture the implementation of a pattern, a layer, a subdomain, or a distribution unit.

- **logical cluster** *n.* any requirements analysis-level or logical design-level cluster used for documenting.
- **physical cluster** *n.* any physical design-level or coding-level cluster used for allocating actual software to hardware.
- **layer** *n.* any large, horizontal cluster used as a strategic architectural unit of design.
- **distribution unit** *n.* any cluster, the members of which are guaranteed to be allocated to a processor or process as a group. Distribution units have the stereotype "location." Members of the same distribution unit communicate locally, whereas members of different distribution units may communicate remotely if distributed to different processors or processes.[14]

---

[14]Distribution units will be listed in drop-down boxes on nodes on deployment diagrams, which are explained later.

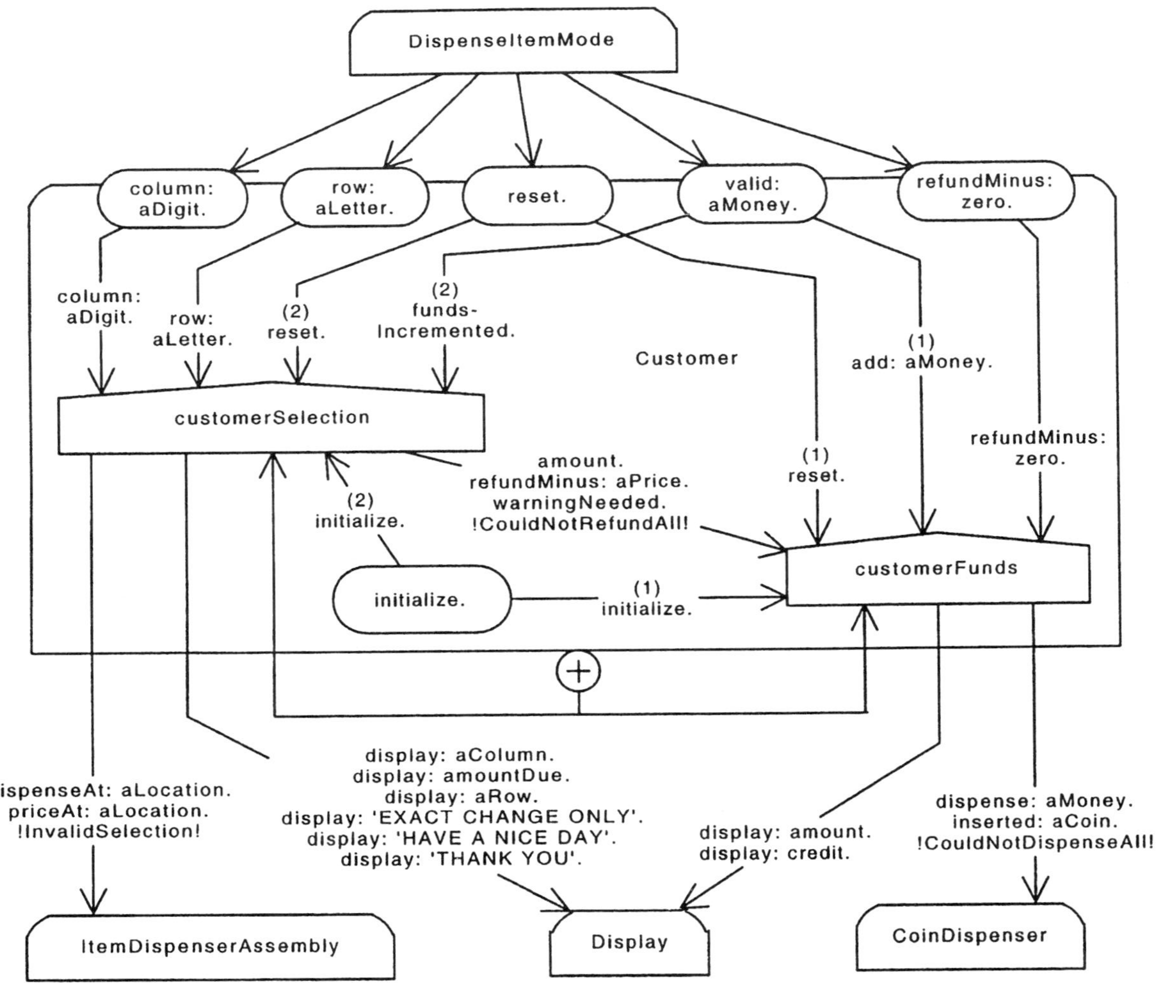

Figure 3.15. Class icons on an internal collaboration diagram.

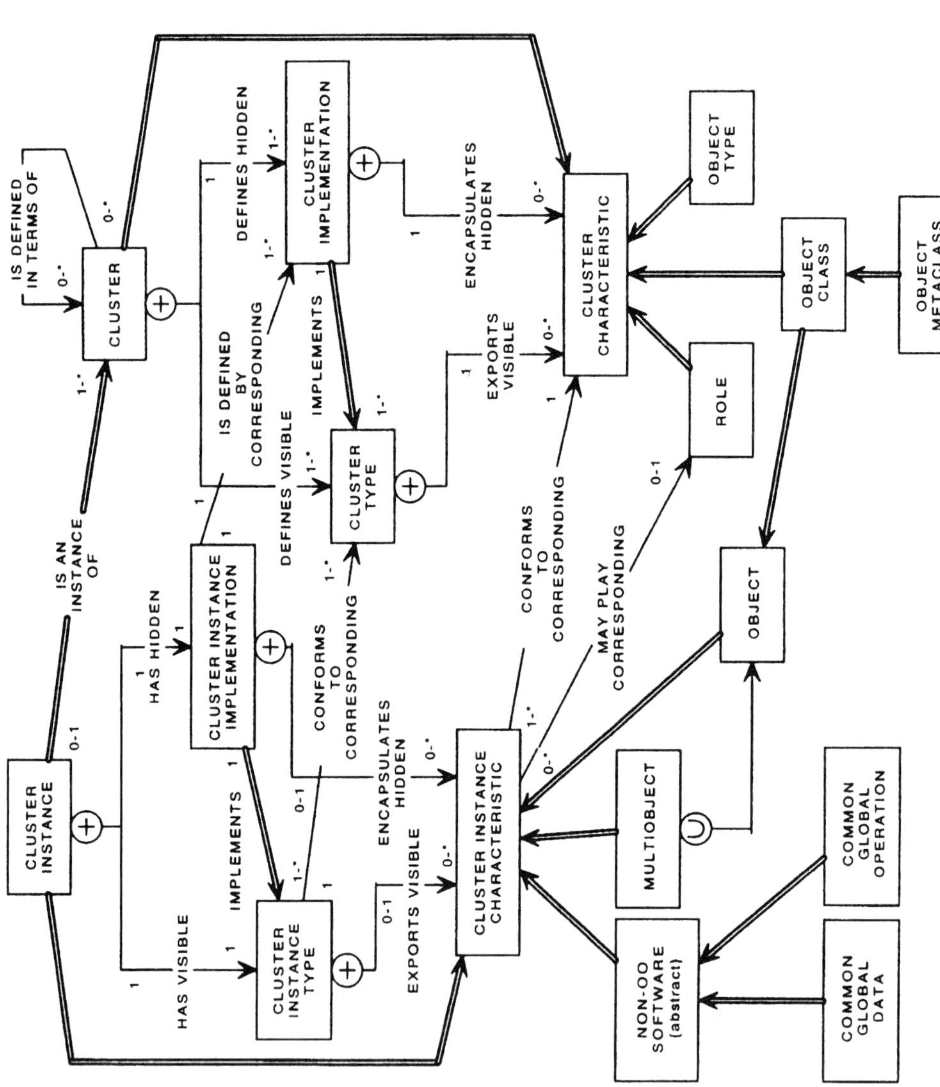

Figure 3.16. Partial metamodel for clusters and their classes and types.

cluster [class] *n.* any class that defines (and optionally can be used to instantiate) clusters (its instances) that have the same or similar characteristics. A cluster class has an interface consisting of one or more cluster types and one or more cluster class implementations that implement these types.[15]

cluster type *n.* any declaration of visible characteristics that form all or part of the interface of a single kind of cluster. A cluster conforms to a cluster type if and only if its interface is consistent with the type (i.e., the set of visible characteristics in the interface of the cluster is a superset of the set of characteristics declared by the type).

cluster class implementation *n.* any declaration of hidden characteristics that form all or part of the implementation of a single kind of cluster.

cluster instance characteristic *n.* any resource or feature (i.e., any object, multiobject, object class, cluster, common global data, common global operation) that makes up the cluster.

cluster [class] characteristic *n.* any specification of a cluster characteristic (i.e., any object class, object type, or role) that makes up the cluster class and defines a kind of cluster instance characteristic.

- **role** *n.* any partial declaration of a kind of object, the declared characteristics of which are required to fulfill a cohesive set of responsibilities. Such an object is said to play the role.

OML Metamodel

Figure 3.16 illustrates a partial OML metamodel documenting the key cluster-level concepts of object-orientation and the semantically important relationships among them. This partial metamodel captures the following information:

- Each cluster instance may have one or more cluster instance types and one or more cluster instance implementations:

    — Each cluster instance type consists of externally visible cluster instance characteristics (and the implicit behavioral dependencies among them) that conform to the corresponding cluster characteristics in the cluster type.

---

[15]Note that the term cluster by itself has historically meant a cluster class and not an instance of a cluster class.

- — Each cluster instance implementation consists of encapsulated (i.e., hidden) cluster instance characteristics that are defined by the corresponding cluster implementation.

- The characteristics of a cluster instance can be objects, multiobjects, object classes, other cluster instances, and non-object-oriented software (i.e., common global data and common global operations).
- Each cluster instance is the instance of one or more clusters, but not all clusters need to have instances.
- Each cluster must have one or more types and one or more cluster implementations that implement the types.

  - — Each cluster type consists of one or more visible exported cluster characteristics.
  - — Each cluster implementation encapsulates zero or more hidden cluster characteristics.

- The characteristics of a cluster can be object classes, object types, other cluster, and roles.
- Each cluster may be defined in terms of zero or more other clusters.
- When instantiating a cluster, each cluster characteristic results in the production of one or more corresponding cluster instance characteristics in the corresponding cluster instance. After instantiation, each resulting cluster instance characteristic conforms to the corresponding cluster characteristic in the cluster:

  - — Each object in the cluster instance either:
    - – is an instance of the corresponding object class in the cluster,
    - – conforms to the corresponding object type in the cluster, or
    - – plays the corresponding role in the cluster.
  - — Each multiobject in the cluster instance is a collection of objects that either:
    - – are instances of the corresponding object class in the cluster,
    - – conform to the corresponding object type in the cluster, or
    - – plays the corresponding role in the cluster.
  - — Each cluster instance in the cluster instance is an instance of the corresponding cluster in the cluster.

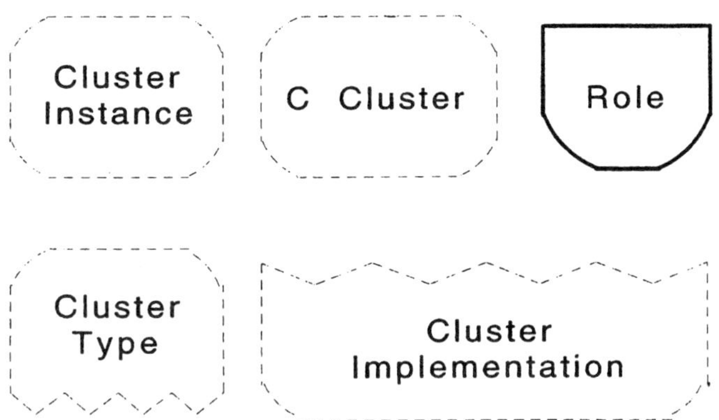

Figure 3.17. Basic cluster-level icons.

COMN Notation

cluster instance. A single cluster instance is represented by a dashed rectangle, the four corners of which are rounded. The label of a cluster instance icon is a character string consisting of the name of the cluster.

cluster. A cluster is represented by a dashed rectangle, the four corners of which are rounded. The label of a cluster icon is a character string consisting of a capital 'C' followed by a space followed by the name of the cluster.

cluster type. A cluster type is represented by a dashed rectangle, the top two corners of which are rounded, and the bottom of which is jagged. The label of a cluster type icon is a character string consisting of the name of the type. Thus, the icon for a cluster type is the top half of the icon of an cluster class, horizontally ripped in two.

cluster implementation. A cluster implementation is represented by a dashed rectangle, the top of which is jagged and the bottom two corners of which are rounded. The label of an cluster implementation icon is a character string consisting of the name of the cluster implementation. Thus, the icon for an cluster implementation is the bottom half of the icon for a cluster class, horizontally ripped in two.

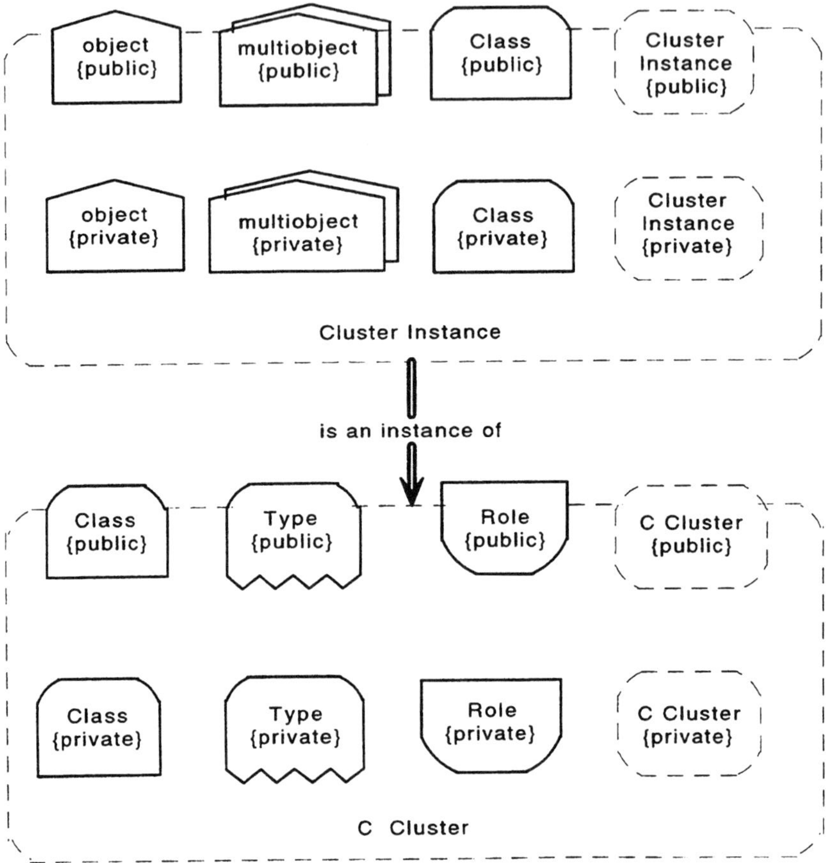

Figure 3.18. Documenting visibility of cluster-level characteristics.

visibility and encapsulation. Throughout COMN, the following technique illustrated in Figure 3.18 is used to distinguish externally visible nodes from hidden ones:

- any icon drawn straddling the boundary of a cluster instance or cluster
  represents a characteristic that is part of the public (i.e., externally visible) interface of the cluster instance or cluster.

- any icon drawn within the boundary of a cluster instance or cluster represents a characteristic that is part of the hidden implementation of the
  cluster instance or cluster.

Clusters and cluster instances form namespaces. The names of object and class characteristics must only be unique within the object or class in which they are encapsulated.

role. A single role is represented by in inverted tablet (i.e., a solid rectangle, the bottom two corners of which are rounded). The label of a role icon is a character string consisting of the name of the role.

Applicable Diagrams

Icons for clusters instances, clusters, cluster types, cluster implementations, and roles can occur on the following kinds of diagrams:

- Context Diagrams
- Layer Diagrams
- Cluster Diagrams
- Software Collaboration Diagrams

Node Parenting Rules

The following node parenting rules document the permitted straddling and nesting of visible and hidden subnodes.

Clusters may:

- export objects, multiobjects, object classes, and clusters.
- hide objects, multiobjects, object classes, and clusters.

Cluster classes may:

- export object classes, the metaclass, cluster classes, roles, and mechanisms.
- hide object classes, the metaclass, cluster classes, roles, and mechanisms.

Usage Guidelines

1. Use clusters to decompose the application into manageable pieces.
2. Base cluster boundaries on coupling, cohesion, and team development considerations.
3. Use roles to document mechanisms and patterns (idioms, design patterns, frameworks).

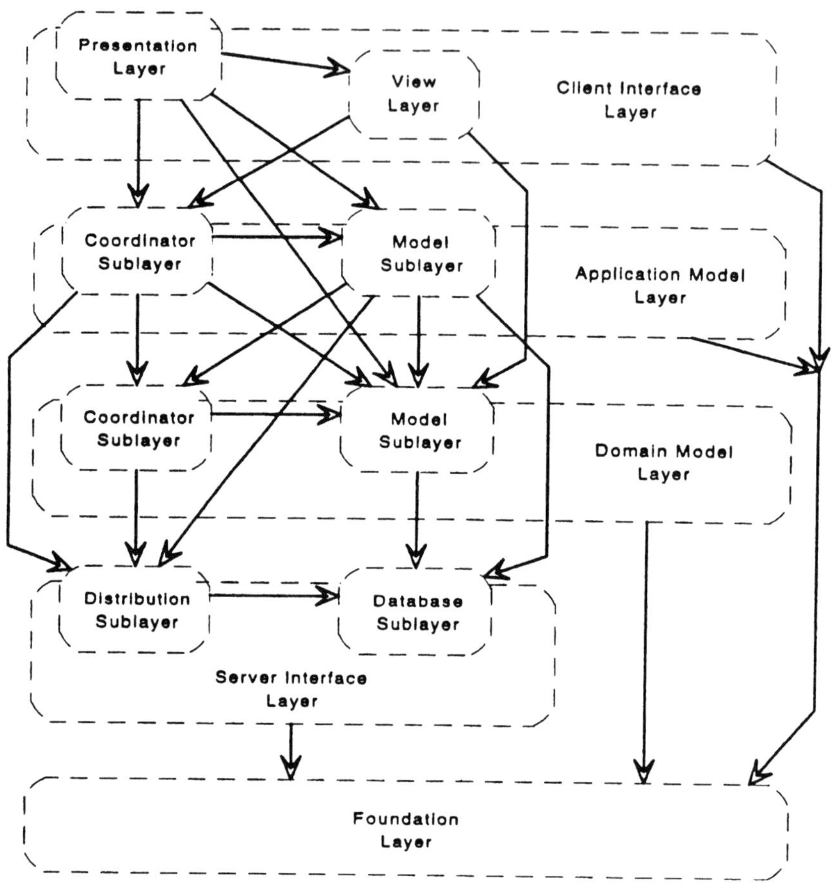

Figure 3.19. Clusters on a layer diagram.

Rationale

In small applications, one typically first identifies objects and classes and then groups them into clusters by drawing a dashed line around them to mark the cluster boundaries. Dashed lines are easy to draw by hand and are easily differentiated from the solid lines used for other nodes in diagrams which allow clusters.

In larger applications, initial clusters are often identified by a project architect; the following clusters are typically identified recursively as part of the iterative, incremental, parallel development cycle.

The use of a rectangle with bottom rounded corners for a role icon is reminiscent of the shape of the medieval masks used by actors in plays.

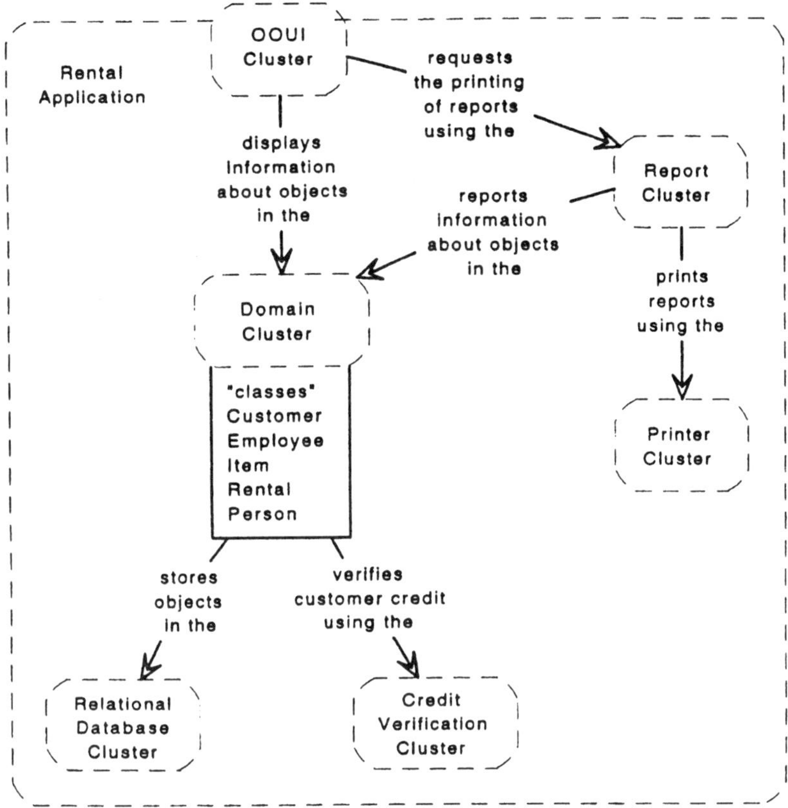

Figure 3.20. Clusters on a configuration diagram for a rental application.

Examples

Figure 3.19 illustrates how cluster icons can be used to document layers in a layer diagram and the dependency relationships between the layers. This can be thought of as akin to the traditional three layer architecture or as an enhancement thereof. Cluster characteristics (e.g., classes, types, roles) in the higher layers typically are built upon and use services provided by characteristics in lower levels, but rarely vice versa. The unlabeled associations can be interpreted as general dependency relationships.

Figure 3.20 illustrates the use of cluster icons on the cluster diagram of a rental application. Only the OOUI cluster is visible externally to clients of the Rental Application cluster. Five other clusters are encapsulated inside the Rental

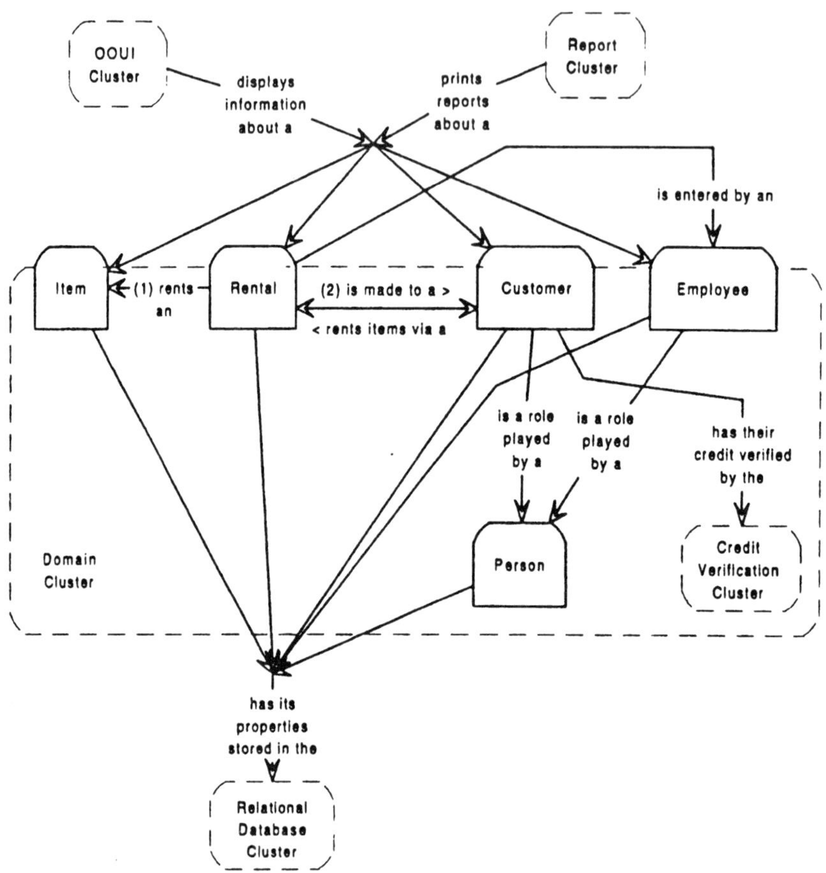

Figure 3.21. Clusters on a cluster diagram for a rental application.

Application cluster, and one of these (Domain Cluster) is documented in more detail using COMN's drop-down box technique. This shows that the Domain Cluster contains the classes Customer, Employee, Item, Rental, and Person.

Figure 3.21 illustrates the use of cluster icons on a cluster diagram documenting the domain model cluster of a rental application. Some clusters are globally visible and interact with each other freely (OOUI, Report, Relational Database, and Domain). On the other hand, the Credit Verification cluster is embedded within the Domain cluster and may not be accessed from outside the Domain cluster.

Figure 3.22 illustrates the use of cluster class icons on an inheritance diagram documenting cluster inheritance. Note that the child cluster class (1) inherits the

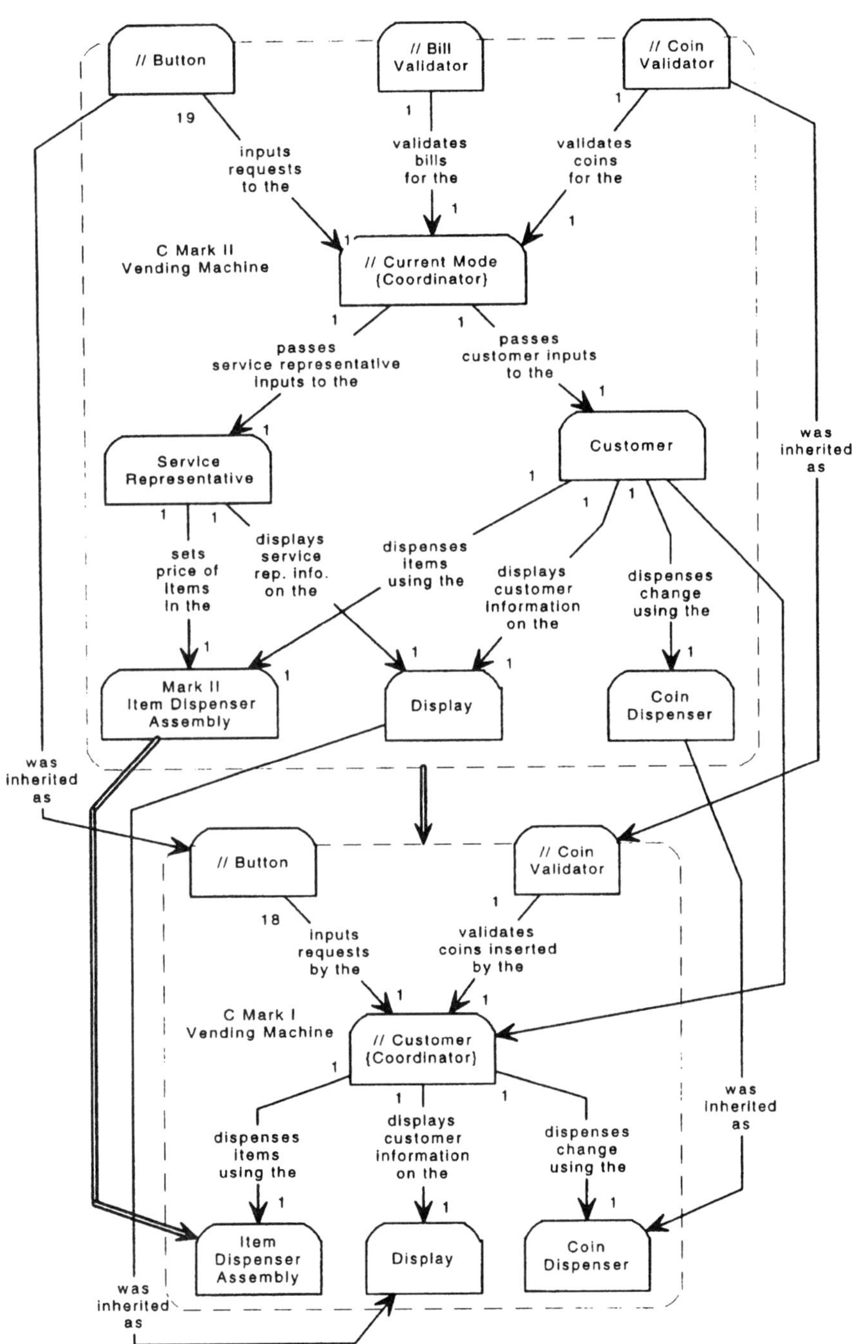

Figure 3.22. Cluster inheritance between cluster classes.

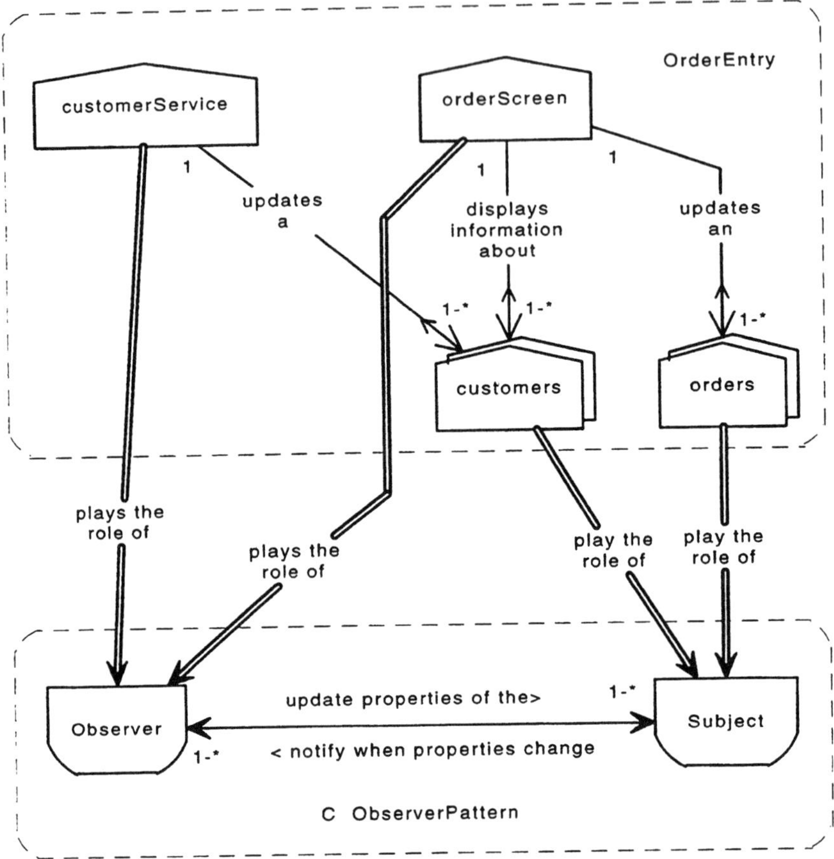

Figure 3.23. Example use of roles to document a pattern.

classes and associations from the parent cluster class, (2) overrides one of the object classes in the parent cluster class with a subclass, and (3) adds additional object classes and associations.

Figure 3.23 illustrates the use of role icons to document the Observer pattern. Both the orderScreen and the customerScreen objects play the Observer role, and customers and orders (both multiobjects) play the Subject role.

3.1.3 Scenarios and their Classes

Definitions

The following definitions provide semantics to the associated partial metamodel:

scenario *n.* any specific, contiguous set of interactions that is not completely implemented as a single operation within an instance or class. any instance of a scenario class.

- **usage scenario** *n.* any scenario that captures a complete functional abstraction that provides something of value to the users of the application.

scenario class *n.* any definition of a functionally cohesive class of scenarios (i.e., one that provides a single functional abstraction). OML recognizes the following kinds of scenario classes:

- **mechanism** *n.* a mid-sized pattern of collaborating roles, the cooperative behavior of which provides a desired functional abstraction.
- **task script** *n.* any scenario class that defines a business process, possibly independent of any application.
- **use case** *n.* any general, requirements-level way of using an application described in terms of interactions between an application as a blackbox and its externals. A class of usage scenarios.

scenario type *n.* any declaration of the externally visible aspects of a scenario class, typically including name, parameters (if any), preconditions, and post-conditions.

path *n.* any contiguous list of instances or classes that are involved in a single scenario. A scenario class may have multiple paths, each of which may be traversed by multiple scenarios of the scenario class.

- **primary path** *n.* any of the more common or important paths through a given scenario class.
- **secondary path** *n.* any of the less common or important paths through a given scenario class. Secondary paths are often variants of a primary path that provide exception handling.

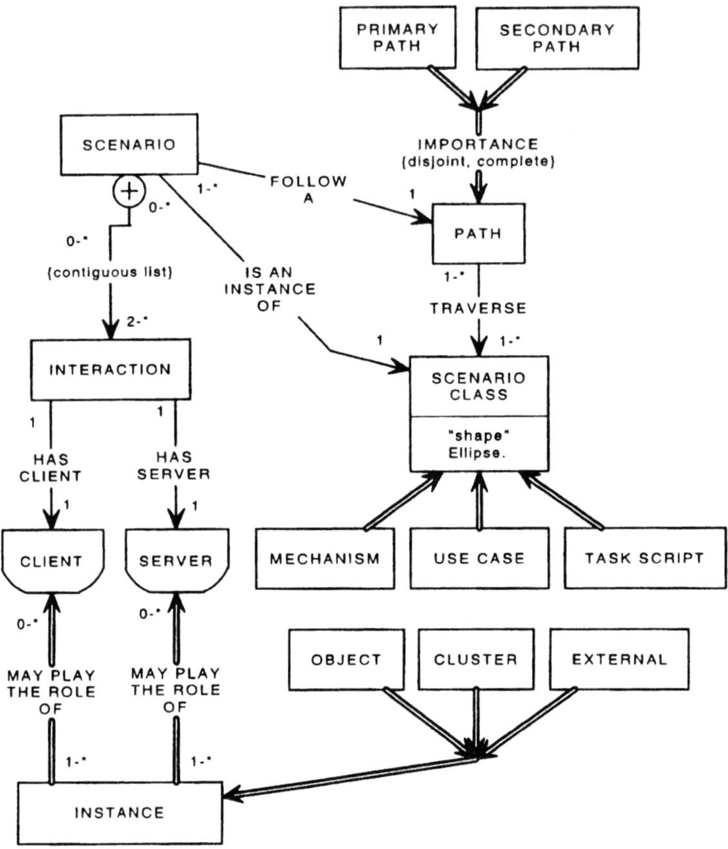

Figure 3.24. Partial metamodel for scenarios and their classes.

OML Metamodel

Figure 3.24 illustrates a partial OML metamodel documenting scenarios, scenario classes, and their relationships. This partial metamodel captures the following information:

- Each scenario is an instance of a single scenario class.
- Each scenario follows a path that traverses the associated scenario class.
- Each path is classified as either primary or secondary based on importance.
- Scenarios can be either mechanisms, use cases, or task scripts.

- Each scenario consists of a list of contiguous[16] interactions connecting clients to servers.
- Objects, clusters, and externals are different kinds of instances that may play the roles of client and server in the interactions that make up scenarios.

Notation

scenario. A scenario is represented by an ellipse. The label of a scenario icon is a character string consisting a capital S followed by a space followed by either:

- the name of the scenario, a space, a colon, a space, and the name of its class (e.g., 'S rental1 : RentItem'),
- the name of the corresponding scenario (e.g., 'S rental') if the class is either unimportant or understood, or
- a colon followed by a space followed by the name of the object's class (e.g., 'S : RentItem') if the name of the scenario is unimportant.

scenario class. A scenario class is represented by an ellipse. The label of a scenario class icon is a character string consisting of a capital 'C' followed by a space followed by the name of the scenario class (e.g., 'C RentItem').

path. A path is represented by an ellipse. The label of a path icon is a character string consisting of a capital 'P' followed by a space followed by the name of the path (e.g., 'P Path1').

visibility. Throughout COMN, the following technique is used to distinguish externally visible nodes from hidden ones:

- Any icon drawn straddling the boundary of a cluster instance or cluster represents a characteristic that is part of the public (i.e., externally visible) interface of the cluster instance or cluster.
- Any icon drawn within the boundary of a cluster instance or cluster represents a characteristic that is part of the hidden implementation of the cluster instance or cluster.

---

[16]Two interactions are contiguous if the server of the first is the client of the second (e.g., if the receiver of a message is the sender of the next message).

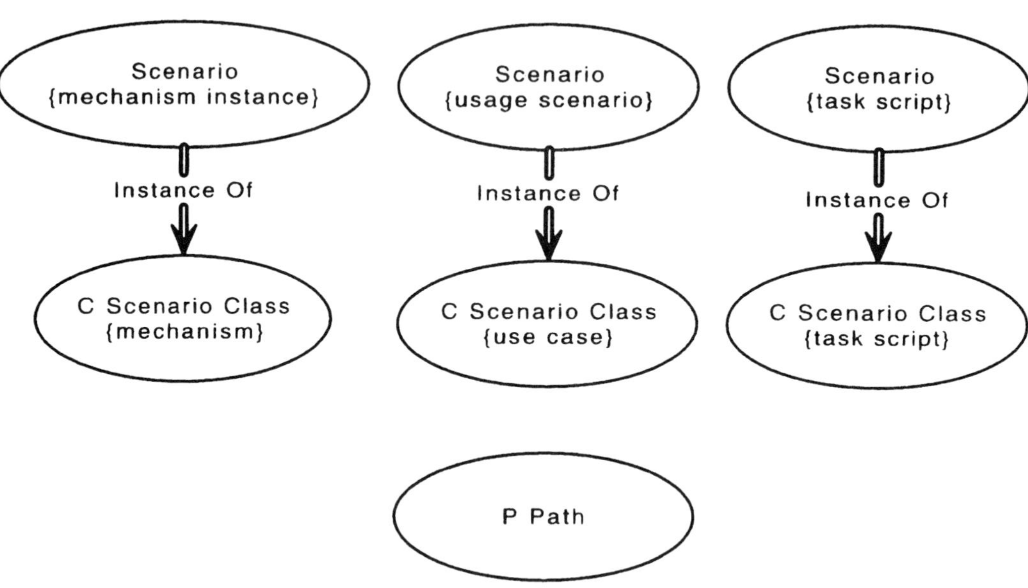

Figure 3.25. Icons for scenarios, scenario classes, and paths.

Stereotypes

Stereotypes of scenario classes include:

- Mechanism vs. Task Script vs. Use Case.
- Partial vs. Complete.

Stereotypes of paths include:

- Primary vs. Secondary.
- Normal vs. Exceptional.

Applicable Diagrams

Icons for scenarios and scenario classes can be used on the following kinds of diagrams:

- Cluster Diagrams
- Scenario Class Diagrams
- Sequence Diagrams

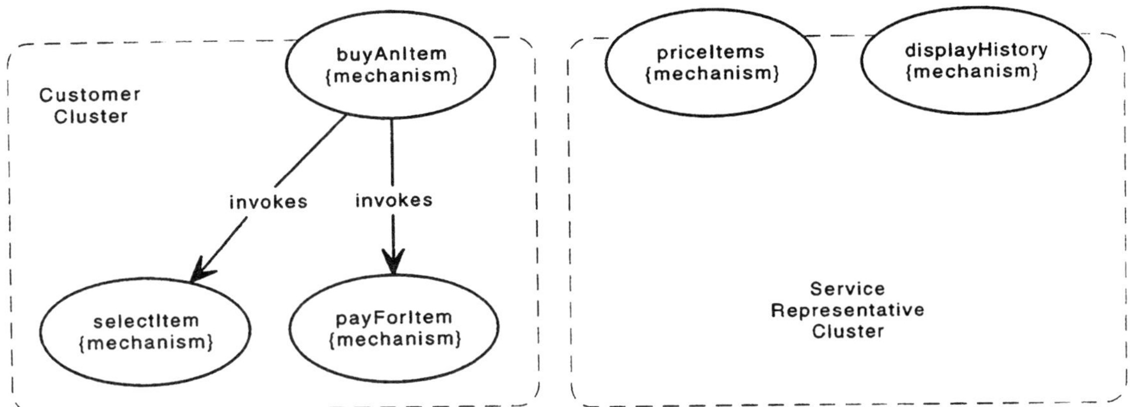

Figure 3.26. Mechanism icons on a cluster diagram of a vending machine application.

Node Parenting Rules

Only drop-down boxes can be children of scenario and scenario class icons.

Usage Guidelines

1. Remember that scenarios, scenario classes, and paths are functional rather than object-oriented and should therefore be used with great care.
2. Avoid functionally decomposing the scenario classes too far or without adequate reason.
3. Use *task scripts* during business process engineering when there is no application per se.
4. Use *use cases* to capture the blackbox requirements of a application.
5. Use *mechanisms* to capture the whitebox behavior of a set of collaborating roles.
6. Use a representative scenario from each path in a set of basis paths as the test cases to test the scenario class.

Rationale

All COMN icons representing functional abstractions are rounded. COMN uses the now traditional ellipse icon, popularized by Ivar Jacobson.

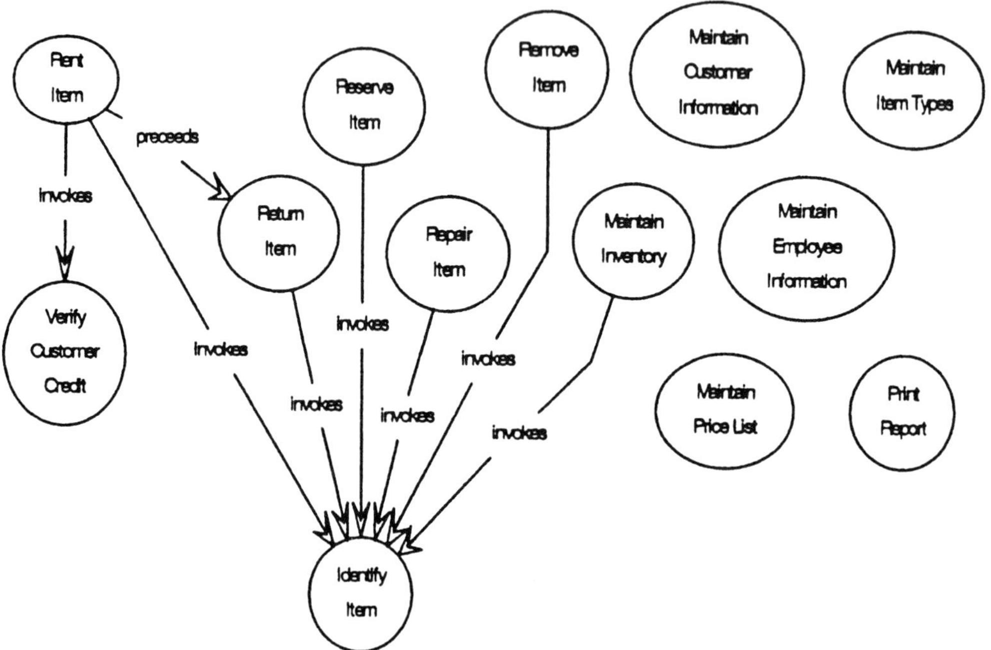

Figure 3.27. Scenario class icons on a task script diagram.

Examples

Figure 3.26 illustrates the use of mechanism icons on a cluster diagram from a vending machine application. Note that the buyAnItem mechanism is visible outside the Customer cluster, but the selectItem and payForItem mechanisms are not.

Figure 3.27 illustrates the use of scenario class icons on a task script diagram. This diagram supports functional abstraction and the functional decomposition of task scripts.

Figure 3.28 illustrates the use of scenario class icons on a sequence diagram. This diagram supports functional abstraction (each use case encapsulates numerous interactions deemed to be at too low of a level of detail to be shown on the sequence diagram).

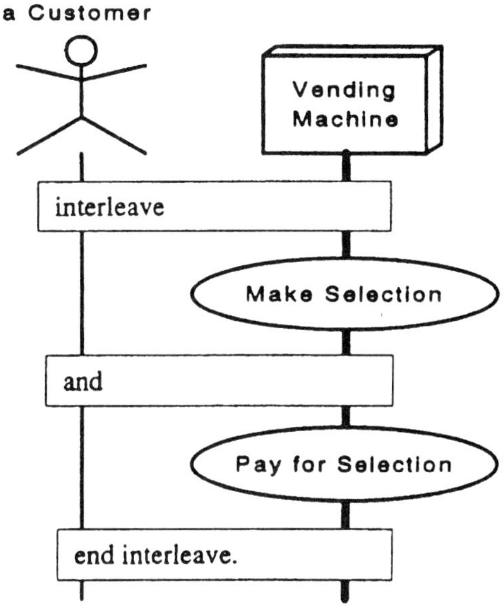

Figure 3.28. Scenario class icons on a sequence diagram.

3.1.4 Drop-Down Boxes

Definitions

The following definitions provide semantics to the partial metamodel documented by Figure 3.29:

drop-down box *n.* any optional rectangular node attached to the bottom outside of its parent node, used to display a subset of the information stored about its parent node based on a selection of traits.

trait *n.* any specific information about a particular modeling element, typically documented in the element's drop-down box (e.g., its description, its responsibilities, its public protocol, its assertions, its characteristics of a class).

trait kind *n.* any general kind of information about a modeling element (e.g., "description," "responsibilities," "public protocol," "assertions," "characteristics," "stereotypes"); a class of traits.

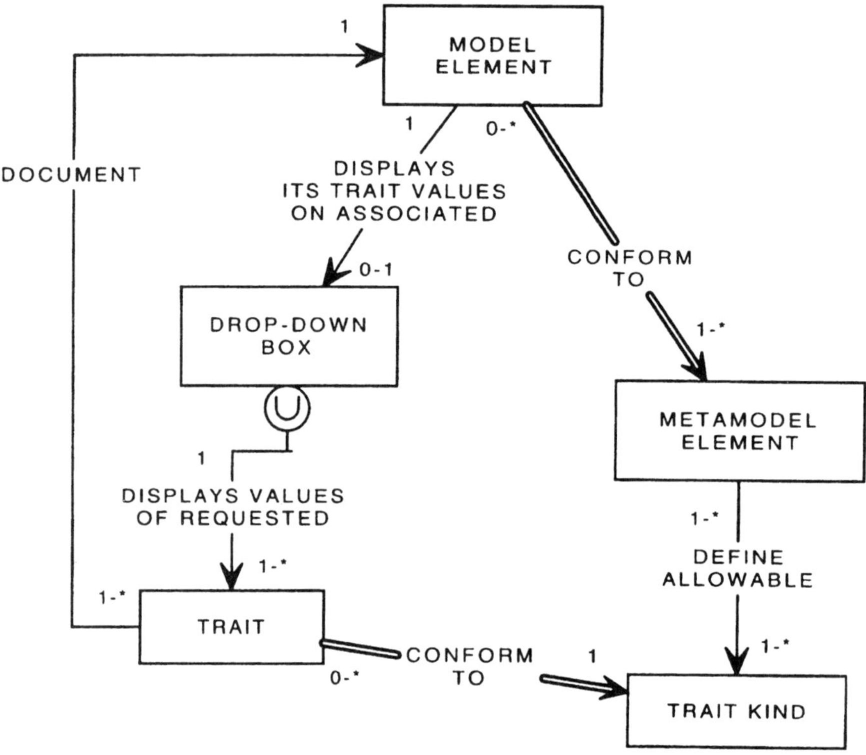

Figure 3.29. Partial metamodel for drop-down boxes.

OML Metamodel

Figure 3.29 illustrates a partial OML metamodel documenting drop-down boxes, traits, and their relationships. This partial metamodel captures the following information:

- Any metamodel element have an optional drop-down box that displays a requested subset of the values of its traits.
- Different kinds of metamodel elements define different allowable kinds of traits.
- The values of the traits document the metamodel elements.

```
┌─────────────────┐        ┌─────────────────┐
│                 │        │                 │
│  "trait kind"   │        │  "trait kind 1" │
│  value 1        │        │  value 1        │
│  value 2        │        │  value 2        │
│                 │        │                 │
└─────────────────┘        ├─────────────────┤
                           │                 │
                           │  "trait kind 2" │
                           │  value 3        │
                           │  value 4        │
                           │                 │
                           └─────────────────┘
```

Figure 3.30. Notation for a drop-down box.

OML Notation

drop-down box. A drop-down box is represented by a rectangle attached to the outside of a node and extending below it. The contents of the drop-down box consist of the trait kind in quotation marks followed by the actual trait values. If a drop-down box is to list the values of multiple kinds of traits, then these collections of traits are separated by horizontal lines. See Figure 3.30, above.

Recommendations for CASE tool Vendors

Drop-down boxes are primarily intended for use with upperCASE tools, but may also be drawn on static paper diagrams. The modeler moves the cursor on top of the node requiring a drop-down box and presses the right mouse button. The CASE tool will display a pop-up list box listing the traits (kinds of information) about the node. The modeler selects one or more traits, and the CASE tool displays the drop-down box containing these traits and if necessary moves arcs accordingly. The drop-down box remains open until explicitly closed by the user. UpperCASE tools may provide a mechanism for closing the drop-down window.

Stereotypes

None.

Applicable Diagrams

Drop-down boxes may be used on all diagrams.

Rules

Allowable parent icons for drop-down boxes include the icons of all modeling elements (both things and relationships) except drop-down boxes.

As far as the arc checking rules for relationships are concerned, a drop-down box represents an extension of its parent node. Therefore, if the parent node is a legitimate node for the client or server end of an arc, then so is a drop-down box of that parent node.

Usage Guidelines

1. Use drop-down boxes to display more information than merely the name but not so much information as to require an entire pop-up window.
2. Use drop-down boxes to show the inherited characteristics of classes in inheritance diagrams so that one can see what characteristics are inherited, made effective, and overridden.
3. Be careful not to select so much information to display on drop-down boxes that one loses track of the forest (i.e., the overall design) for the trees (i.e., the information on the drop-down boxes).

Rationale

The amount and kind of information about a icon that should be displayed on diagrams varies over time due to the appropriate current level of abstraction, the increasing knowledge gained during development, and the purpose of the diagram. Drop-down boxes were designed to support this elaboration of information over time and the need to be able to choose the desired level of abstraction.

For example, a modeler may initially know nothing more meaningful than the name of a class. A textual definition of the class is then produced to ensure that everyone understands the abstraction captured by the class and to ensure that different people do not use the name to mean different things. Public responsibilities are then allocated to the class before getting down to the level of the messages in the public protocol(s) that implement these responsibilities. Only towards the end of detailed design should decisions regarding attributes and hidden operations be made; after all, a logical attribute could be stored as a physical attribute, calculated by an operation, stored in a database, or provided by a server in response to a delegated message.

Clearly, one size does not fit all. We need a flexible way to display the right kind and amount of information on an "as needed" basis.

The question is how much to display and when. If too little information is displayed (e.g., only the name and type of node), assumptions and miscommunication may result. If too much information is displayed on the nodes, then (1) this information overloads the reader, who loses track of the overall picture and either (2) some nodes takes up too much space or (3) a magnifying glass is required to read the information about these nodes.

Drop-Down boxes are a standard technique for providing a small amount of information of a specific kind about any kind of modeling element without cluttering up the diagram. It formalizes the notation of selective visibility introduced by MOSES (a predecessor of OPEN and OML).

Dividing icons into multiple compartments (as in OMT and UML) was rejected as non-workable because it does not scale well. The number and combination of compartments is essentially indefinite, restricted only by the number of different kinds of traits and the developer's inventiveness.

Examples

Figure 3.31 illustrates several possible uses of drop-down boxes. A drop-down box can be attached to any icon and always consists of a heading stating the kind of trait being presented followed by a list of items of this trait kind. When the display of more than one kind of trait is desired, then a horizontal line separates the groups of traits.

Figure 3.32 illustrates several different uses of drop-down boxes on class icons. Drop-down boxes for classes are similar to those shown in Figure 3.31. Each individual entry under each kind of trait is separated by a period. Information on return types (as in the last example) may be useful here.

Figure 3.33 illustrates several different uses of drop-down boxes on external icons.

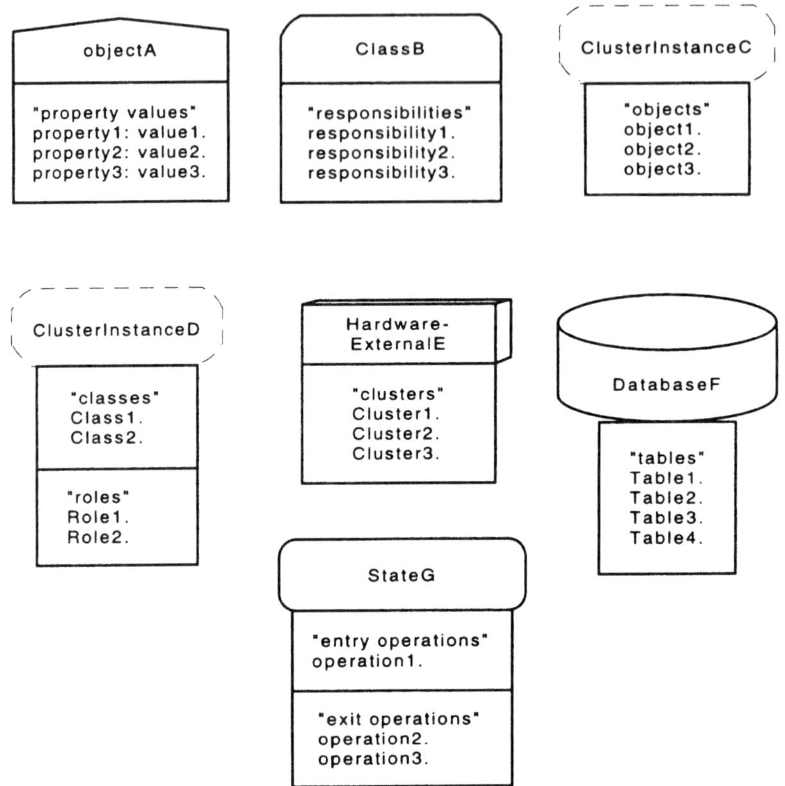

Figure 3.31. Example drop-down boxes.

Figure 3.34 illustrates the use of drop-down boxes to show the parallel nature of instances and classes.

Figure 3.35 illustrates the use of drop-down boxes to explain an inheritance hierarchy. The trait kind "interface" lists the visible characteristics of the class and also assists in understanding which services are newly defined, refined, etc. Note that one subclass delegates to three other subclasses.

Allowable Contents

Object Drop-Down Boxes. The permitted choice of traits for object drop-down boxes includes the following:

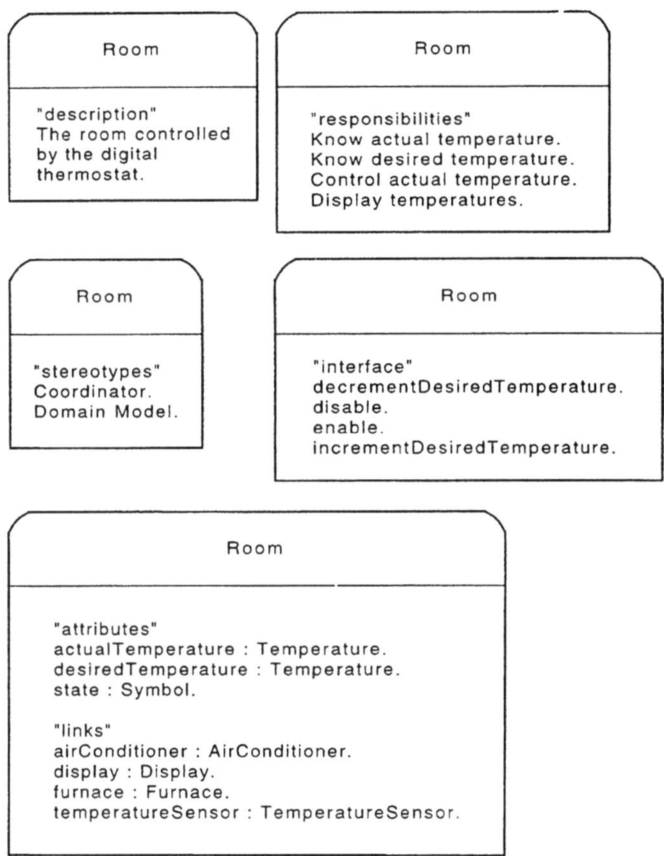

Figure 3.32. Class drop-down boxes.

- Description

  A one sentence description capturing the abstraction of the object.
- Responsibilities
- Property values

Class Drop-Down Boxes. The permitted choice of traits for object class drop-down boxes includes the following:

- Description

  A one sentence description capturing the abstraction of the class.

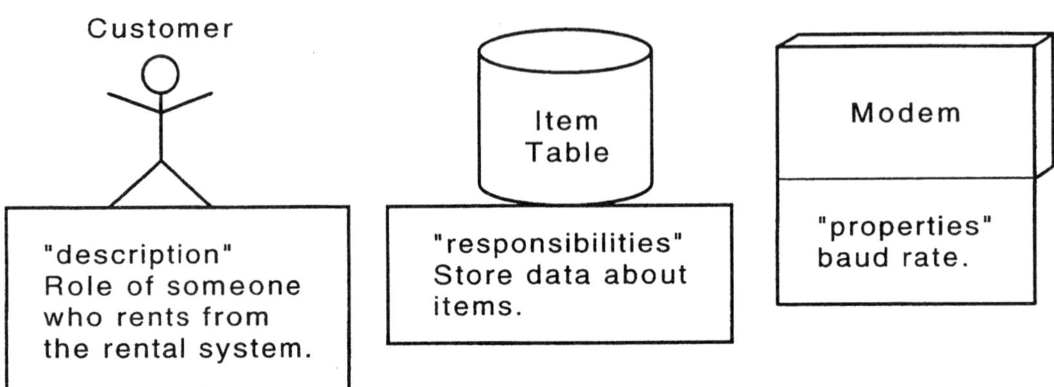

Figure 3.33. Drop-down boxes for externals.

- Public Responsibilities
- Stereotypes

  A character string of enumeration type that either conceptually classifies a class independently from inheritance or provides some other important information about it.

- Class Implementations(s)
- Class Characteristics

  This will include instance level operations, attributes, invariants based on class properties, and exceptions raised by instances of the class.

- Instance Operations
- Instance Attributes
- Instance Rules (i.e., assertions)
- Class Operations
- Class Attributes
- Class Characteristics

Type Drop-Down Boxes. The permitted choice of traits for type drop-down boxes includes the following:

- Description

  A one sentence description capturing the abstraction of the class.

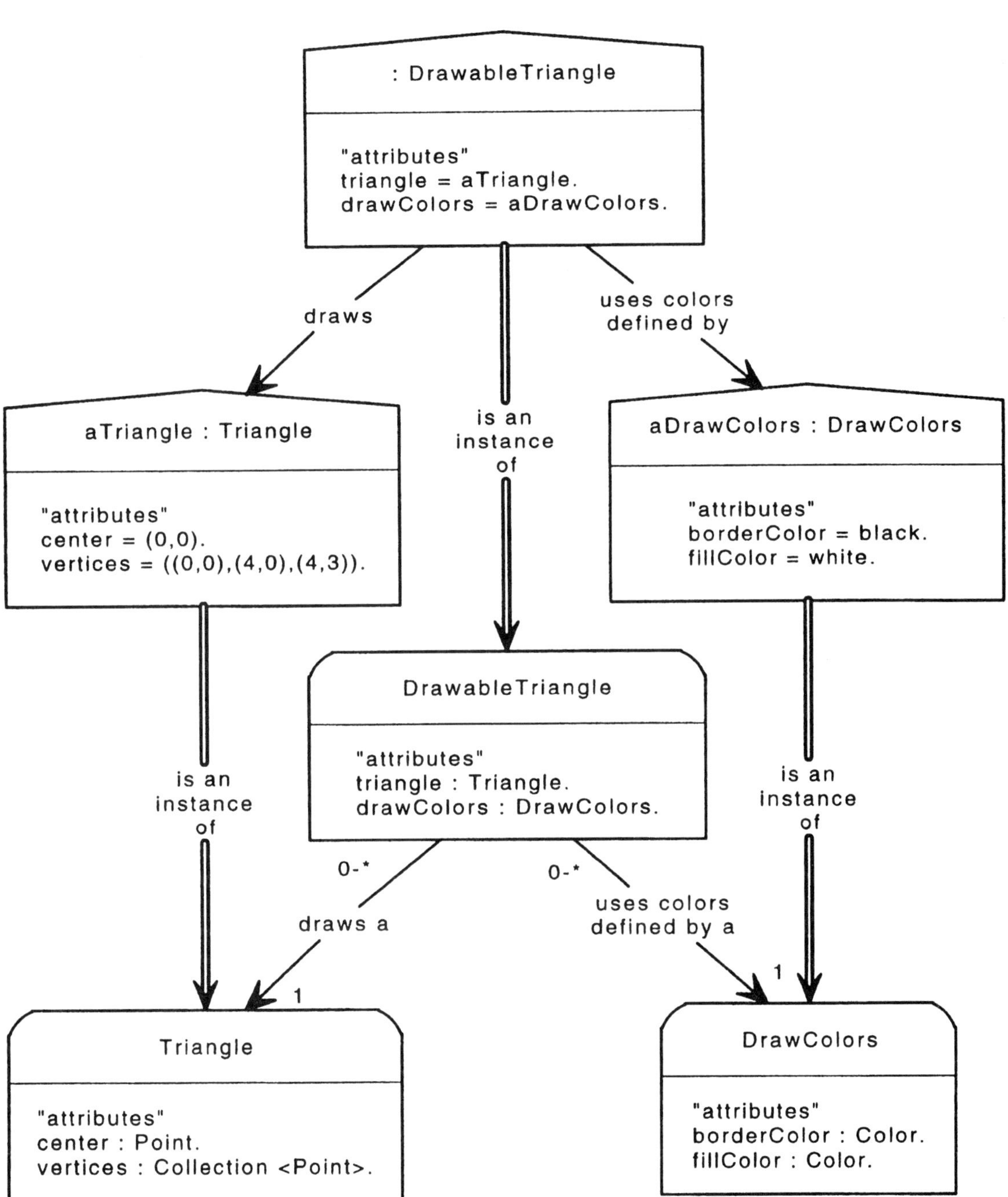

Figure 3.34. Object drop-down boxes.

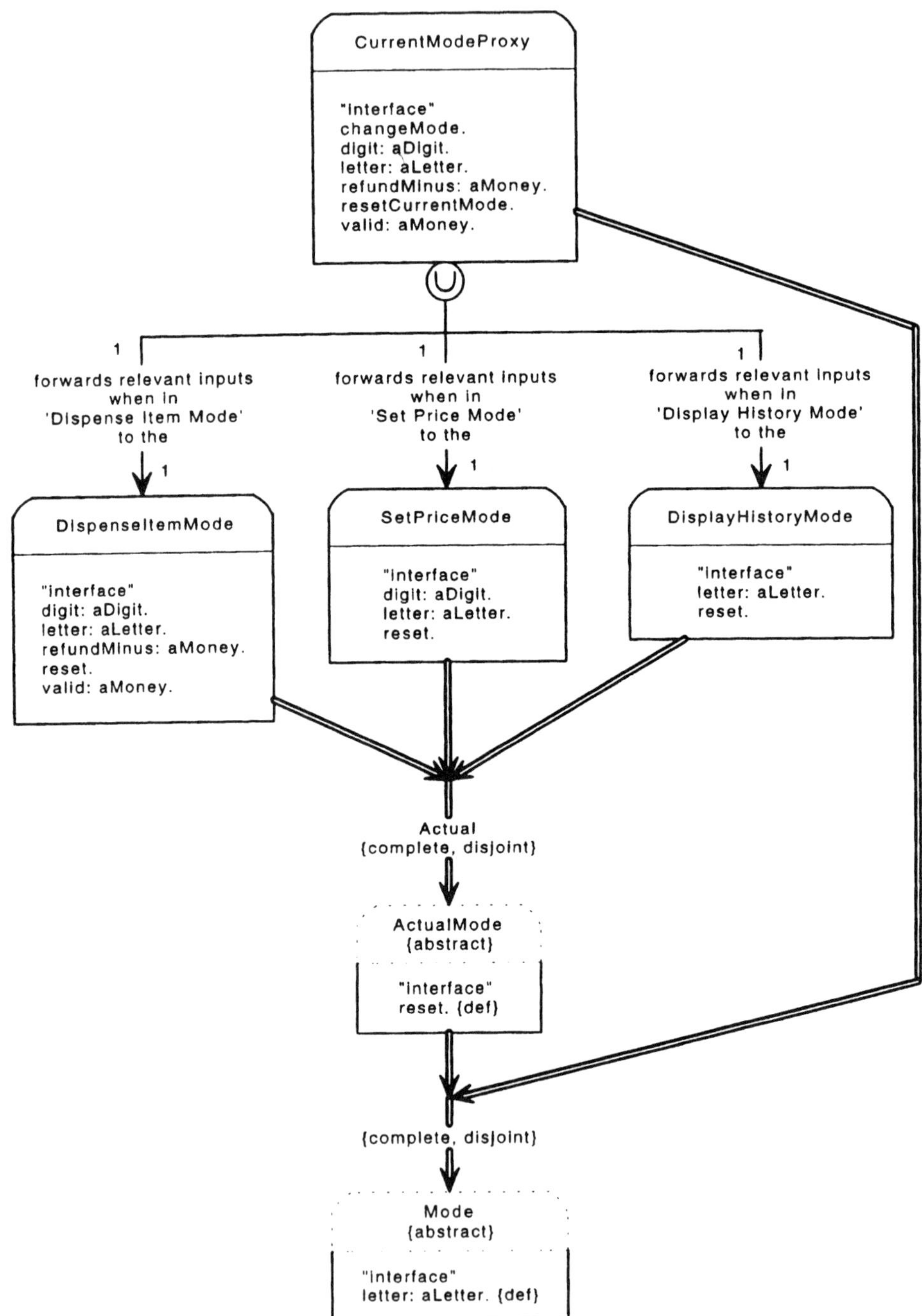

Figure 3.35. Drop-down box for inheritance.

- Public Responsibilities
- Stereotypes

  Examples include: Parameterized; Metaclass; View, Domain, or Foundation.

- Public Protocols

  This will include message signatures, possibly including assertions and exceptions.

Cluster Drop-Down Boxes. The permitted choice of traits for cluster drop-down boxes includes the following:

- Description

  A one sentence description capturing the abstraction of the class.

- Characteristics
- Layer
- Responsibilities

State Drop-Down Boxes. The permitted choice of traits for state drop-down boxes includes the following:

- Operations listed in the drop-down box of a state begin and end in that state. They may also be qualified as entry or exit operations.

Transition Drop-Down Boxes. The permitted choice of traits for transition drop-down boxes includes the following:

- Operations listed in the drop-down box of a transition begin in the pre-transition state and complete execution in the post-transition state.

3.1.5 Non-OO Modeling Elements

Definitions

The following definitions provide semantics to the partial metamodel documented in Figure 3.36:

common global data *n.* any application-internal data that is not stored as a property of some object.

common global operation *n.* any application-internal operation that is not stored as an operation of some object.

common global operations *n.* any logically or physically cohesive collection of common global operations.

internal non-OO database *n.* any application-internal non-object-oriented (e.g., relational, network, hierarchical) database, database table, file, etc.

note *n.* any developer-defined text providing a comment or listing a constraint about a specific modeling element.

OML Metamodel

Figure 3.36 illustrates a partial metamodel for the optional non-OO modeling elements and captures the following information:

- All non-OO modeling elements are things.
- Internal non-OO databases, common global data, collections of common global operations, and common global operations are different kinds of non-OO modeling elements.
- Common global operations are collections of two or more common global operations.

COMN Notation

common global data. Common global data are represented by a traditional data store icon consisting of two parallel horizontal lines. The label of the common global data icon is a character string placed between the horizontal lines.

internal database. An internal non-object-oriented database is represented by a cylinder. The label of the internal database icon is a character string placed on the side of the cylinder. In order to differentiate internal from external databases, internal databases are annotated with the stereotype "{internal}."

common global operation. A common global operation is represented by an oval (i.e., two horizontal parallel lines capped with half circles on each end). The label of a common global operation icon is a verb or verb phrase character string starting with a lower case letter that is placed within the oval.

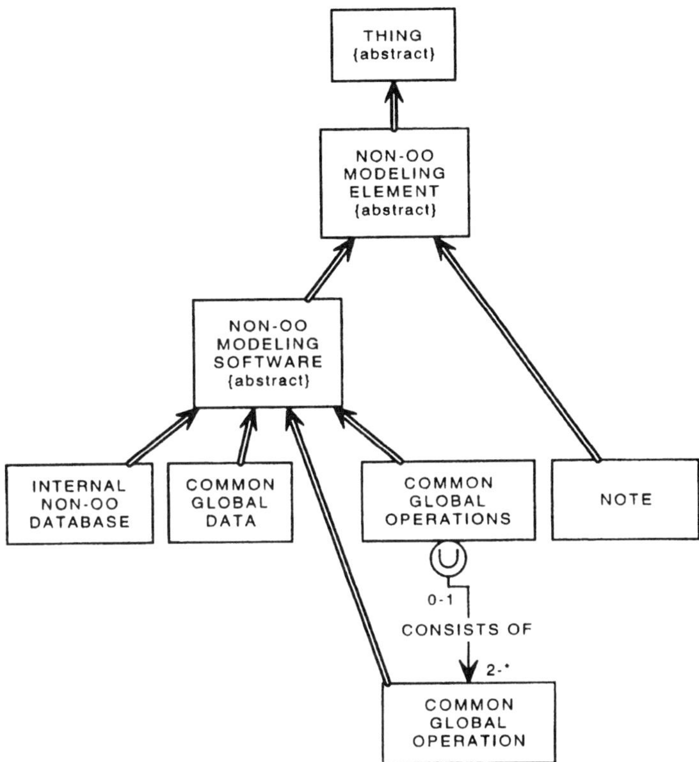

Figure 3.36. Partial metamodel for non-OO modeling elements.

common global operations. Common global operations are represented by two ovals, one behind, above, and to the right of the other. The label of a common global operations icon is a plural noun or noun phrase character string starting with a lower case letter that is placed within the front oval.

note. A note is represented by a rectangle with the upper left corner turned over. The label of a note is any character string.

Applicable Diagrams

Icons for non-object-oriented software can occur on the following kinds of diagrams:

- Cluster Diagrams
- Collaboration Diagrams

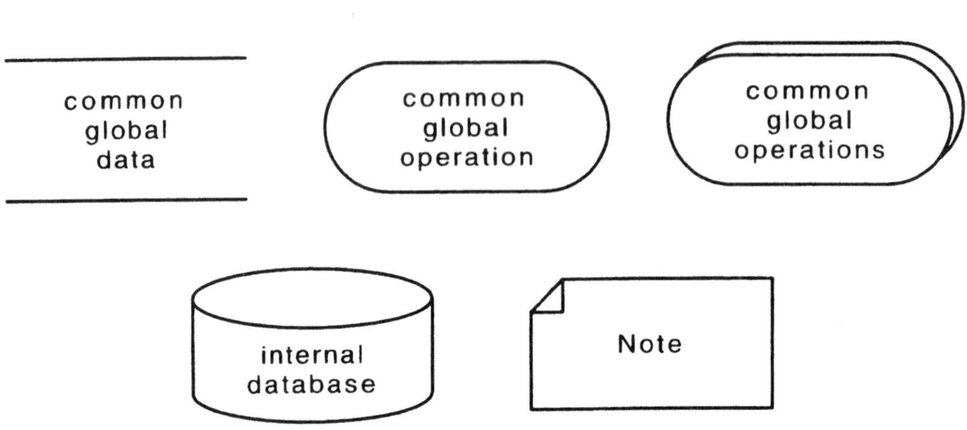

Figure 3.37. Notation for non-OO modeling elements.

Icons for notes can occur on all diagrams.

Usage Guidelines

1. Avoid using the non-OO modeling elements during the logical design of new object-oriented software.
2. Only use non-OO modeling elements when:
   - developing the physical design of hybrid (e.g., C++, Ada95) software that contains non-OO components.
   - reverse engineering hybrid software that contains non-OO components.
   - using a non-OO database as an internal[17] part of a new application.

Rationale

The traditional data store icon was retained to represent common global data.

A cylinder was chosen to represent an internal non-OO database because that is the traditional icon for databases and persistent memory. It is also consistent with the use of a cylinder to represent an external database.

---

[17]Context can be used to differentiate an internal non-OO database from a persistent memory external, even though they use the same icon.

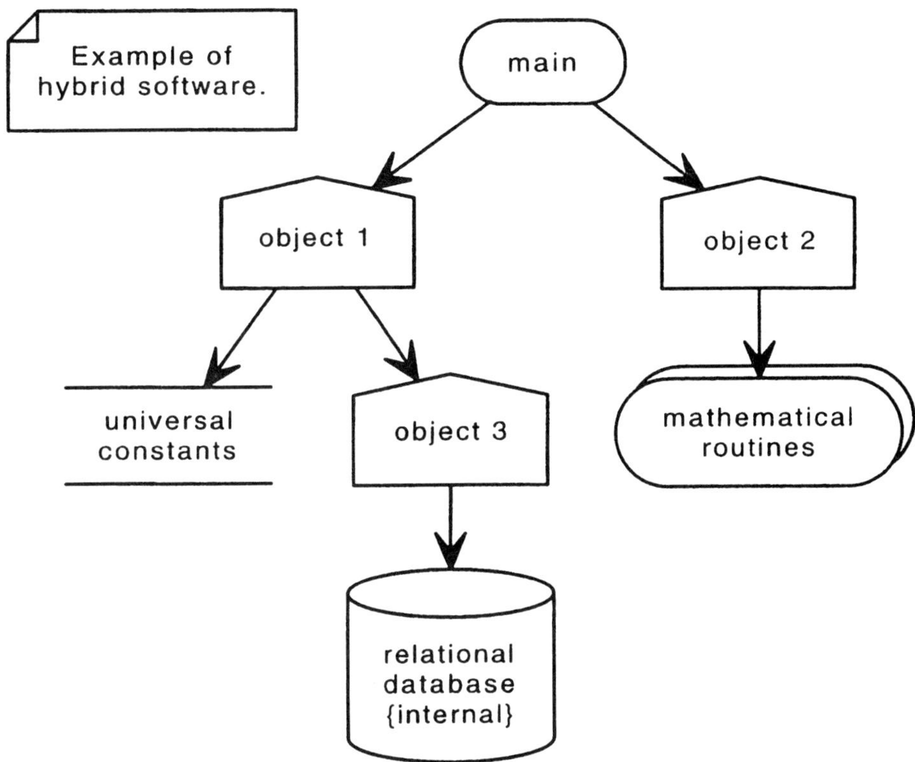

Figure 3.38. Example physical design of hybrid software.

The oval was chosen to represent a common global operation because COMN uses rounded icons for operations (e.g., ellipse for use case) and the parallel top and bottom edges of the icon are reminiscent of the common global data icon.

A pair of ovals was chosen to represent multiple common global operations because it is intuitive and consistent with the multiobject icon.

Example

Figure 3.38 illustrates the physical design of a hybrid applet that uses common global data, common global operations, a relational database, and is labeled with a note.

3.2   Common Relationship Arcs

Definitions

The following definitions provide semantics to the partial metamodel documented in Figure 3.39:

binary unidirectional dependency relationship $n.$ any relationship between two model elements that is directed in the direction of dependency from client to server.

- **definitional relationship** $n.$ any binary unidirectional dependency relationship from one modeling element to another whereby one modeling element depends on the definition provided by another.

- **referential relationship** $n.$ any binary unidirectional dependency relationship whereby one modeling element refers to (i.e., has visibility to) another.

- **scenario relationship** $n.$ any relationship involving a scenario or scenario class.

- **transitional relationship** $n.$ any relationship in which one modeling element transitions or transforms into another.

client $n.$ the role at the start of any binary unidirectional dependency relationship played by the modeling element that depends on the role at the end of the relationship.

server $n.$ the role at the end of any binary unidirectional dependency relationship played by the modeling element, on which the role at the start of the relationship depends.

OML Metamodel

Figure 3.39 illustrates a partial metamodel for OML relationships that captures the following information:

- All modeling elements are completely and disjointedly partitioned into either binary unidirectional dependency relationships (arcs) or things (nodes).

- Each binary unidirectional dependency relationship connects one client to one server, which are roles played by things.

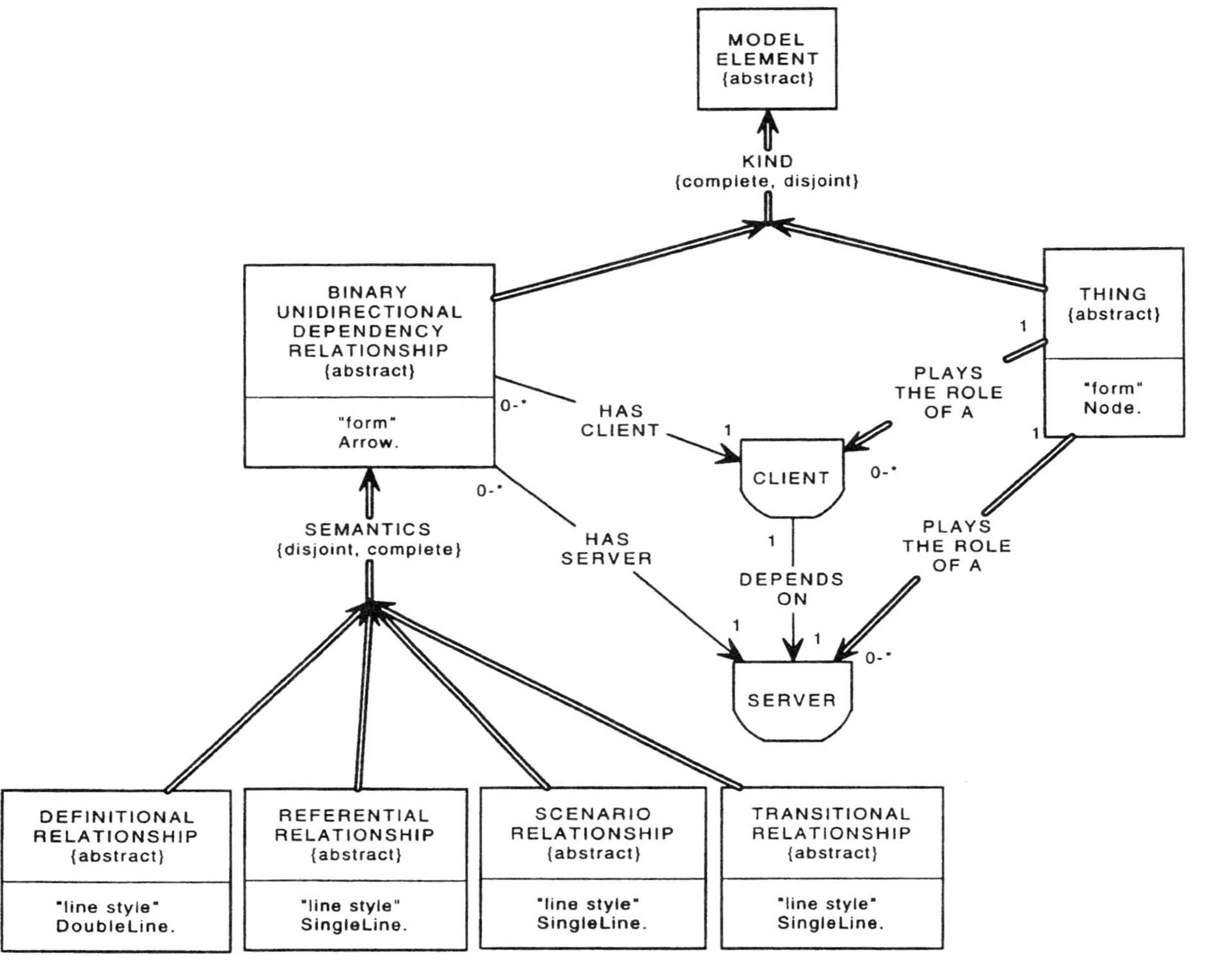

Figure 3.39. Partial metamodel for OML relationships.

- A client depends on its server via the binary unidirectional dependency relationship between them.
- Binary unidirectional dependency relationships are arrows whereas things are nodes.
- Binary unidirectional dependency relationships are completely and disjointedly partitioned into definitional relationship, referential relationship, scenario relationships, or transitional relationships.

COMN Notation

binary unidirectional dependency relationship. A binary unidirectional dependency relationship is represented by a directed arc, drawn in the direction of dependency from the client to the server with some kind of arrow head on the server end.

definitional relationships. All definitional relationships will be denoted by two parallel lines.

referential relationships. Referential relationships will be denoted by only a single line.

scenario relationships. Scenario relationships will be denoted by only a single line.

transitional relationships. Transitional relationships will be denoted by only a single line.

In COMN, the choice of straight lines, connected line segments, or curved lines for relationships has no semantic meaning and is a matter of stylistic convention or personal taste.[18]

Rationale

All object-oriented relationships between modeling elements are binary unidirectional dependency relationships. Therefore, all OML relationships arcs[19] are

---

[18]However, we do recommend that a consistent style be used within a single project or organization.

[19]The two exceptions to this rule are: 1) "bi-directional" association/linkage arcs which have arrowheads at both ends because they represent two unidirectional associations/linkages that are semi-strong inverses of one another so that each end points to the server of one of the unidirectional arcs; and 2) TBD association/linkage arcs for which the direction has not yet been determined.

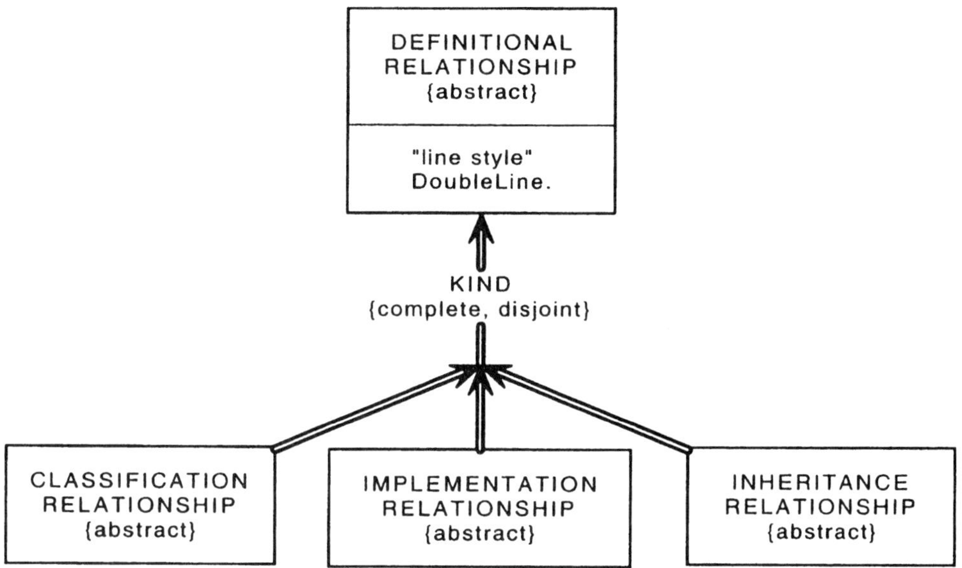

Figure 3.40. Partial metamodel for definitional relationships.

drawn from the client to the server and have an arrowhead at the server end that points to the server (i.e., in the direction of dependency).

All definitional relationships will be denoted by two lines because of the strong coupling they imply

3.2.1 Definitional Relationships

Definitions

The following definitions provide semantics to the partial metamodel documented in Figure 3.40:

definitional relationship *n.* any binary unidirectional dependency relationship from one modeling element to another whereby one modeling element depends on the definition provided by another.

- **classification relationship** *n.* the "is a" definitional relationship from an instance to one of its class(es), type(s), or the roles it plays.

- **implementation relationship** *n.* the definitional relationship whereby one modeling element provides the implementation of another.
- **inheritance relationship** *n.* the definitional relationship from a child to its parent(s), whereby the child is a new definition created from one or more existing definitions.

OML Metamodel

Figure 3.40 illustrates a partial metamodel for definitional relationships that captures the following information:

- Each definitional relationship is either a classification relationship, an implementation relationship, or an inheritance relationship.

COMN Notation

definitional relationships. All definitional relationships will be represented by two parallel lines.

Rationale

Two parallel lines are used for all definitional relationships because of the strong coupling they imply.

There is no need to use a different notation for the three different kinds of definitional relationships because each connects a different kind of modeling element.

3.2.1.1 CLASSIFICATION RELATIONSHIPS

Definitions

The following definitions provide semantics to the partial metamodel documented in Figure 3.41:

classification relationship *n.* any "is a" definitional relationship[20] from an

---

[20]Classification relationships represent "is a" relationships because the instance 'is an' instance of the class, conformer to the type, and player of the role. Classification relationships should not be confused with inheritance relationships that often are used to capture a "kind of" relationships. For example, Spot (an instance) *is a* dog, and dogs are a *kind of* mammal.

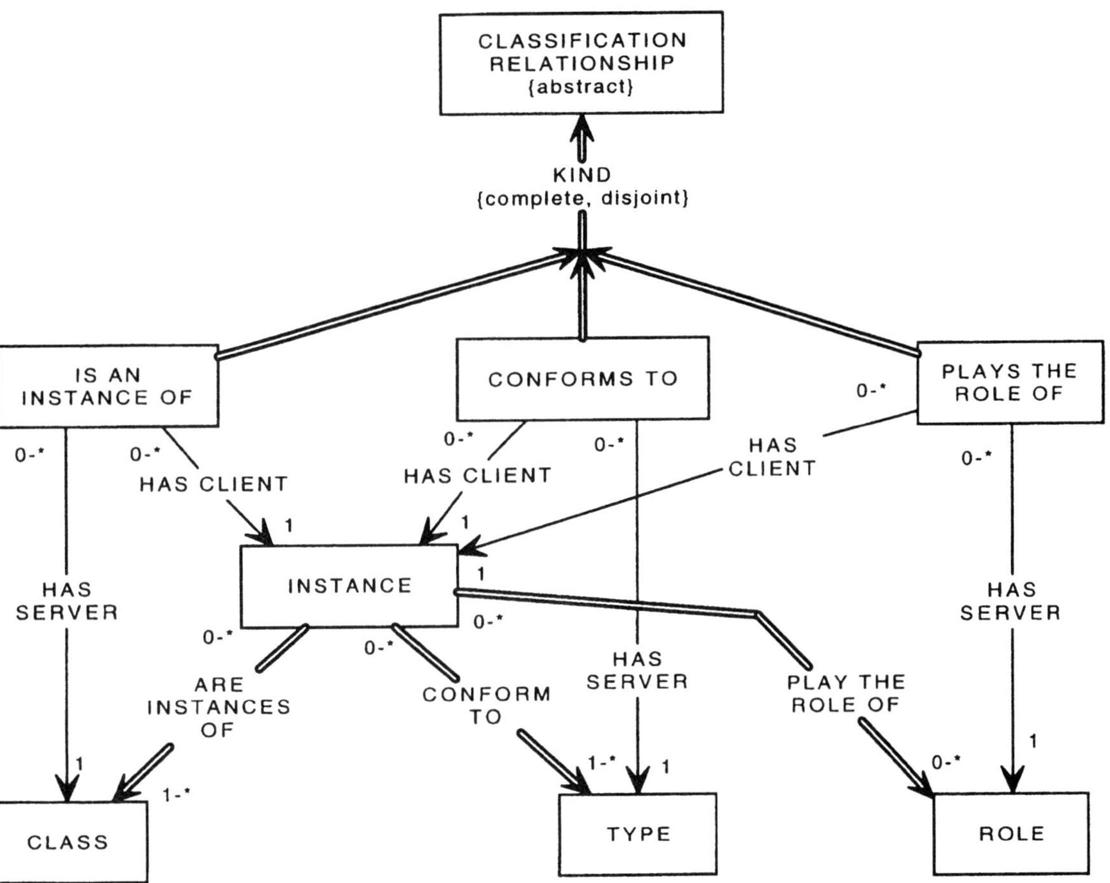

Figure 3.41. Partial metamodel for classification relationships.

instance to one of its class(es), type(s), or the roles it plays.

- **is an instance of** n. the classification relationship from an instance to one of its classes whereby the instance is consistent with the complete definition provided by the class. An instance is an instance of a class if and only if its interface conforms to each of the types of the class and its implementation is defined by the class implementations of the class.

- **conforms to** n. the classification relationship from an instance to one of its types whereby the interface of the instance is consistent with the type.

An instance conforms to an type if and only if its interface is consistent with the type (i.e., the set of characteristics in the interface of the instance is a superset of the set of characteristics declared by the type).

- **plays the role of** n. the classification relationship from an instance to one of its roles whereby the instance fulfills the responsibilities defined by the role.

OML Metamodel

Figure 3.41 illustrates a partial metamodel for classification relationships that captures the following information:

- Each definitional relationship is either an 'instance of' relationship, a 'conforms to' relationship, or a 'plays the role of' relationship.

- Each 'is an instance of' relationship connects one instance to one class, but each instance may be an instance of multiple classes (i.e., multiple classification is supported) via multiple 'is an instance of' relationships.

- Each 'conforms to' relationship connects one instance to one type, but each instance may conform to multiple types (i.e., multiple typing and interfaces are supported) via multiple 'conforms to' relationships.

- Each 'plays the role of' relationship connects one instance to one role, but each instance may play multiple roles.

COMN Notation

classification relationships. As illustrated in Figure 3.42, all classification relationships will be represented by two lines. Labels are character strings and optional.

Applicable Diagrams

Icons for classification arcs can be used on Cluster Diagrams and Collaboration Diagrams.

Rules

All classification relationships are:

- asymmetric. If A is an instance of B, then B cannot be an instance of A. If A conforms to B, then B cannot conform to A. If A plays the role of B, then B cannot play the role of A.

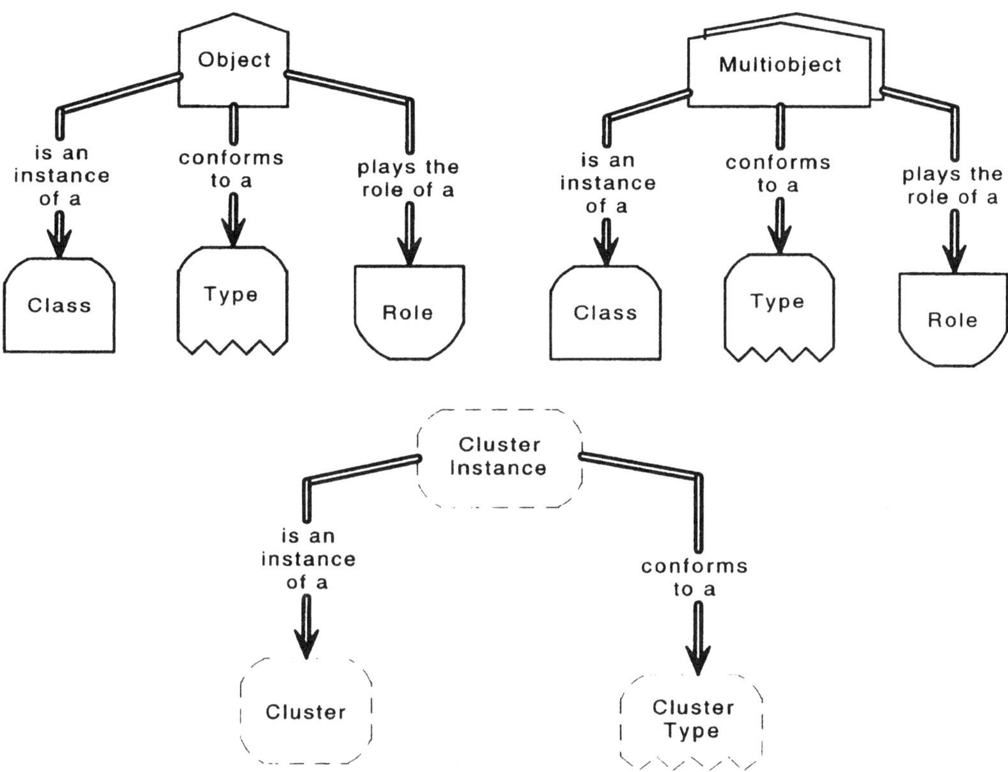

Figure 3.42. Icons for classification relationships.

- irreflexive. No instance can be an instance of itself. No instance can conform to itself, because instances are not types. No instance can play the role of itself, because instances are not roles.

A *is an instance of* arc may connect:

- a cluster to a cluster class.
- an object to an object class.
- a multiobjects to a object class.

A *conforms to* arc may connect:

- a cluster to a cluster type.
- an object to an object type.
- a multiobject to an object class.

A *plays the role of* arc may connect:

- an object to a role.
- a multiobject to a role.

Usage Guidelines

- Where feasible, draw the instances (a) consistently above their classes, types, and roles so that all dependency relationships point downwards, or (b) consistently below their classes, types, or roles so that all dependency relationships point upwards.

Rationale

Two parallel lines are used for all classification relationships because of the strong coupling they imply.

There is no need to label or use different notations for the three different kinds of classification relationships because each connects an instance to a different kind of modeling element (i.e., class, type, and role).

Examples

Figure 3.43 illustrates the use of classification notation for objects. Figure 3.44 illustrates the use of classification notation for clusters.

3.2.1.2 IMPLEMENTATION RELATIONSHIPS

Definitions

The following definitions provide semantics to the partial metamodel documented in Figure 3.45:

implementation relationship *n.* any definitional relationship whereby one modeling element provides the implementation of another.

- **implements** *n.* the implementation relationship from a class implementation to one of the types of the corresponding class whereby the instances of the class conform to the type.

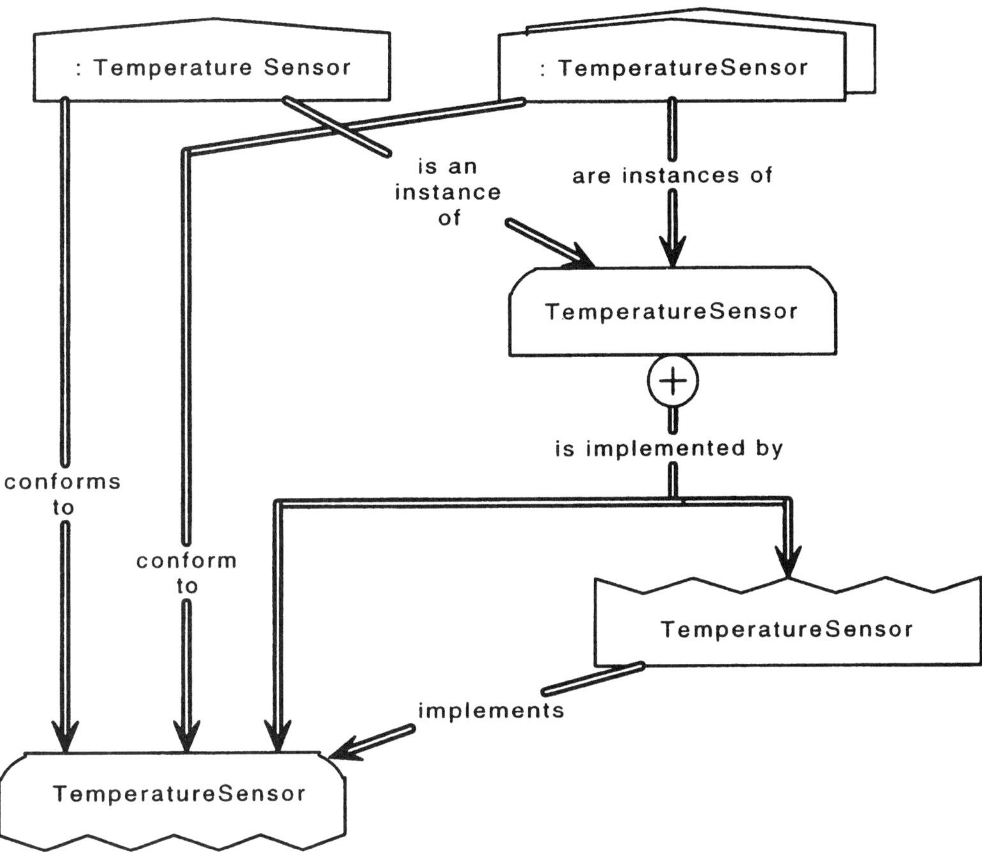

Figure 3.43. Classification notation for objects.

- **is implemented by** n. the implementation relationship from a class to one of its types or class implementations whereby the class is the combination of its types and implementations.

OML Metamodel

Figure 3.45 illustrates a partial metamodel for implementation relationships that captures the following information:

- Each implementation relationship is either an 'implements' relationship or an 'is implemented by' relationship.

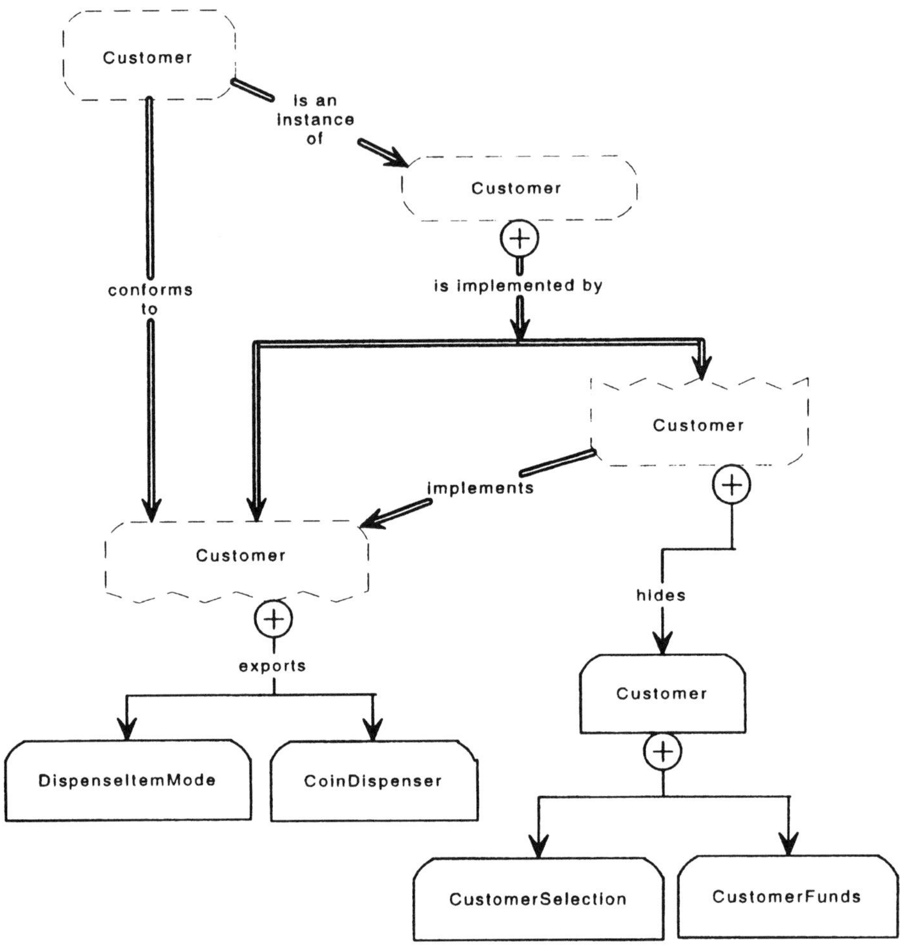

Figure 3.44. Classification notation for clusters.

- Each 'implements' relationship connects one class implementation to one class type, whereby each class implementation implements one or more class types and each class type has zero or more class implementations.

- Each 'is implemented by' relationship connects one class to either one class type or one class implementation, whereby each class has one or more class types and zero or more class implementations and each class type or implementation implements zero or more classes.

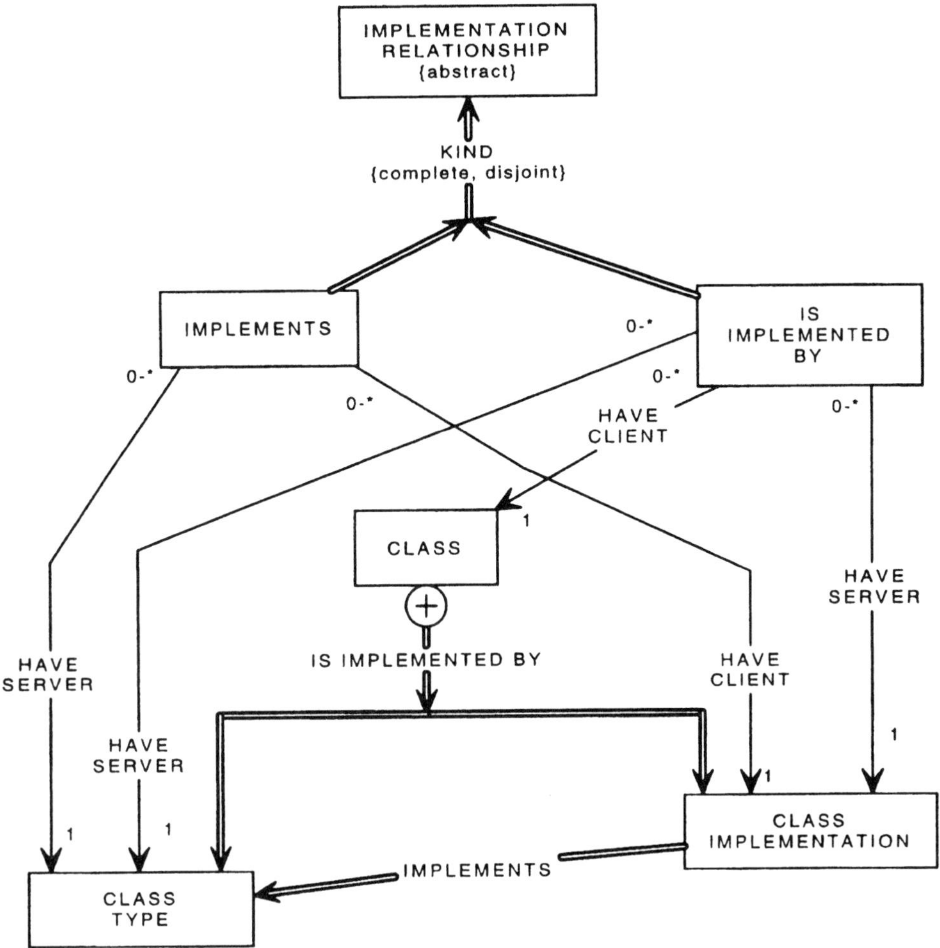

Figure 3.45. Partial metamodel for implementation relationships.

COMN Notation

implementation relationships. As illustrated in Figure 3.46, all implementation relationships will be represented by two lines. Labels are character strings and optional.

is implemented by relationships. All 'is implemented by' relationship arcs will have an aggregation symbol (a circle around a large plus sign) drawn on the tail (i.e., class) end of the relationship arc.

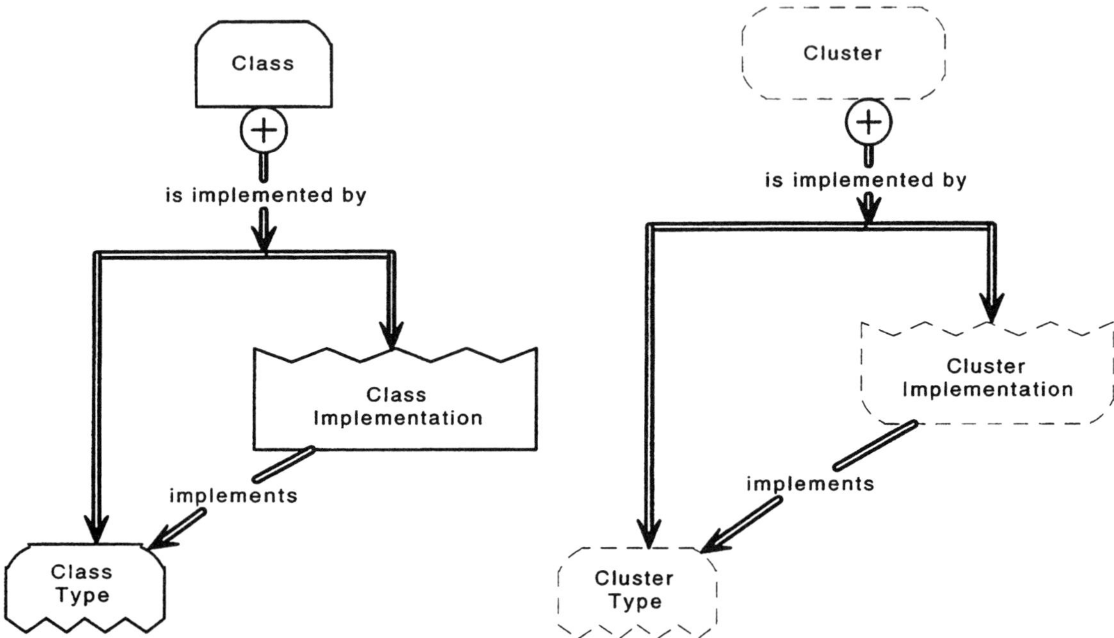

Figure 3.46. Notation for implementation relationships.

Applicable Diagrams

Icons for implementation arcs can be used on Cluster Diagrams and Collaboration Diagrams.

Rules

All implementation relationships are:

- asymmetric. If A implements B, then B cannot implement A. If A is implemented by B, then B cannot be implemented by A.
- irreflexive. No class type, class type, or class implementation can implement itself or be implemented by itself.

An *implements* arc may connect a class implementation to a class type.

An *is implemented by* arc may connect:

- a class to a class type.
- a class to a class implementation.

Usage Guidelines

1. Where feasible, draw the instances above their classes, types, and roles so that all dependency relationships point downwards.
2. The labels on implementation arcs are optional and may be left if they tend to clutter up a diagram.

Rationale

Two parallel lines are used for all implementation relationships because of the strong coupling they imply.

An aggregation symbol is placed at the class end of "is implemented by" arcs because the class can be considered an aggregation of its types and implementations.

There is no need to label or use different notations for the two different kinds of implementation relationships because each connects a different pair of modeling elements.

Examples

Figure 3.43 illustrates the use of implementation notation for objects.

3.2.1.3 INHERITANCE RELATIONSHIPS

Definitions

The following definitions provide semantics to the partial metamodel documented in Figure 3.47:

inheritance relationship *n.* any definitional relationship from a child to one of its parents, whereby the child is a new definition created from one or more existing definitions provided by the parent(s).

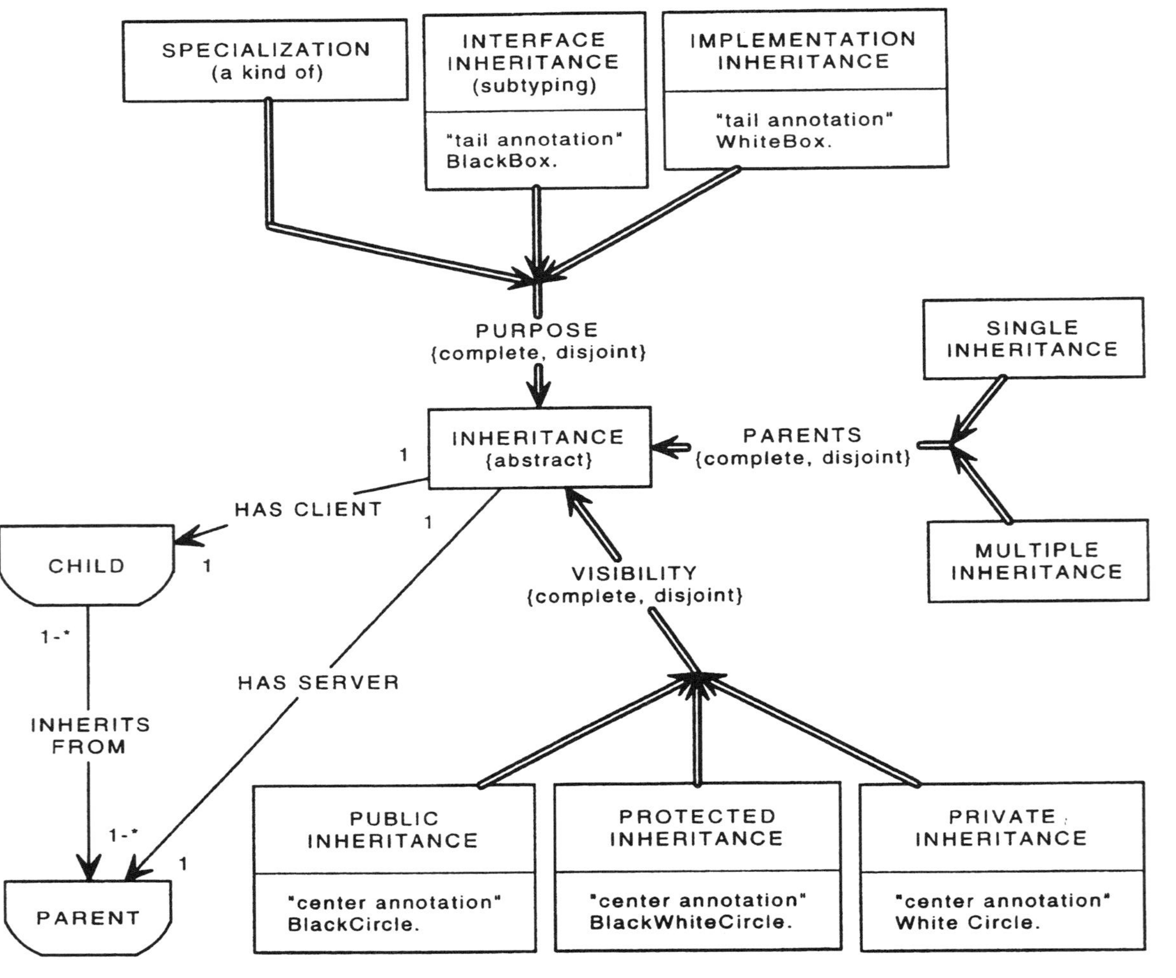

Figure 3.47. Partial metamodel of inheritance relationships.

Inheritance relationships can be partitioned into the following three kinds:

- **specialization** *n.* (1) the definitional relationship from a more specialized node (child) to a more general node (parent), whereby the child is "a kind of" its parent(s). (2) any specialized node at the child end of a specialization arc.

- **interface inheritance (a.k.a., blackbox inheritance, subtyping)** *n.* the inheritance relationship that implies only interface conformance, but not specialization.

- **implementation inheritance (a.k.a., whitebox inheritance)** *n.* the inheritance relationship that implies neither specialization nor interface conformance. The primary purpose of implementation inheritance is to reuse the class implementation.

Inheritance relationships can be partitioned into the following two kinds:

- **single** *n.* the inheritance whereby a single class or type inherits from only a single parent.

- **multiple** *n.* the inheritance whereby a single class or type inherits from multiple parents.

Inheritance relationships can be partitioned into the following three kinds:

- **public** *n.* the inheritance whereby the visibility of characteristics in the parent is retained in the child.

- **protected** *n.* the inheritance whereby public characteristics in the parent become protected in the child.

- **private** *n.* the inheritance whereby public and protected characteristics in the parent become private in the child.

child *n.* the client role at the start of an inheritance relationship.

parent *n.* the server role at the end of an inheritance relationship.

generalization *n.* any generalized node at the parent end of a specialization arc.

discriminant *n.* any value of a property of the parent class that is used to differentiate the members of a partition of child classes.

Inheritance relationships partition classes into the following three kinds:

- **abstract class** *n.* any incomplete class that therefore cannot be used to instantiate semantically meaningful instances.

- — **deferred class** *n.* any abstract class that declares the existence of one or more characteristics that must be implemented by its descendants prior to instantiation of its descendants.
- **concrete class** *n.* any complete class that therefore can be used to instantiate semantically meaningful instances.

Inheritance relationships partition classes by position in the hierarchy into the following three kinds:

- **root class** *n.* any class that does not inherit from any other class.
- **branch class** *n.* any class that both inherits from and is inherited from other classes.
- **leaf class** *n.* any class that is not inherited from by any other class.

Inheritance relationships partition characteristics into the following five kinds:

- **deferred characteristic** *n.* any characteristic that does not have a complete current implementation.
- **effective characteristic** *n.* any characteristic that has a complete current implementation.
- **overridden characteristic** *n.* any characteristic, the current implementation of which supersedes a previous implementation.
  - — **replaced characteristic** *n.* any overridden characteristic, the current implementation of which replaces its previous implementation without using it.
  - — **refined characteristic** *n.* any overridden characteristic, the current implementation of which delegates to its previous implementation (e.g., using the Smalltalk and Java pseudovariable super).

OML Metamodel

Figure 3.47 illustrates a partial metamodel for inheritance relationships and captures the following information:

- Inheritance can be partitioned by purpose into the following three kinds: specialization, interface inheritance, and implementation inheritance.
- Inheritance can be partitioned by the number of parents into the following two kinds: single inheritance and multiple inheritance.

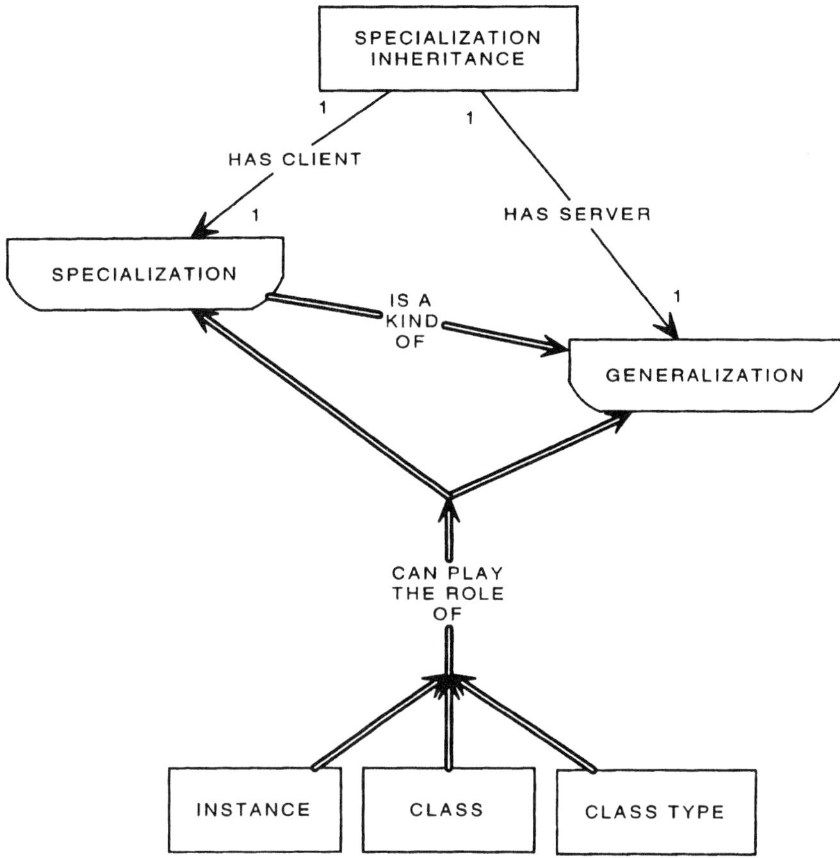

Figure 3.48. Partial metamodel of specialization inheritance relationships.

- Inheritance can be partitioned by visibility into the following three kinds: public inheritance, protected inheritance, and private inheritance.
- Each inheritance relationship connects a single child to a single parent, whereby the child role inherits from parent role.
- A child can have one or more parents, and a parent can have zero or more children.

Figure 3.48 illustrates a partial metamodel for specialization inheritance relationships and captures the following information:

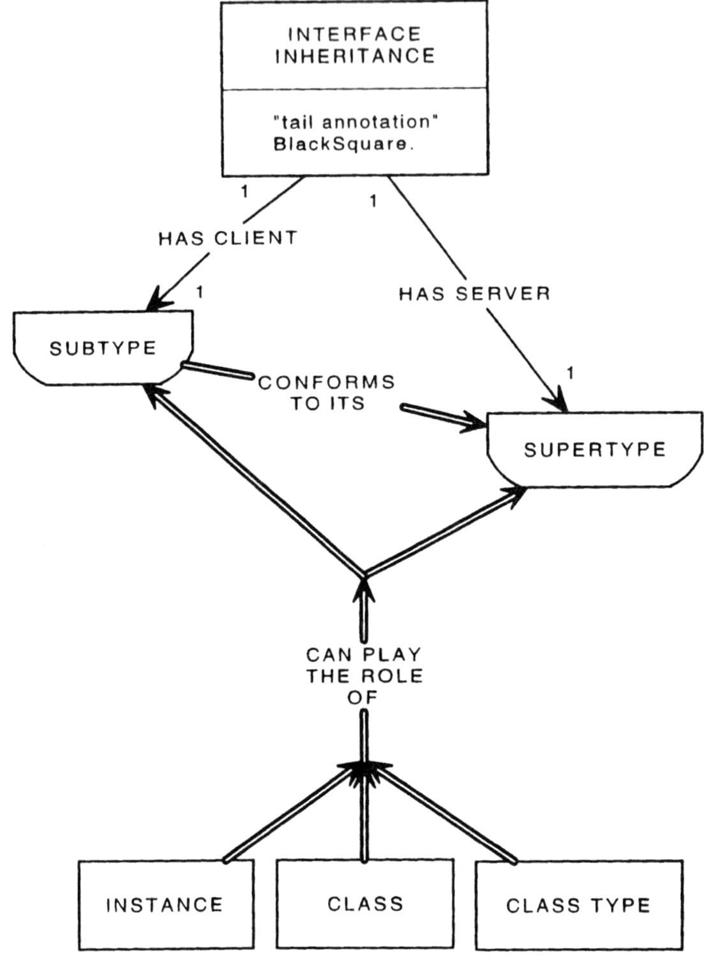

Figure 3.49. Partial metamodel of interface inheritance relationships.

- Each specialization inheritance connects one specialization to one generalization, whereby the specialization is a kind of the generalization.
- The specialization and generalization roles may be played by instances, classes, and class types.

Figure 3.49 illustrates a partial metamodel for interface inheritance relationships and captures the following information:

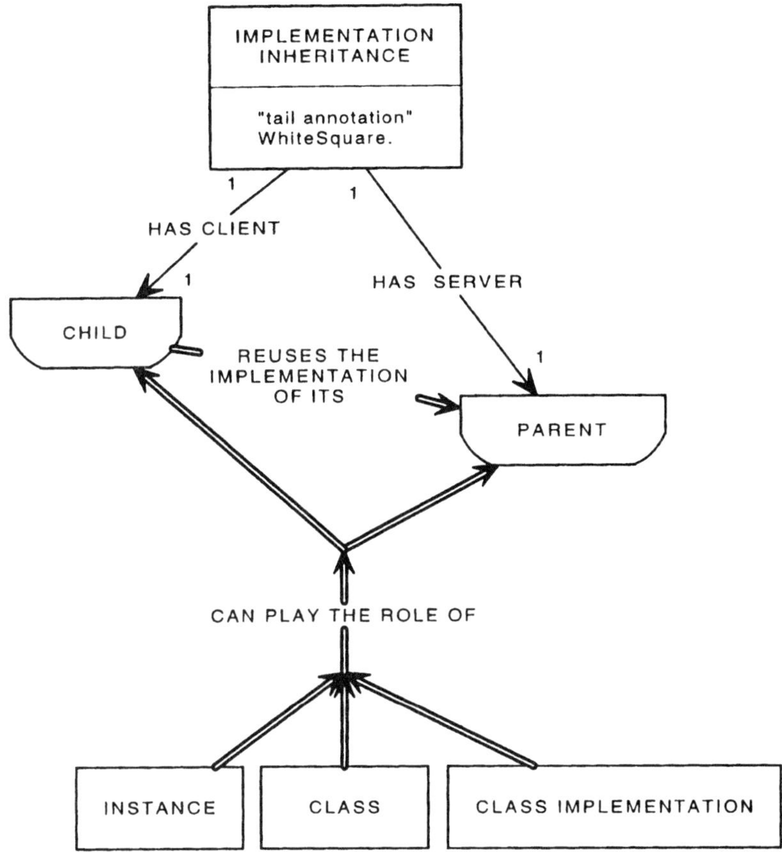

Figure 3.50. Partial metamodel of implementation inheritance relationships.

- Each interface inheritance connects one subtype to one supertype, whereby the subtype conforms to the supertype.
- The subtype and supertype roles may be played by instances, classes, and class types.

Figure 3.50 illustrates a partial metamodel for implementation inheritance relationships and captures the following information:

- Each implementation inheritance connects one child to one parent, whereby the child reuses the implementation of the parent.

- The child and parent roles may be played by instances, classes, and class implementations.

COMN Notation

inheritance. Inheritance is represented by a directed arc made up of two solid parallel lines with the arrowhead at the parent end.

- **specialization inheritance.** Specialization inheritance is represented by a directed arc made up of two solid lines with the arrowhead at the generalization end.
- **interface inheritance.** Interface (blackbox) inheritance is represented by a small black (i.e., filled in) square on the child end of the arc.
- **implementation inheritance.** Implementation (whitebox) inheritance is represented by a small white (i.e., not filled in) square on the child end of the arc.
- **public inheritance.** Public inheritance is represented by a small black (i.e., filled in) circle on the inheritance arc, midway from the child to the parent.
- **protected inheritance.** Protected inheritance is represented by a small black and white (i.e., half filled in and half not filled in) circle on the inheritance arc, midway from the child to the parent.
- **private inheritance.** Implementation inheritance is represented by a small white (i.e., not filled in) circle on the inheritance arc, midway from the child to the parent.

partition. Inheritance arcs from members of the same partition joined together before continuing on to the parent, and the combined arc is labeled with the discriminant. Optionally, the kind of partition can be labeled with the stereotypes "complete" or "incomplete" and "disjoint" or "overlapping." If unlabeled, the assumed default is incomplete and disjoint.

abstract class. Abstract classes may optionally be represented with a dotted outline.

Stereotypes

The following definitional stereotypes have the following optional annotations:

Abstract Class. An abstract class should be annotated with the character string "{abstract}" or "{abs}" placed at the end of the class label. Because of its importance, an abstract class may be optionally drawn with a dotted outline.

Deferred Class. A deferred class should be annotated with the character string "{deferred}" or "{def}" placed at the end of the class label.

Concrete Class. A concrete class requires no label because concrete is the assumed default.

Deferred Characteristic. A deferred characteristic should be annotated with the character string "{deferred}" or"{def}" placed at the end of the characteristic signature.

Effective Characteristic. An effective characteristic may be <u>optionally</u> annotated with the character string "{effective}" or "{eff}" placed at the end of the characteristic signature. Effective is the default, and characteristics should be assumed to be effective unless otherwise annotated.

Overridden Characteristic. An overridden characteristic should be annotated with the character string "{overridden}" or "{ovr}" placed at the end of the characteristic signature.

Replaced Characteristic. A replaced characteristic should be annotated with the character string "{replaced}" or "{rep}" placed at the end of the characteristic signature.

Refined Characteristic. A refined characteristic should be annotated with the character string "{refined}" or "{ref}" placed at the end of the characteristic signature.

Applicable Diagrams

Icons for inheritance arcs can be used on Semantic Nets and Collaboration Diagrams.

Rules

All inheritance relationships are:

- asymmetric. If A inherits from B, then B cannot inherit from A.
- irreflexive. Nothing can inherit from itself.

A *specialization inheritance* arc may connect:

- an object to an object.
- a class to a class.
- a class type to a class type.

An *interface inheritance* arc may connect:

- an object to an object.
- a class to a class.
- a class type to a class type.

An *implementation inheritance* arc may connect:

- an object to an object.
- a class to a class.
- a class implementation to a class implementation.

Usage Guidelines

1. Merge inheritance arcs from multiple children if they belong to the same partition. Line up all members of the same partition.

2. There is no semantic meaning to the placement of children relative to their parents. Organize the nodes to best fit the diagram and minimize the crossing of relationship arcs. However, where practical, consistently use one of following approaches:

   - Place parents above children. This is the traditional placement in both computer science and, for example, genealogical trees. It has the advantage of familiarity, especially for experienced software professionals. It is also easy to add new subclasses at the base since most people begin to draw on paper from the top downwards.
   - Place parents to the left of children. This mirrors the use of indentation found in single-inheritance browsers.
   - Place children above their parents. Advantages of this approach include:
     - All arcs (linkages, association, aggregation, classification, inheritance) run downhill from client to server (in the direction of dependency), making it easier to determine the overall dependency structure of the nodes so that dependency-based development and testing can be used.
     - It is more intuitive because reuse has traditionally been considered to be bottom-up, and inheritance supports reuse. Children classes are built on the foundation of parent (a.k.a., base) classes. Inheritance trees grow like normal trees with their roots in the ground and leaves in the air.

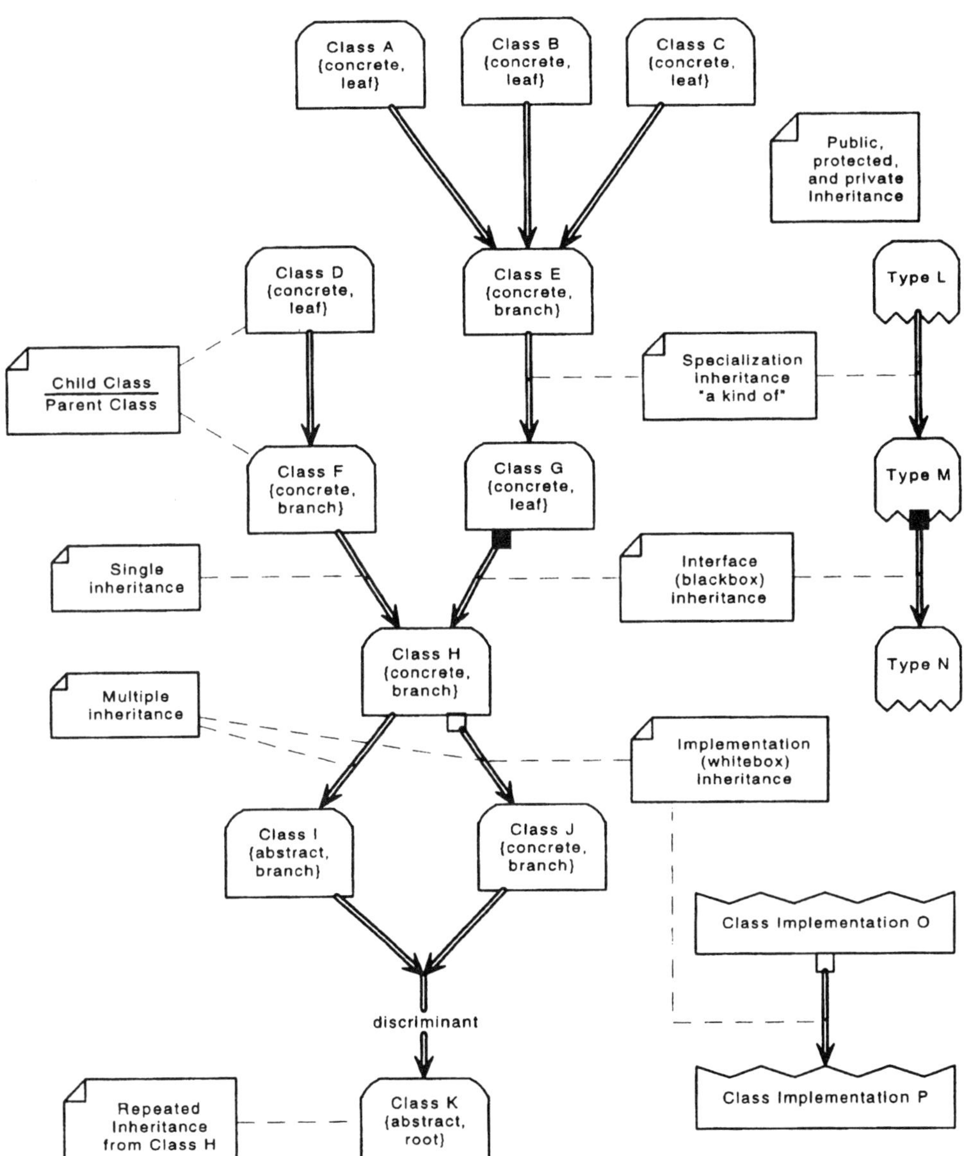

Figure 3.51. Inheritance icons.

3. Whenever practical, use specialization inheritance. Beware of interface inheritance, which supports polymorphic substitutability but may lead to misunderstandings. Replace implementation inheritance with specialization inheritance because implementation inheritance violates abstraction and does not guarantee polymorphic substitutability which is typically expected.

Rationale

An inheritance arc is drawn from the child to its parent because the child strongly depends on (i.e., is defined in terms of) its parent.

A double lined arrow is used to represent inheritance to emphasize the very strong coupling of the child to its parents.

The inheritance arcs from children forming a partition are joined into a single arc so that:

- the partition can be recognized,
- the partition can be labeled with the discriminant and stereotypes (e.g., complete vs. incomplete, disjoint vs. overlapping), and
- the discriminant need be listed only once on the arc from the join point to the parent.

A black square intuitively represents interface (blackbox) inheritance, and a white square intuitively represents implementation (whitebox) inheritance.

No special symbol is used to represent specialization because this should be the default case (in order to support polymorphic substitutability and a kind of taxonomies).

Braces are used instead of parentheses to delineate all stereotypes so that stereotypes will not be confused with parameters.

The class inheritance annotations come from the Eiffel programming language.

Examples

Figure 3.52 illustrates a relatively simple inheritance hierarchy. Because drop-down boxes are not used, this diagram only documents the inheritance structure and not what is inherited, deferred, and overridden. Notice the use of a dotted outline to signify abstract classes.

Figure 3.53 illustrates the use of drop-down boxes with classes to document the actual characteristics inherited, deferred, and overridden.

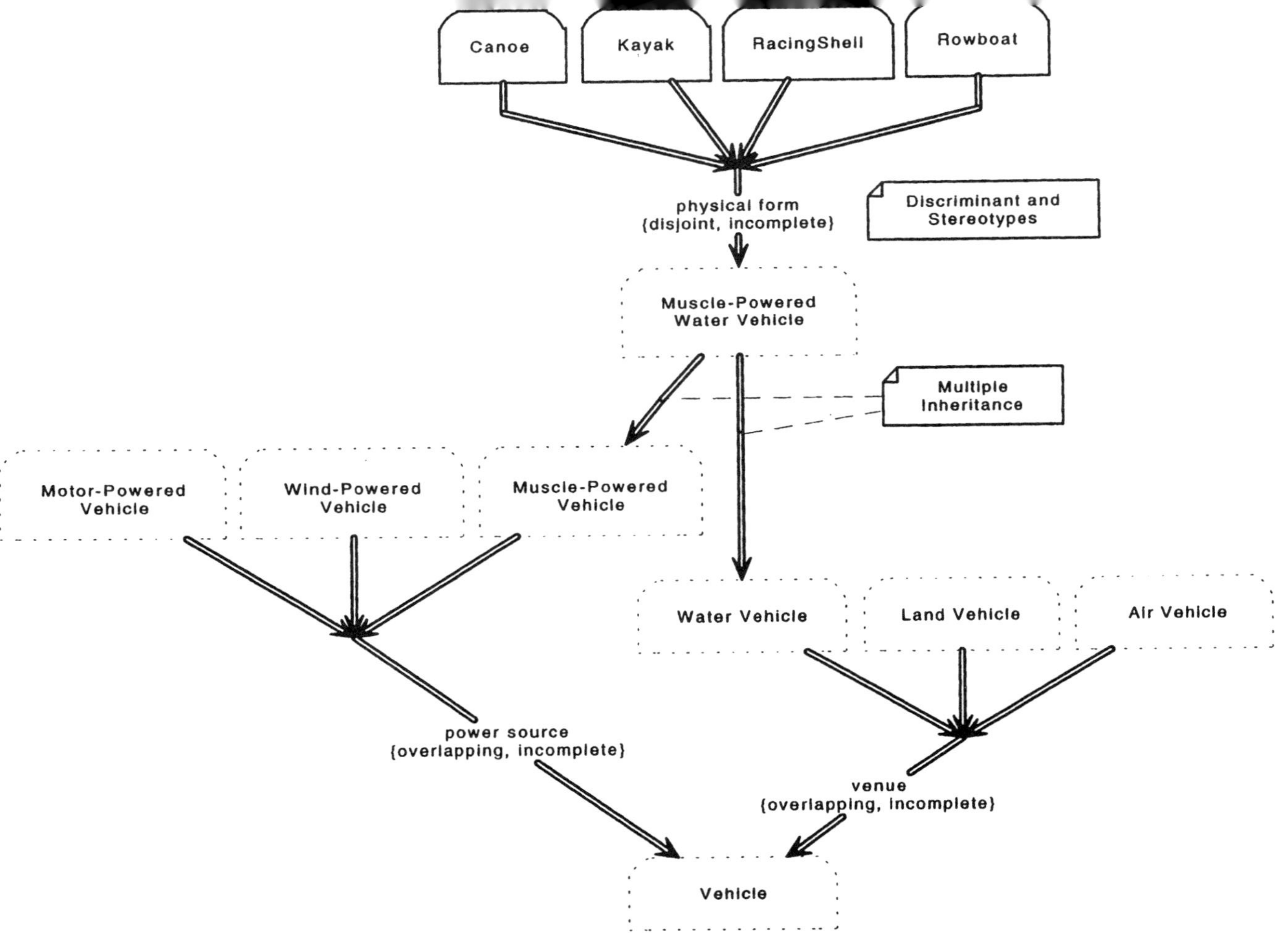

Figure 3.52. Example inheritance graph.

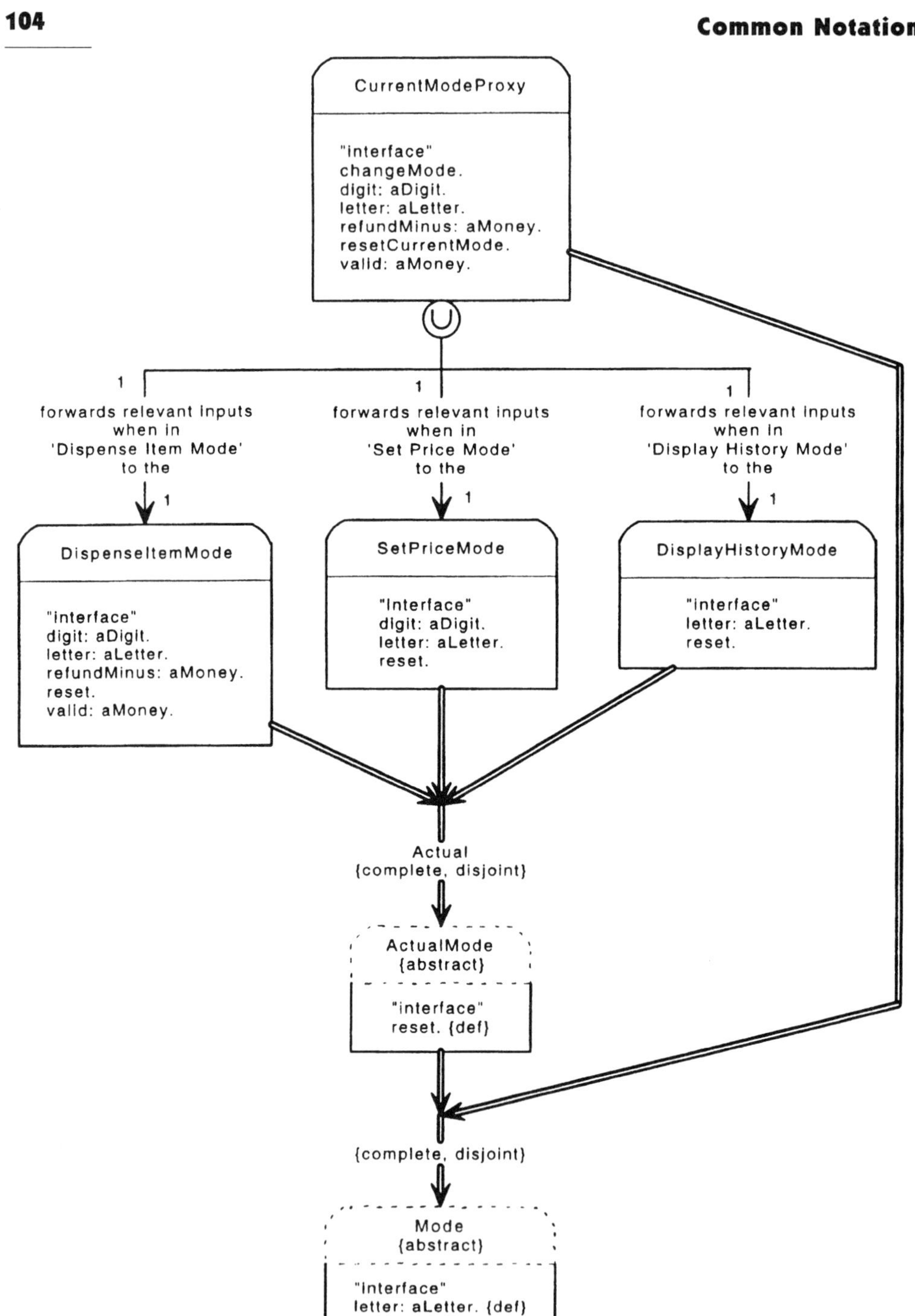

Figure 3.53. Example of inheritance using drop-down boxes and Smalltalk syntax.

3.2.2 Referential Relationships

Definitions

The following definitions provide semantics to the partial metamodel documented in Figure 3.54:

referential relationship *n.* any binary unidirectional dependency relationship from one modeling element to another whereby one modeling element refers to another.

- **linkage relationship** *n.* the referential relationship connecting one instance to another, representing a specific structural dependency of the first instance on the second.

- **association relationship** *n.* the referential relationship from one kind (class, type, or role) to another, representing a general structural dependency of the first kind on the second. An association consists of a class of linkages between the associated instances.

- **aggregation relationship** *n.* the referential relationship that captures the logical relationship that exists from an aggregate (structure) to one of its component part.

- **containment relationship** *n.* the referential relationship that captures the logical relationship that exists from a container to one of its entries.

OML Metamodel

Figure 3.54 illustrates a partial metamodel for referential relationships that captures the following information:

- Referential relationships are completely and disjointedly partitioned by metatypes into relationships between nodes of the same metatype and relationships between nodes of different metatypes.

- Referential relationships between nodes of the same metatype are completely and disjointedly partitioned by level into associations and linkages, whereby each linkage is an instance of an association and each association may have zero or more linkages as instances.

- Referential relationships between nodes of the same metatype may also be whole-part relationships.

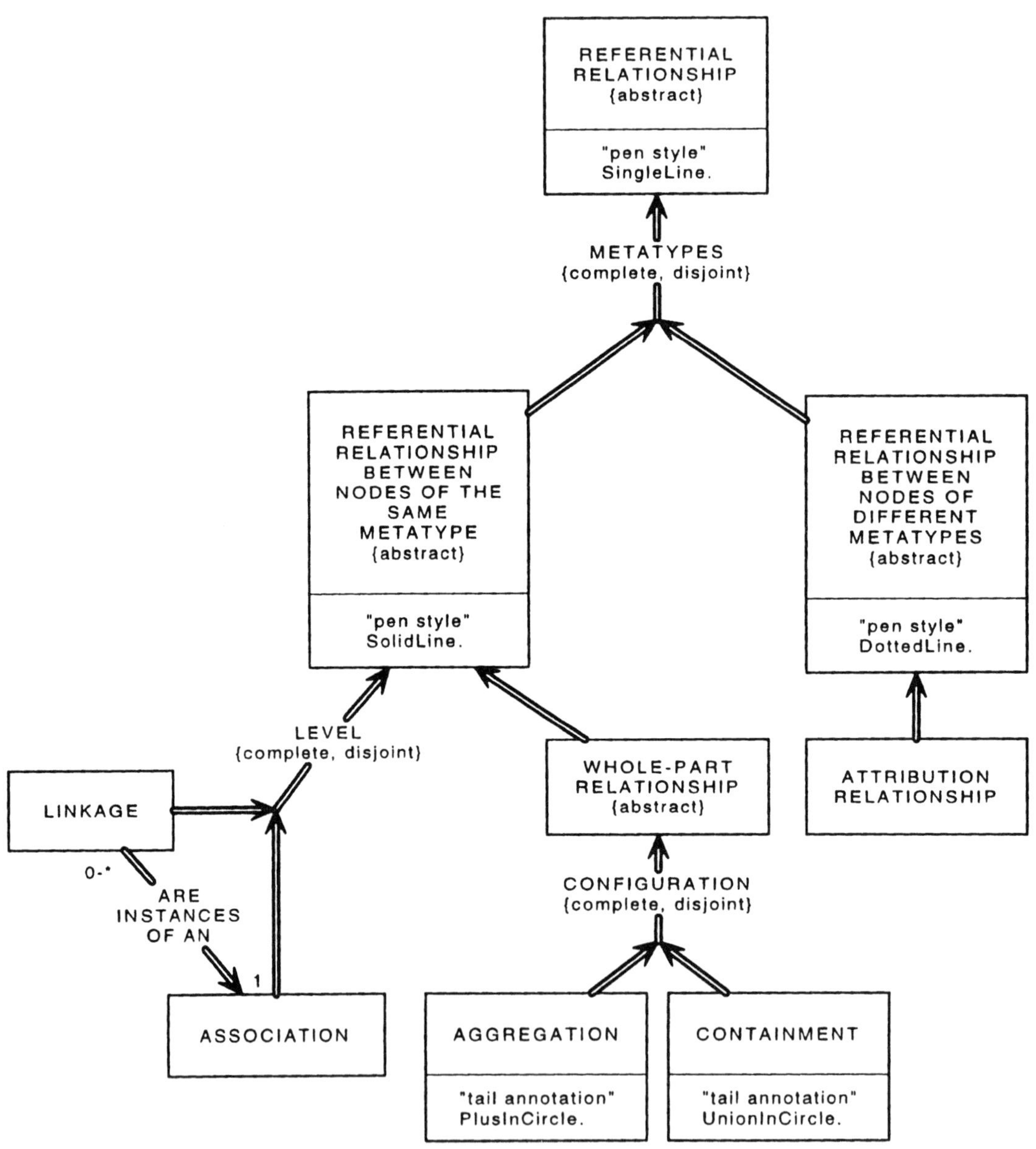

Figure 3.54. Partial metamodel for referential relationships.

- Whole-part relationships are completely and disjointedly partitioned by configuration into aggregation relationships and containment relationships.
- Referential relationships between nodes of different metatypes may also be attribution relationships.

COMN Notation

referential relationships. All referential relationships will be represented by one line.

referential relationships between nodes of the same metatype. All referential relationships between nodes of the same metatype will be represented by solid lines.

referential relationships between nodes of different metatypes. All referential relationships between nodes of different metatypes will be represented by dotted lines.

Rationale

Referential relationships are drawn with a single solid line because the most common relationship should be drawn with the simplest relationship icon.

3.2.2.1 ASSOCIATION AND LINKAGE RELATIONSHIPS

Definitions

The following definitions provide semantics to the partial metamodel documented in Figures 3.55 and 3.56:

linkage *n.* the referential relationship connecting one instance to another, representing a specific structural dependency of the first instance on the second.

- **unidirectional linkage** *n.* any one-way linkage from a client to a server.[21] It is implemented as a link property of the client and is maintained by operations of the client.
- **bi-directional linkage** *n.* the short hand way of expressing the combination of two one-way linkages between peers, whereby each of the corre-

---

[21]The client and the server may be the same.

sponding uni-directional links is the semi-strong inverse of the other and the corresponding operations in the peers ensure referential integrity.

- **observer linkage** *n.* the specialized kind of bi-directional linkage which captures the Observer pattern from the patterns book by the Gang of Four.[22]
- **TBD linkage** *n.* any linkage, the directionality of which has yet to be determined (TBD).

association *n.* the referential relationship from one kind (class, type, or role) to another, representing a general structural dependency of the first kind on the second. An association consists of a class of linkages between the associated instances.

- **unidirectional association** *n.* any class or type of unidirectional linkages.
- **bi-directional association** *n.* any class or type of bi-directional linkages.
- **observer association** *n.* any class or type of observer linkages.
- **TBD association** *n.* any class or type of TBD linkages.

peer *n.* with regard to another role, any role that (1) depends on the other role and (2) on which the other role depends.

associative class *n.* any class that is a reification of an association.

- **N-ary association** *n.* any associative class representing an "association" among 3 or more classes, types, or roles.

semi-strong inverse *n.* describing two referential relationships going in opposite directions between peers that together map an object into a set of objects that contains the first object. For example, *author of* and *written by* are semi-strong inverses of one another. The set of authors of the set of books written by a given author contains that author. Similarly, the set of books written by the set of authors of a given book includes that book.

responsibility *n.* any purpose, obligation, or required capability of an object, class, type, or role, typically provided as a cohesive set of one or more public services.

---

[22]*Design Patterns: Elements of Reusable Object-Oriented Software* by Erich Gamman, Richard Helm, Ralph Johnson, and John Vlissides (Addison-Wesley, 1995).

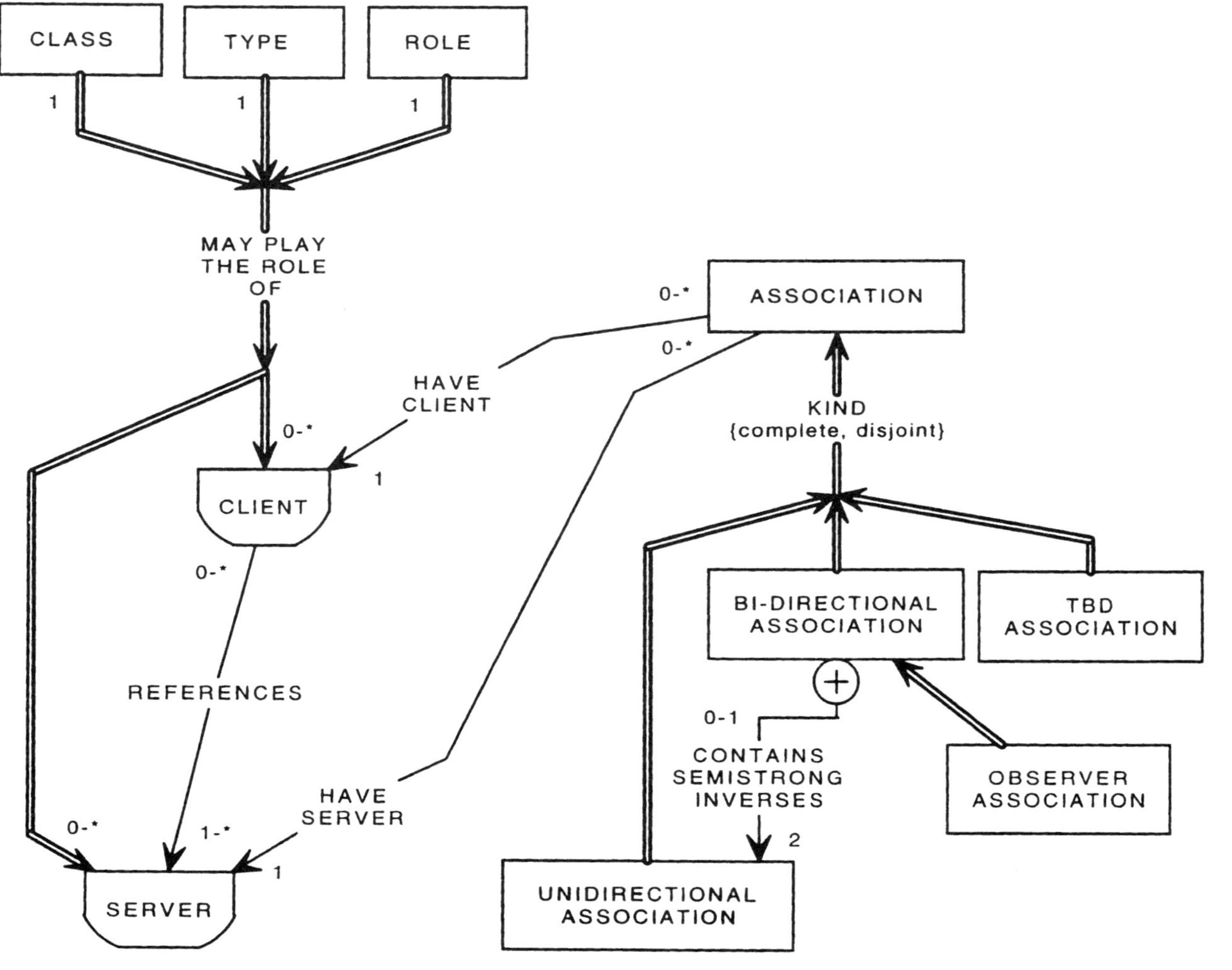

Figure 3.55. Partial metamodel for association relationships.

OML Metamodel

Figure 3.55 illustrates a partial metamodel for association relationships that captures the following information:

- Associations can be completely and disjointedly partitioned into unidirectional associations, bi-directional associations, or TBD associations.
- Bi-directional associations consist of two unidirectional associations that are semi-strong inverses of one another.
- Observer associations are a kind of bi-directional association.
- Each association connects a client to a server, whereby the client references the server.
- The clients and servers of an association are roles that may be played by classes, types, and roles.

Figure 3.56 illustrates a partial metamodel for linkage relationships and captures the following information:

- Linkages can be completely and disjointedly partitioned into unidirectional linkages, bi-directional linkages, or TBD linkages.
- Bi-directional linkages consist of two unidirectional linkages that are semi-strong inverses of one another.
- Observer linkages are a kind of bi-directional linkage.
- Each linkage connects a client to a server, whereby the client references the server.
- The clients and servers of a linkage are roles that may be played by instances.

COMN Notation

unidirectional association. A unidirectional association from a client to a server is represented as a single solid line between them with an arrowhead on the server end pointing at the server. The label of a unidirectional association is either:

- optional,[23]

---

[23]Labeling association or linkage arcs is optional because some members of the OPEN Consortium do not see their necessity and do not always use them. Other members feel that it is important to document not just that such a relationship exists but also to document its meaning by providing a meaningful label. The label can then be used to help identify responsibilities of the server and messages that will eventually be sent along the relationship arc to the server. Because the OML arcs are unidirectional, the label can provide some of the same meaning (in verb form) as the now unnecessary role names of UML.

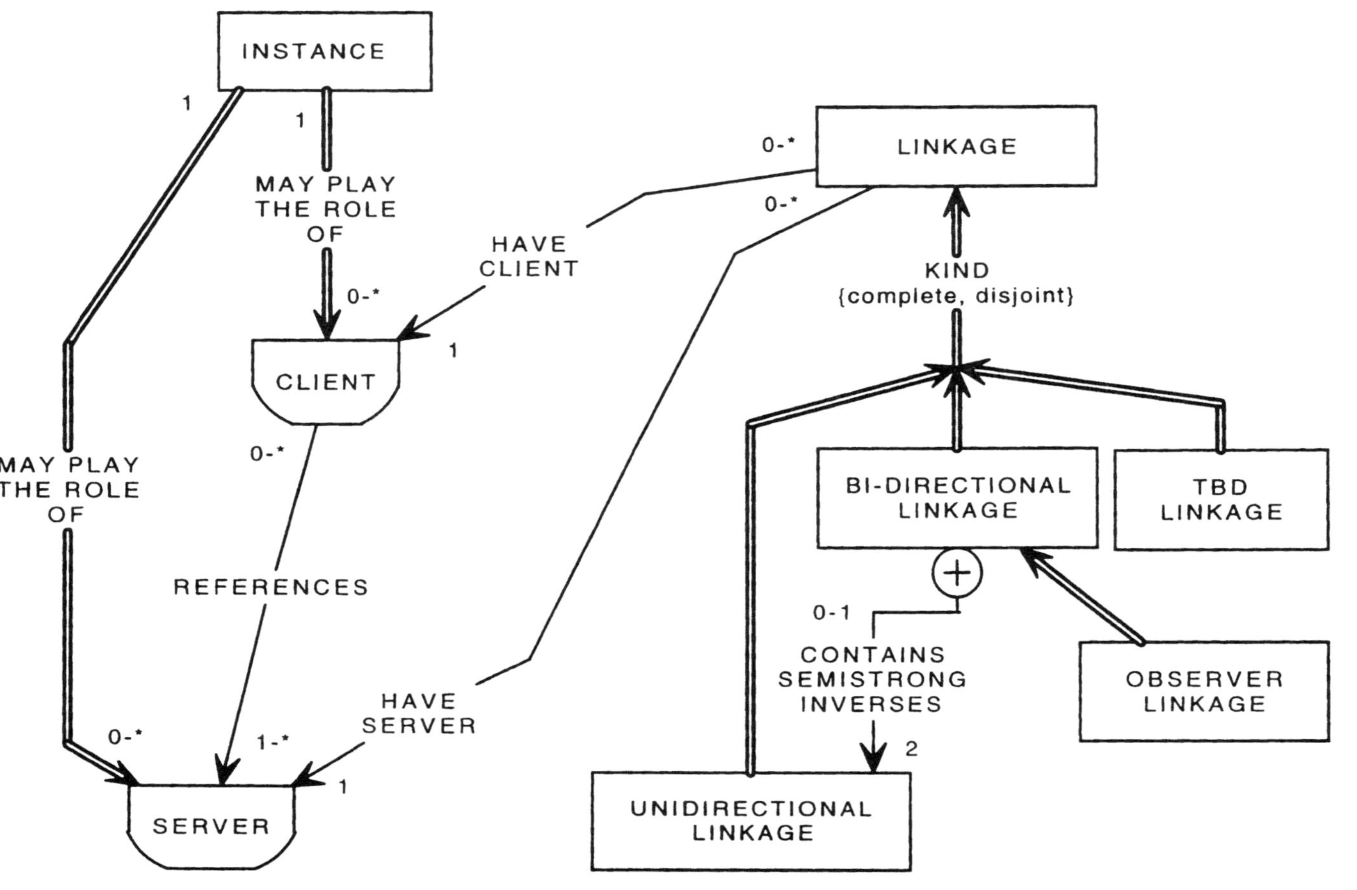

Figure 3.56. Partial metamodel for linkage relationships.

- a character string that is typically a verb phrase that forms an natural language sentence when preceded by the client label and followed by the server label,

- a list of the responsibilities of the server requested by the client, or

- a list of interactions (i.e., messages sent to the server, exceptions raised by the server) documented using the syntax of the selected programming language.

bi-directional association. A bi-directional association between two peers is represented as a single solid line between the peers with an arrowhead on both ends as a shorthand for two unidirectional associations. A bi-directional association requires two labels, one for each of the two implied unidirectional associations. On bi-directional associations, the two labels of the corresponding unidirectional associations are annotated (1) with a direction symbol (">") representing the direction of interpretation, dependency, visibility, and navigability and (2) placed on the port (i.e., left) side of the line when viewed in the direction of dependency. The direction symbol is placed on the side of the label closer to the end of the arc that it points to.

observer association. An observer association is represented as a single solid line with an arrowhead on the subject (i.e., server) end and a one-third size arrowhead, located nearer the observer (i.e., client) than the subject pointing towards the observer. Only the label of the association from the observer to the subject need be included on observer associations.

TBD association. A TBD association is represented as a simple line without arrowheads. Although no label is required for TBD associations, the arrowhead(s) and labels should be added once the directionality is determined.

unidirectional linkage. A unidirectional linkage from a client to a server is represented as a single solid line between two instances with an arrowhead on the server end pointing at the server. The label of a unidirectional linkage is either:

- optional,

- a character string that is typically a verb phrase that forms an natural language sentence when preceded by the client label and followed by the server label,

- a list of the responsibilities of the server requested by the client, or

- a list of interactions (i.e., messages sent to the server, exceptions raised by the server) documented using the syntax of the selected programming language.

bi-directional linkage. A bi-directional linkage between peers is drawn as a single solid line with an arrowhead on both ends as a shorthand for two unidirectional linkages. A bi-directional linkage requires two labels, one for each of the two implied unidirectional linkages. On bi-directional linkages, the two labels of the corresponding unidirectional linkages are annotated (1) with a direction symbol (">") representing the direction of interpretation, dependency, visibility, and navigability and (2) placed on the port (i.e., left) side of the line when viewed in the direction of dependency. The direction symbol is placed on the side of the label closer to the end of the arc that it points to.

observer linkage. An observer linkage is represented as a single solid line with an arrowhead on the subject (i.e., server) end and a one-third size arrowhead, located nearer the observer (i.e., client) than the subject pointing towards the observer. Only the label of the linkage from the observer to the subject need be included on observer linkages.

TBD linkage. A TBD linkage is represented as a simple line without arrowheads. Although no label is required for TBD linkages, the arrowhead(s) and labels should be added once the directionality is determined.

As illustrated in Figure 3.60, when an association among two or more classes is reified as an associative class with multiple binary associations to the original classes, then the resulting arcs may optionally be numbered to clarify the logical order in which they should be read.

Applicable Diagrams

Icons for associations and linkages can occur on the following kinds of diagrams:

- Semantic Nets:
    - Context Diagrams
    - Cluster Diagrams
    - Inheritance Diagrams
    - Deployment Diagrams
    - Layer Diagrams
- Sequence Diagrams:
    - Blackbox Sequence Diagrams
    - Whitebox Sequence Diagrams

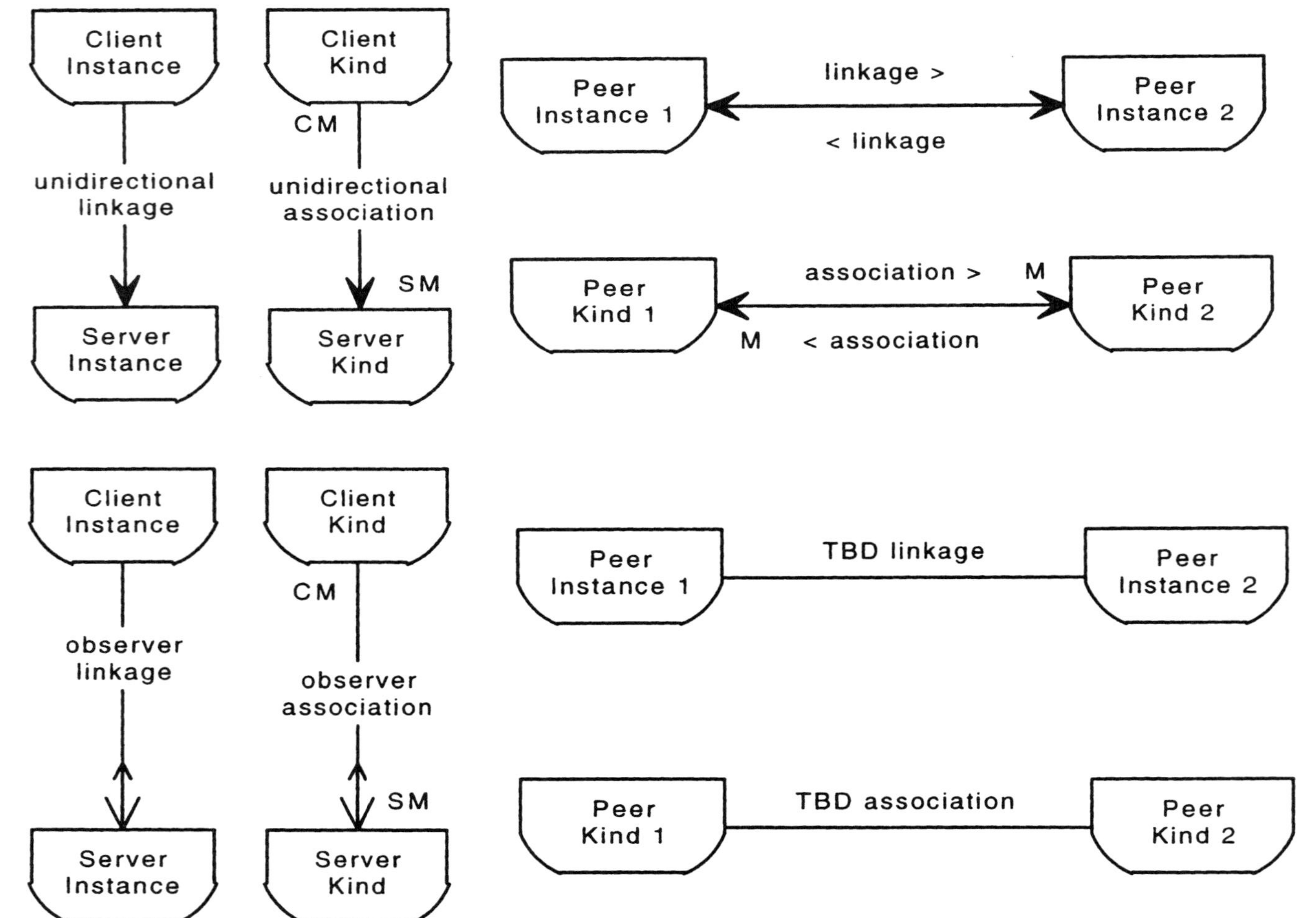

Figure 3.57. Icons for associations and linkages. (CM stands for client multiplicity; SM stands for server multiplicity; and M stands for peer multiplicity.)

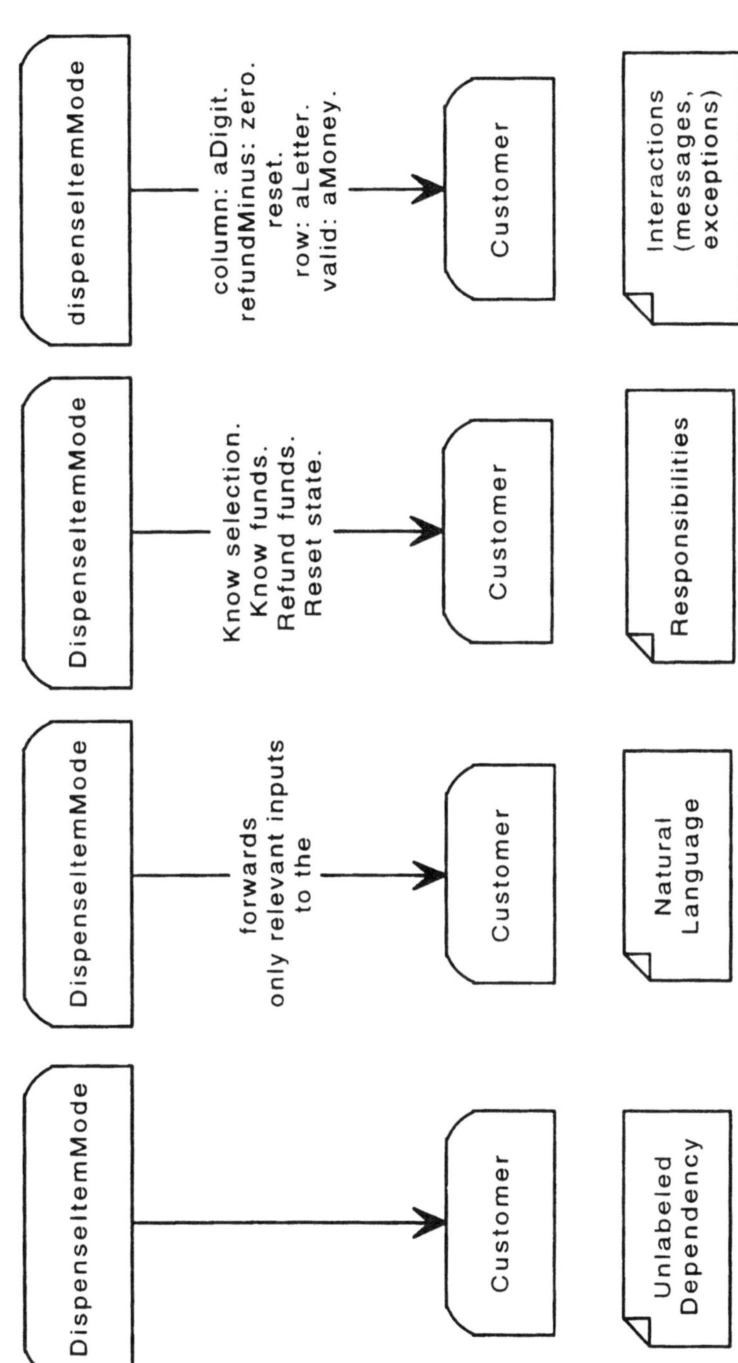

Figure 3.58. Example labels for associations and linkages.

Stereotypes

Associations and linkages have the following stereotypes:

- mutable vs. immutable.
- reflexive vs. irreflexive.
- symmetric vs. asymmetric vs. antisymmetric.
- transitive vs. intransitive.
- uses vs. knows.

Arc Compatibility Rules

Linkage arcs may connect:

- instances (clusters, objects, multiobjects) to instances.

Association arcs may connect:

- classes, types, and roles to classes, types, and roles.

Usage Guidelines

1. Organize the nodes to best fit the diagram and minimize the crossing of relationship arcs. However, where practical, draw clients above servers and draw peers[24] side by side so that the overall control flow is as top-down as is practical.

2. Use the singular form of the verb phrase for labels of linkages and associations if the client has a multiplicity of zero, one, or zero or one. Use the plural form of the verb phrase if the client has a multiplicity of one or more.

Rationale

Using arrowheads is intuitive for directionality. Not using arrowheads is intuitive for lack of (i.e., unknown) directionality.

Because association and linkage are the most commonly drawn relationships, they have the simplest arcs (solid single line with arrowhead). The small backwards pointing arrowhead on the Observer pattern intuitively represents the notification of the observer by the subject when the subject's property values change.

---

[24]Two nodes are peers if each has a dependency relationship on the other.

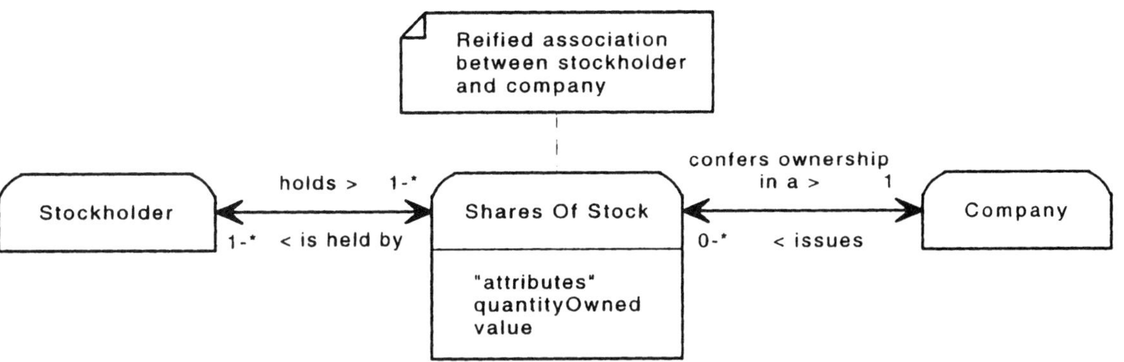

Figure 3.59. Example reification of an association with characteristics.

Examples

Figure 3.59 illustrates the use of classes to reify associations with characteristics. This is useful only when the association is in face a concept and has properties and behavior of its own. In general, reification of associations requires care to be taken since most associations will NOT reify successfully.

Figure 3.60 illustrates the use of classes to reify n-ary associations. In this case, OML supports the structure shown rather than a ternary association.

Figure 3.61 illustrates the COMN use of inheritance instead of the "or" associations of UML.

Figure 3.62 illustrates the use of "bi-directional" associations (i.e., two unidirectional associations that are semi-strong inverses of one another). It also reifies the roles of Employee and Spouse as classes, and reifies the concept of marriage as a class.

Figure 3.63 illustrates the use of linkages on a cluster diagram showing the domain objects involved in a typical automatic teller machine application. Although most of the linkages are unidirectional, three observer linkages implement the Observer pattern to decouple the interrupt-driven input devices from the current customer and one implements the Observer pattern to decouple the current transaction from the bank proxy. Notice also that several of the objects are concurrent because they must be able to handle simultaneous inputs from multiple external sources.

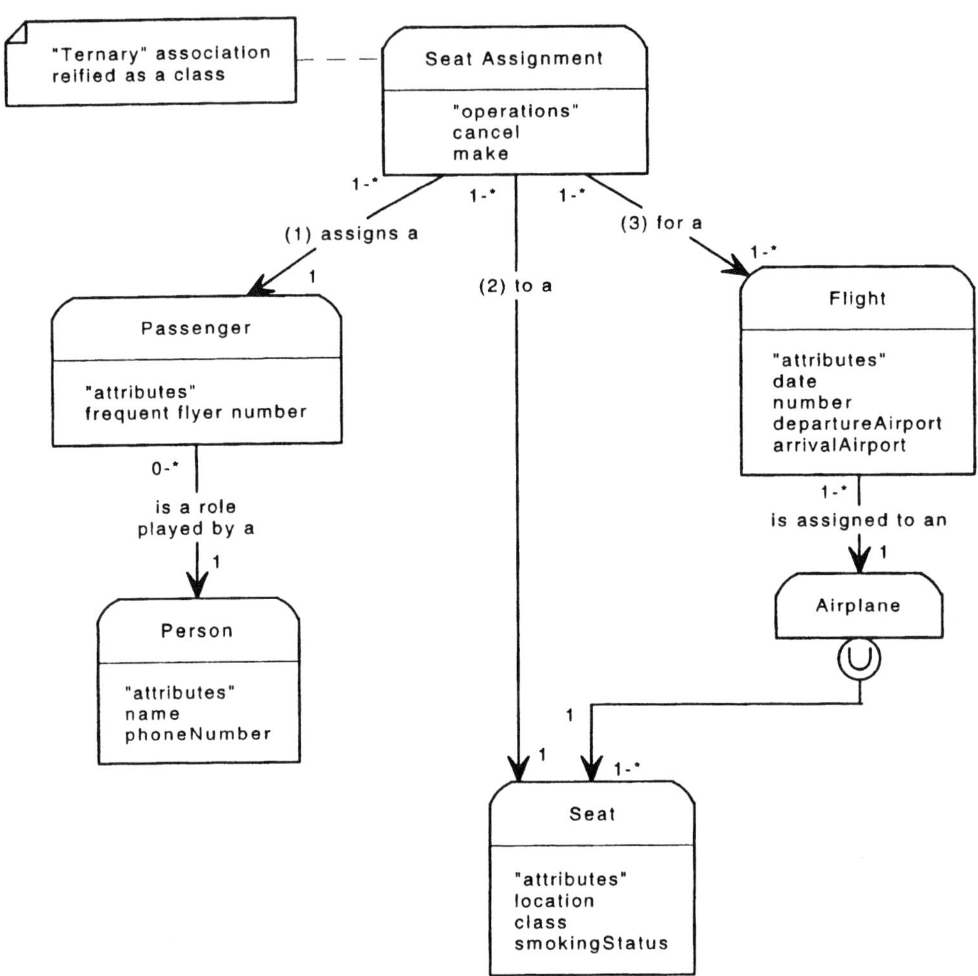

Figure 3.60. Ternary association reified as an associative class.

3.2.2.2 AGGREGATION RELATIONSHIPS

Definitions

The following definitions provide semantics to the partial metamodel documented in Figure 3.64:

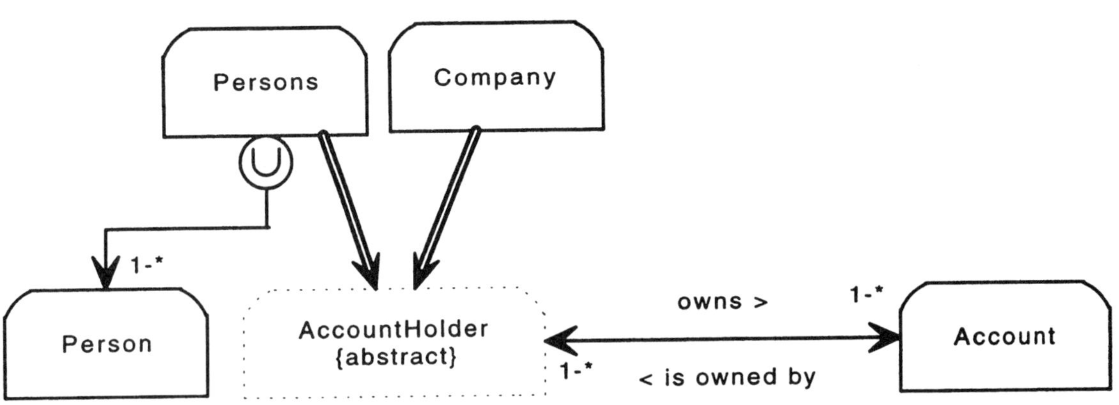

Figure 3.61. No "or" associations.

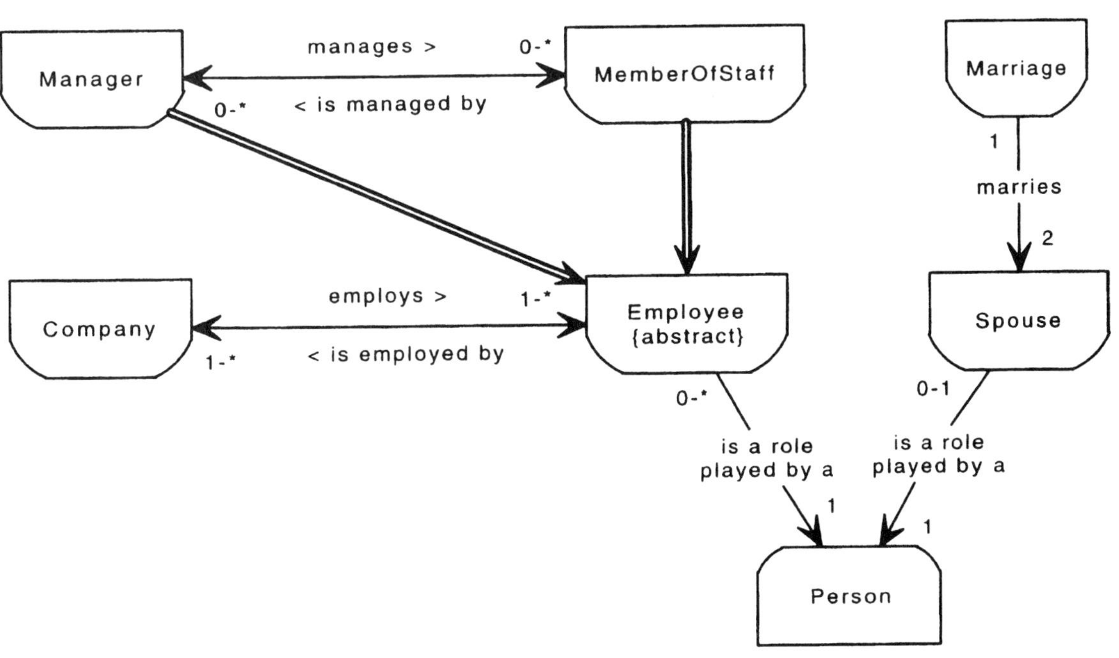

Figure 3.62. Example associations.

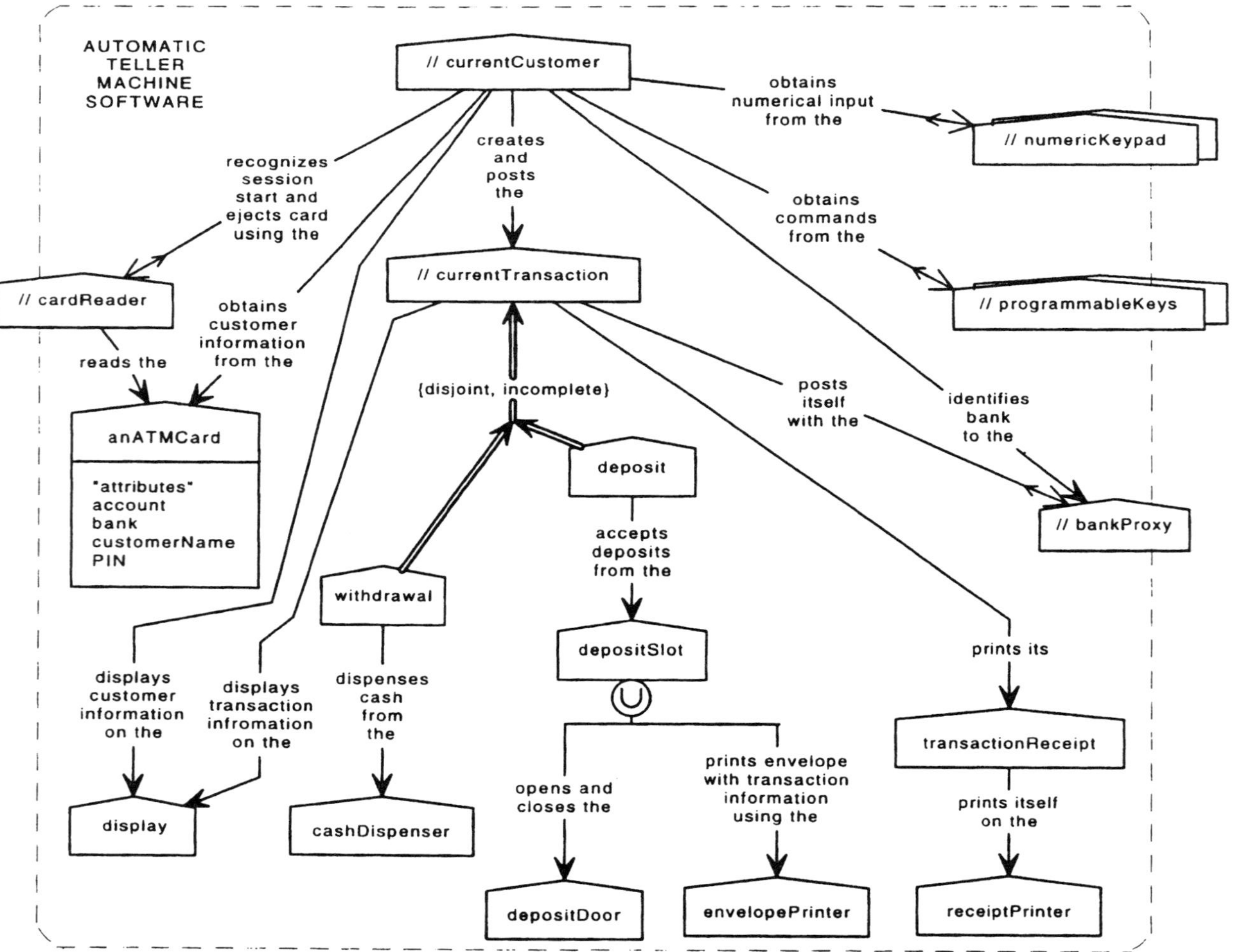

Figure 3.63. Example associations on a cluster diagram of an ATM machine.

aggregate *n.* any modeling element that has other modeling elements of the same metatype as collaborating parts that form a structure.

For example, a car engine consists of pistons, cylinders, spark plugs, etc. and these component parts have specific interpart relationships.

Contrast the term "aggregate" with the term "container" (e.g., car trunk) which contains relatively independent entries.

part *n.* any modeling element that is a component of another modeling element of the same metatype.

The aggregate usually, but not always, hides its component parts. For example, the switch on a motor as a visible, public part of the motor.

The life of a part is usually, but not always, confined to that of its aggregate. As a counterexample, a car engine may be reused meaning that it may exist after the first car exists but before the second car exists.

aggregation *n.* the special form of association and linkage that captures the logical relationship that exists from an aggregate (whole) to one of its component parts.

Because the aggregate is [partially] defined in terms of its component parts in the object paradigm, the parts are visible to the aggregate and the aggregate can therefore delegate some of its responsibilities to its parts (i.e., one can navigate from the aggregate to its parts).

Aggregations provide an example of the practical use of abstraction. Initially, the modeler can work at a higher, blackbox level of abstraction, deferring consideration of the encapsulated, lower level parts until later.

bi-directional aggregation *n.* the shorthand convention representing the rare case in which a unidirectional aggregation relationship and a semi-strong inverse association/linkage exists, allowing the part to know about and navigate to the aggregate.

Bi-directional aggregation is used in the Mediator pattern. Note that bi-directional aggregation does not mean that the part contains the aggregate, but merely that there is a reason to model a semi-strong inverse relationship (i.e., is a part of) back to the aggregate.

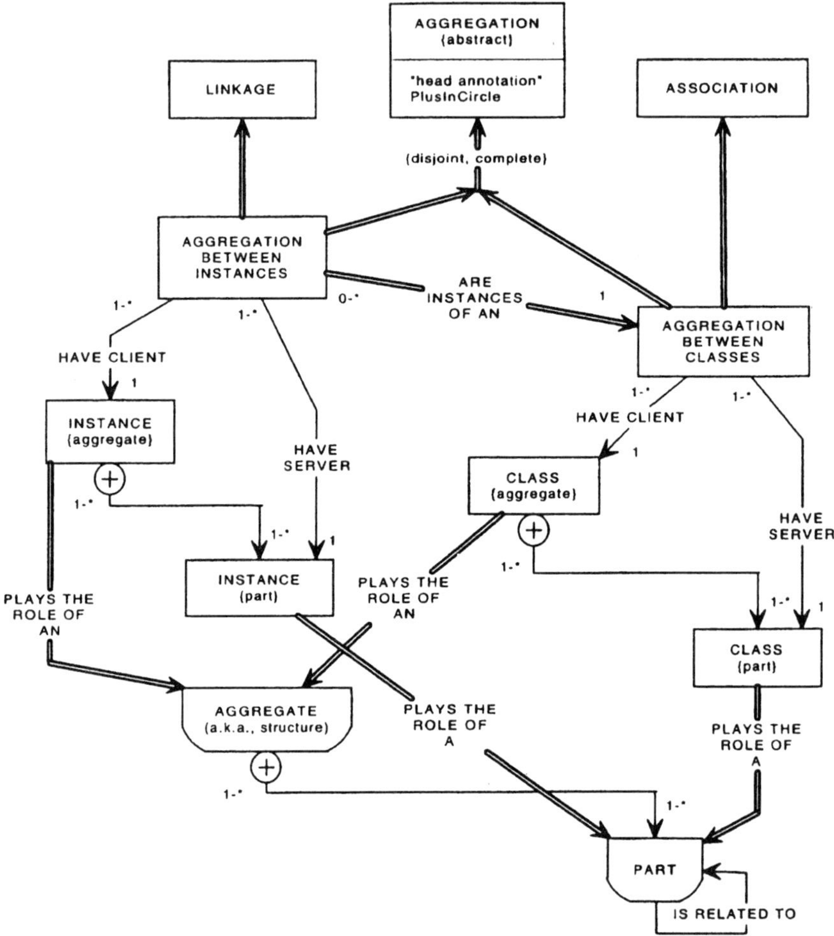

Figure 3.64. Partial metamodel for aggregation relationships.

OML Metamodel

Figure 3.64 illustrates a partial metamodel for aggregation relationships and captures the following information:

- Aggregation can be completely and disjointedly partitioned into aggregation between instances and aggregation between classes, whereby each aggregation between instances relationship is an instance of an aggregation between classes relationship.

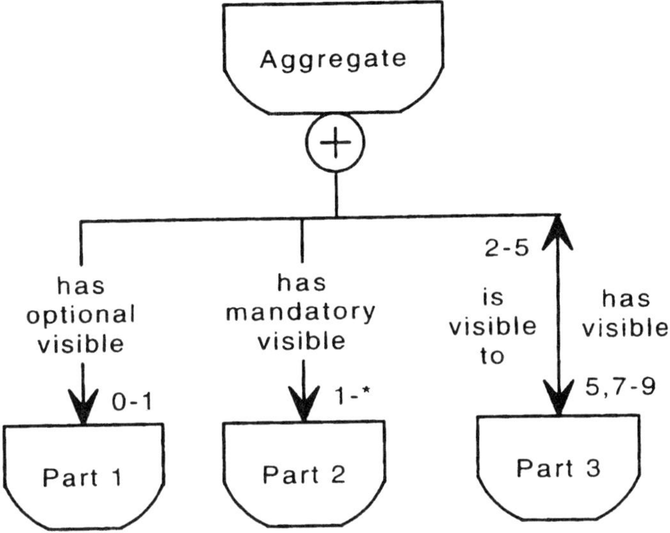

Figure 3.65. Aggregation notation.

- Aggregation between instances is a kind of linkage, and aggregation between classes is a kind of association. Therefore, an aggregation relationship between instances is an instance of an aggregation relationship between classes.

- Each aggregation relationship connects an aggregate to a part, whereby aggregate and part are roles that may be played by either instances or classes.

- The aggregate structure includes its parts.

- An aggregates forms a structure because relationships exist among its parts.

COMN Notation

aggregation. As illustrated by Figure 3.65, aggregation is represented by:

- the vertical aggregation arc consisting of the aggregation symbol (a circle around a large plus sign) drawn at the aggregate end of a line segment from the aggregate to the aggregation yoke,

- the horizontal aggregation yoke[25] between the aggregate and its parts, and

- the vertical association/linkage arcs from the aggregation yoke to the individual parts.

---

[25]The horizontal aggregation yoke is optional if the number of part nodes is one.

Although the standard cardinality notation of association/ linkage arcs is supported, the default cardinality at the aggregate end of the arc is one and assumed if not explicitly noted otherwise.

unidirectional aggregation. Unidirectional aggregation is represented by using the unidirectional association/linkage arc from the aggregation yoke to the part.

bi-directional aggregation. Bi-directional aggregation is represented by using the bi-directional association/linkage arc from the aggregation yoke to the part.

Applicable Diagrams

Icons for aggregation associations and linkages can occur on the following kinds of diagrams:

- Semantic Nets:
    - Context Diagrams
    - Cluster Diagrams
    - Inheritance Diagrams
    - Deployment Diagrams
    - Layer Diagrams
- Interaction Diagrams

Stereotypes

Aggregation has the following stereotypes:

- mutable vs. immutable.
- transitive vs. intransitive.
- symmetric vs. asymmetric vs. antisymmetric.

Arc Compatibility Rules

Aggregation is irreflexive. That is, an aggregate may not have itself as a part of itself. Because there are different kinds of aggregation, aggregation is usually (but not always!):

- *transitive.* If A has part B and B has part C, then logically A indirectly has part C.
- *antisymmetric.* If A has part B, then B cannot have part A.

However, the recursive use of aggregation does require it to be transitive and antisymmetric.

Because the aggregate must have visibility to its parts, the "TBD" form of association/linkage is not permitted.

Aggregation linkage arcs may connect:

- actors to actors.

  Example: A patient (mother) can contain another patient (fetus).

- clusters to clusters.

- hardware externals to hardware externals or software externals.

- objects to objects.

- persistent memory externals to persistent memory externals.

  Example: A database is an aggregation of database tables.

- roles to roles.

- software externals to software externals.

Aggregation association arcs may connect:

- actor classes to actor classes.

  Example: A patient (mother) can contain another patient (fetus).

- cluster classes to cluster classes.

- hardware external classes to hardware external classes or software external classes.

- object classes to object classes.

- persistent memory external classes to persistent memory external classes.

  Example: A database is an aggregation of database tables.

- software external classes to software external classes.

Usage Guidelines

1. Use association or linkage instead of aggregation if it is not clear that the relationship represents a whole/part relationship.

2. Use containment rather than aggregation if the parts do not form a structure (i.e., have interrelationships).

3. Use unidirectional association/linkage arcs to connect the aggregate with its parts except in the atypical situation in which the parts must also have visibility to the aggregate.

4. Consider not showing the parts of an aggregate if the aggregate is best viewed as a blackbox and thus documented at a higher level of abstraction.

Rationale

As noted by Grady Booch and others, aggregation is a specialized form of association and linkage. Therefore, its notation inherits the normal notation for association and linkage. The aggregation symbol includes a plus sign and is on the aggregation end of the association/linkage arc because the whole is [more than [26]] the *sum* of its parts. The aggregation symbol can also be viewed as a Philips screw head, holding together the aggregate's parts. As illustrated in Figure 3.65, the aggregation symbol is drawn touching the outside of the icon for the aggregate so that the association/linkage arcs can form the traditional fork structure. Although bidirectional aggregation is rare, it is sometimes required for navigability, as in the Mediator pattern.

Because most parts are parts of only one aggregate, the default cardinality at the aggregate end of the association/linkage arc is one.

Examples

As illustrated in Figure 3.66, a Polygon is an aggregate that consists of three or more line segments as component parts. In this case, the class Polygon is also an abstract class which forces the designer to create subclasses in order to specify the exact polygon (e.g., square, pentagon) desired.

An aggregate may consist of component parts that are of the same type as the aggregate. This leads to the pattern and example instance in Figure 3.67.

3.2.2.3 CONTAINMENT RELATIONSHIPS

Definitions

The following definitions provide semantics to the partial metamodel documented in Figure 3.68:

---

[26]The aggregate object also has descriptive attributes and links to other objects in addition to its component parts.

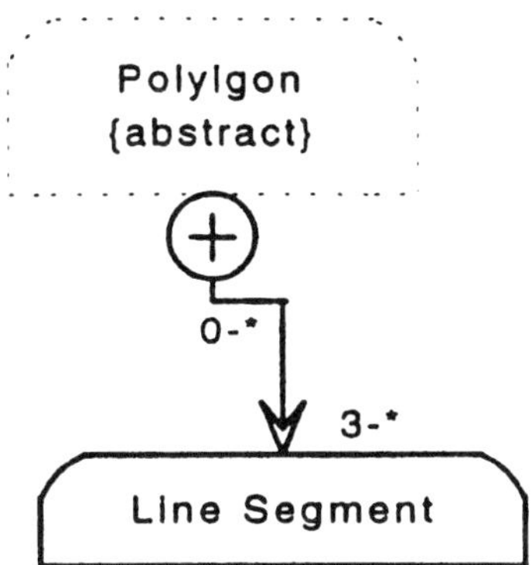

Figure 3.66. Example of simple aggregation.

container *n.* any modeling element that contains other modeling element of the same metatype that do not form a structure.

For example, a car trunk (boot) can contain many items and these items do not have relationships.

- **homogeneous container** *n.* any container that contains entries of a single type.
- **heterogeneous container** *n.* any container that contains entries of multiple types.

entry *n.* any modeling element contained in a container.

containment *n.* the special form of association and linkage that captures the logical relationship that exists from container to its component entries.

Because the container holds its entries in the object paradigm, the entries are visible to the container.

OML Metamodel

Figure 3.68 illustrates a partial metamodel for containment relationships and captures the following information:

- Containment can be completely and disjointedly partitioned into containment between instances and containment between classes, whereby each containment between instances relationship is an instance of a containment between classes relationship.

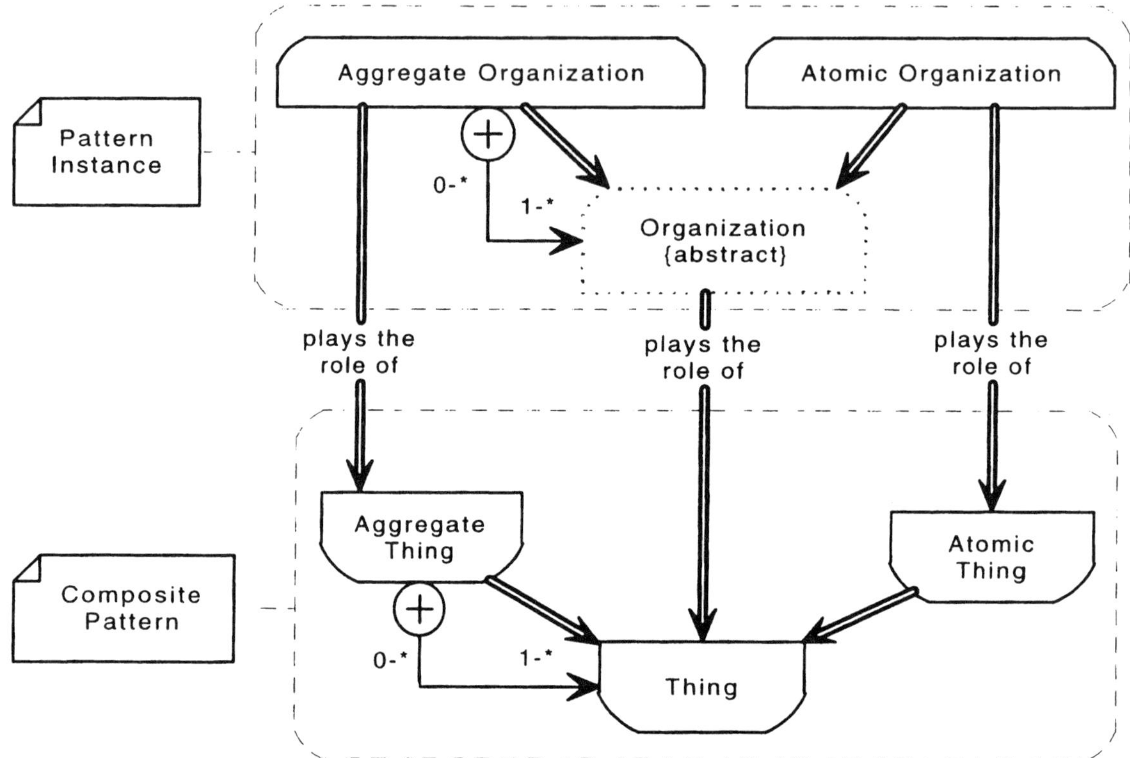

Figure 3.67. Example of recursive aggregation in the composite pattern.

- Containment between instances is a kind of linkage, and containment between classes is a kind of association. Therefore, a containment relationship between instances is an instance of a containment relationship between classes.

- Each containment relationship connects a container to an entry, whereby container and entry are roles that may be played by either instances or classes.

- The container contains its entries.

- Unlike an aggregate, a container does not form a structure because relationships do not exist among its entries.

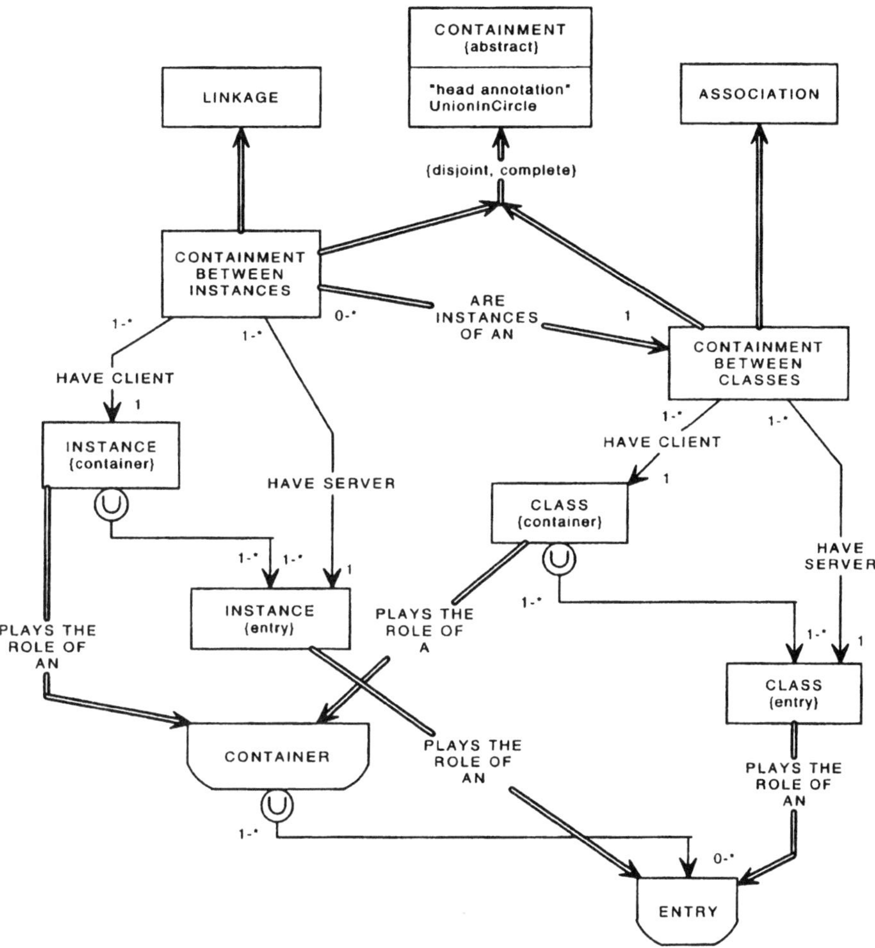

Figure 3.68. Partial metamodel of containment relationships.

COMN Notation

containment. As illustrated on Figure 3.69, containment is represented by:

- the vertical containment arc consisting of the containment symbol (a circle around a large "U" or union sign) drawn at the container end of a line segment from the container to the containment yoke,

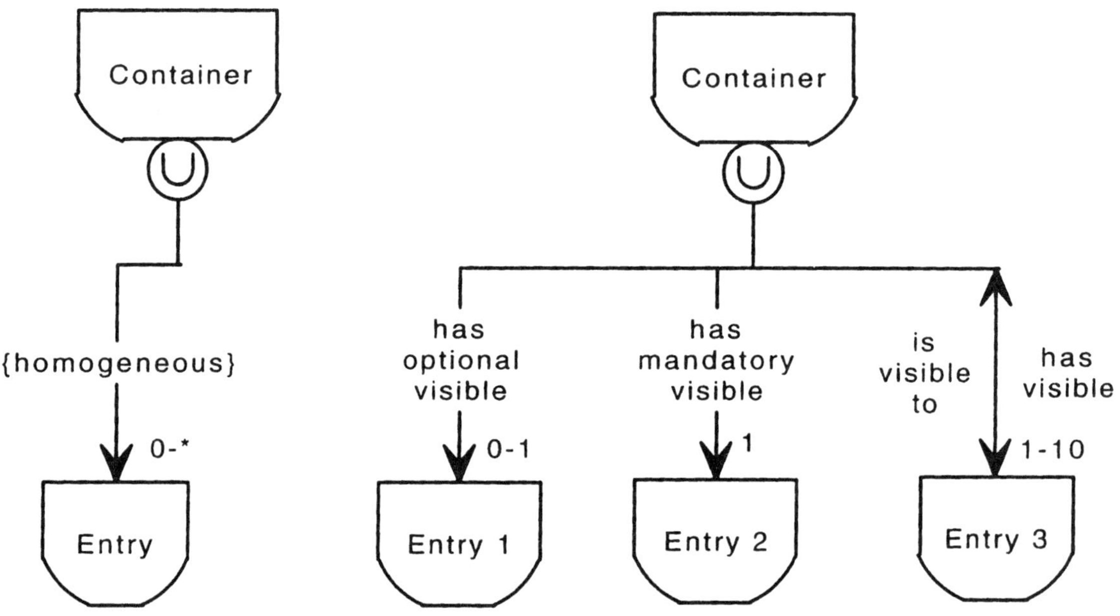

Figure 3.69. Containment notation.

- the horizontal containment yoke[27] between the container and its entries, and
- the vertical association/linkage arcs from the containment yoke to the entries.

The standard cardinality notation of association/linkage arcs is supported. However, the default cardinality at the containment end of the association/linkage arc is one and assumed unless explicitly annotated.

unidirectional containment. Unidirectional containment is represented by using the unidirectional association/linkage arc from the containment yoke to the entry.

bi-directional containment. Bi-directional containment is represented by using the bi-directional association/linkage arc from the containment yoke to the part.

---

[27]The horizontal containment yoke is optional if the number of entry nodes is 1.

Applicable Diagrams

Icons for containment associations and linkages can occur on the following kinds of diagrams:

- Semantic Nets:
    - Context Diagrams
    - Cluster Diagrams
    - Inheritance Diagrams
    - Deployment Diagrams
    - Layer Diagrams
- Interaction Diagrams

Stereotypes

Containment has the following stereotypes:

- mutable vs. immutable.
- transitive vs. intransitive.
- symmetric vs. asymmetric vs. antisymmetric.

Containers have the following stereotypes:

- bag vs. set vs. list vs. queue vs. stack, etc.

Arc Compatibility Rules

Containment is irreflexive. That is, an container may not contain itself. Because there are different kinds of containment, containment is usually (but not always!):

- *transitive.* If A has entry B and B has entry C, then logically A indirectly has entry C.
- *antisymmetric.* If A has entry B, then B cannot have entry A (i.e., entries cannot contain their containers).

However, the recursive use of entry does require it to be transitive and antisymmetric.
   Containment linkage arcs may connect:

- hardware externals to hardware external or software externals.
- objects or multiobjects to objects.
- roles to roles.

Containment association arcs may connect:

- hardware external classes to hardware external classes.
- object classes to object classes.

Usage Guidelines

1. Use unidirectional association/linkage arcs to connect the container with its entries except in the atypical situation in which the entries must also have visibility to their container.
2. Containers are often implemented by generic/template classes in C++ and by container classes in Smalltalk.

Rationale

Because containment is a specialized form of association and linkage, its notation inherits the normal notation for association and linkage. The containment symbol is a U-shaped container (cup) at the container end of the association/linkage arc. As illustrated in Figures 3.69 and 3.70, the containment symbol is drawn touching the outside of the icon for the container so that the association/linkage arcs can form the traditional fork structure.

Because most entries are entries of only one container, the default cardinality at the containment end of the association/linkage arc is one.

Examples

Figure 3.70 illustrates an example of containment. Note that the multiobject icon can be used to summarize the containment relationship between a container and its entries. Note also that an iterator message (i.e., price) to a container is often polymorphically passed through to its entries.

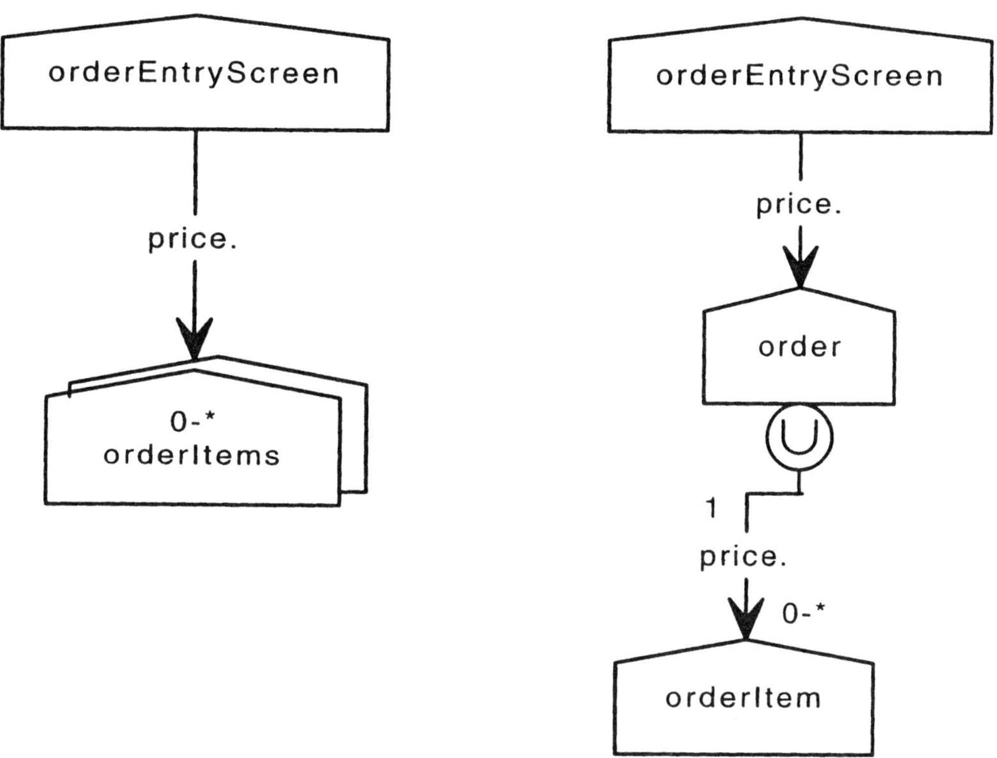

Figure 3.70. Examples of containment including polymorphic call-through.

3.2.2.4 MESSAGE PASSING AND EXCEPTION RAISING

Definitions

The following definitions provide semantics to the partial metamodel documented in Figure 3.71:

interaction *n.* (1) at the software level, either the passing of a message or the raising of an exception. (2) at the system level, a single communication.

exception *n.* any object which models an exceptional or error condition raised by an operation in order to notify a client that the condition has occurred.

message *n.* the normal unit of communication sent by one object to another.

Messages can be completely and disjointedly partitioned by concurrency semantics into the following three kinds of messages:

- **sequential message** *n.* any message (e.g., Smalltalk, C++) involving only one thread of control that is temporarily passed from the sender to the receiver, thereby blocking the sender until the receiver's operation is completed.
- **synchronous message** *n.* any message (e.g., Ada rendezvous) that synchronizes two threads of control, thereby potentially blocking either the sender or the receiver until both are ready to communicate.
- **asynchronous message** *n.* any message involving two threads of control that do not synchronize during message passing so that neither the sender nor the receiver is blocked by having to wait for the other.

Messages can be completely and disjointedly partitioned by reference semantics into the following three kinds of messages:

- **normal message** *n.* any message that is not sent along either an aggregation or containment linkage.
- **aggregation message** *n.* any message that is sent along an aggregation linkage.
- **containment message** *n.* any message that is sent along a containment linkage.

sender *n.* the client role that sends messages.

receiver *n.* the server role that receives the messages sent by the sender.

raiser *n.* the server role that raises exceptions.

handler *n.* the client role that handles exceptions raised by the raiser.

OML Metamodel

Figure 3.71 illustrates a partial metamodel for interaction relationships and captures the following information:

- Messages and exceptions are kinds of interactions.
- Senders send messages to receivers, whereby senders are a kind of client and receivers are a kind of server.
- Messages can be completely and disjointedly partitioned by the kind of linkage traversed into normal messages, aggregation messages, and containment messages.

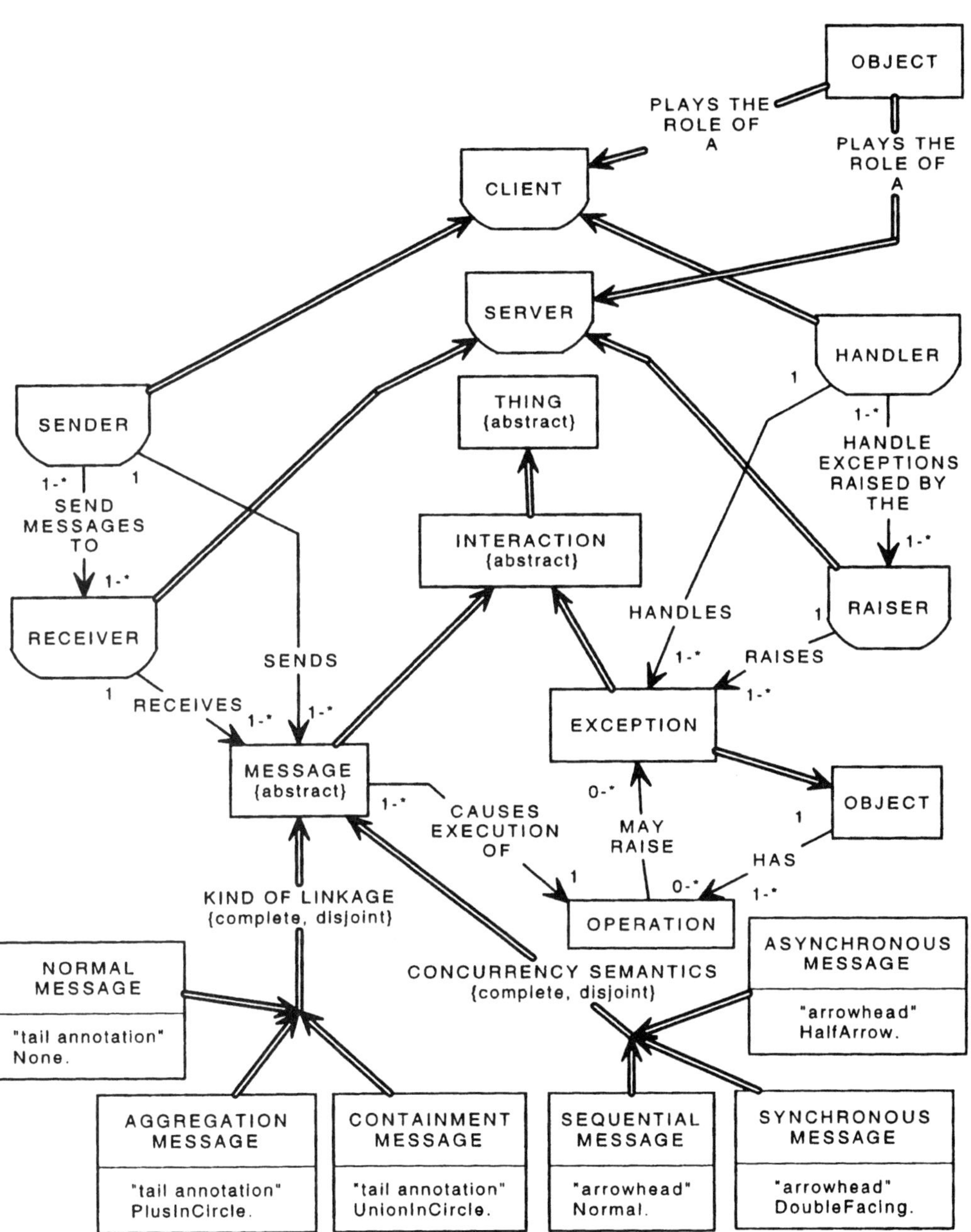

Figure 3.71. Partial metamodel for message passing and exception raising.

- Messages can be completely and disjointedly partitioned by concurrency semantics into sequential messages, synchronous messages, and asynchronous messages.
- Messages cause the execution of operations in objects, and these operations may raise exceptions.
- Exceptions are a kind of object.
- Raisers raise exceptions to handlers which handle them, whereby raisers are a kind of server and handlers are a kind of client.

COMN Notation

message. A message is represented by a solid line connecting the sender to the receiver. The label of a message is the signature of the message, typically in the intended programming language and optionally including associated exception and return type.

- *sequential message.* A sequential message is denoted by a normal arrowhead on the receiver end.
- *synchronous message.* A synchronous message is denoted by double facing arrowheads (i.e., two open arrowheads pointing at each other) near the receiver end.
- *asynchronous message.* An asynchronous message is denoted by a half arrowhead on the port (left) side of the receiver end.
- *normal message.* A normal message requires no annotation on the sender end.
- *aggregation message.* An aggregation message is denoted by an aggregation symbol (i.e., large plus sign in a circle) on the sender end.
- *containment message.* A containment message is denoted by a containment symbol (i.e., a union symbol in a circle) on the sender end.
- Exceptions are denoted by an exclamation mark before and after the name of each exception.

As illustrated in Figure 3.72, on collaboration diagrams:

- All messages of the same kind and exceptions are listed on the same message arc.
- The signature of each message is terminated by the normal terminator in the implementation language (e.g., by a period in Smalltalk).

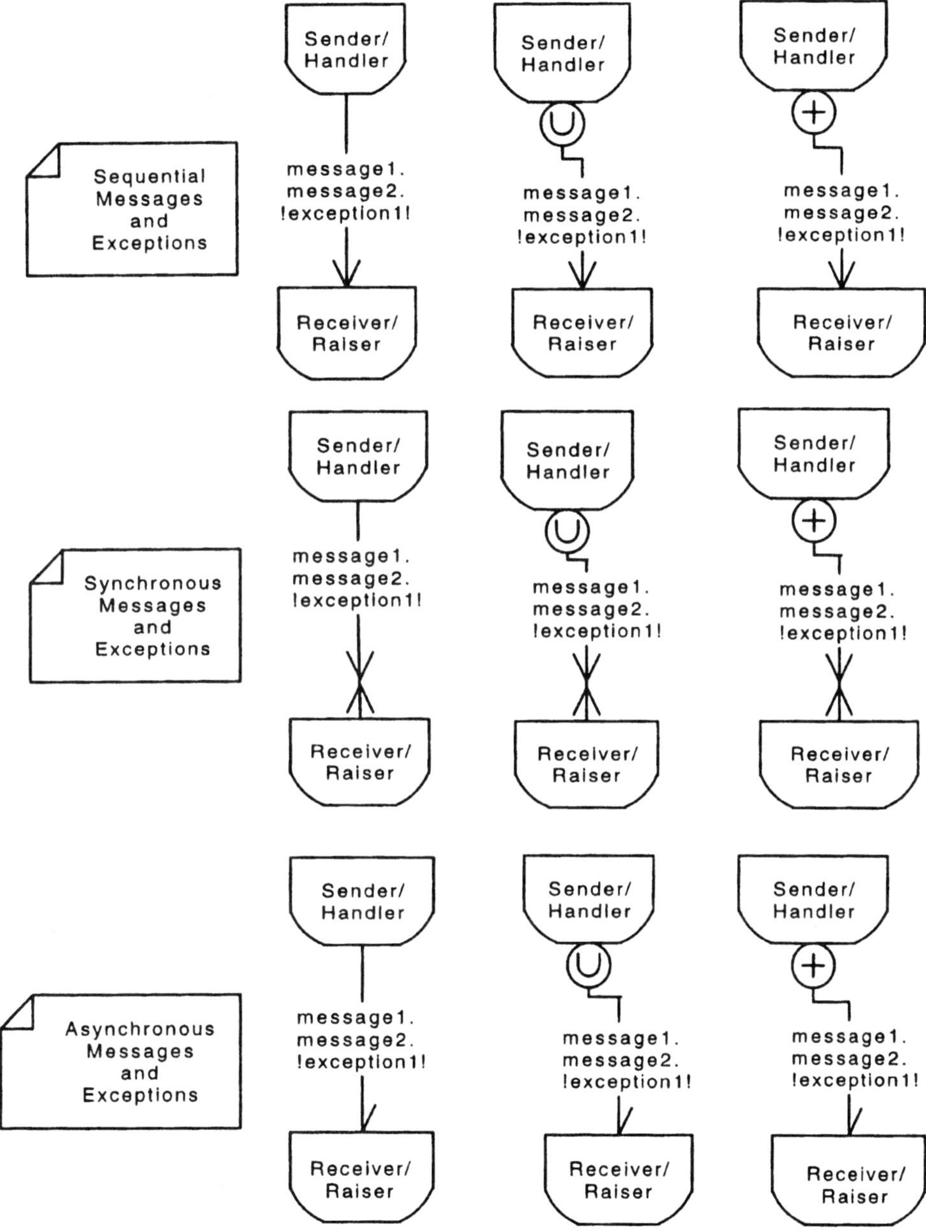

Figure 3.72. Messages and exceptions on collaboration diagrams.

- If the collaboration diagram is used instead of a sequence diagram to represent a specific sequence of interactions, then the messages and exceptions can be labeled with a sequence number. In a single thread, the order of the interaction can optionally be represented by a positive integer surrounded by parentheses preceding the interaction. Multiple threads can be indicated by preceding the number with a lower-case letter representing the thread.

As illustrated on Figure 3.73, on sequence diagrams:

- All messages and exceptions are drawn horizontally between time lines.
- An exception is represented by a dashed line drawn from the raiser to the handler with an arrowhead on the handler end.

Applicable Diagrams

Icons for message and exception arcs can be used on Interaction Diagrams.

Rules

Messages arcs from sender to receiver may connect:

- object to object.
- timeline to timeline.

Exception arcs from raiser to handler may connect:

- object to object.
- timeline to timeline.

Usage Guideline

1. On collaboration diagrams, draw senders above receivers so that the overall control flow of the diagram is clear.

Rationale

If associations and linkages are viewed as one-way roads connecting objects, then messages can be viewed as the primary traffic on those roads and exceptions can

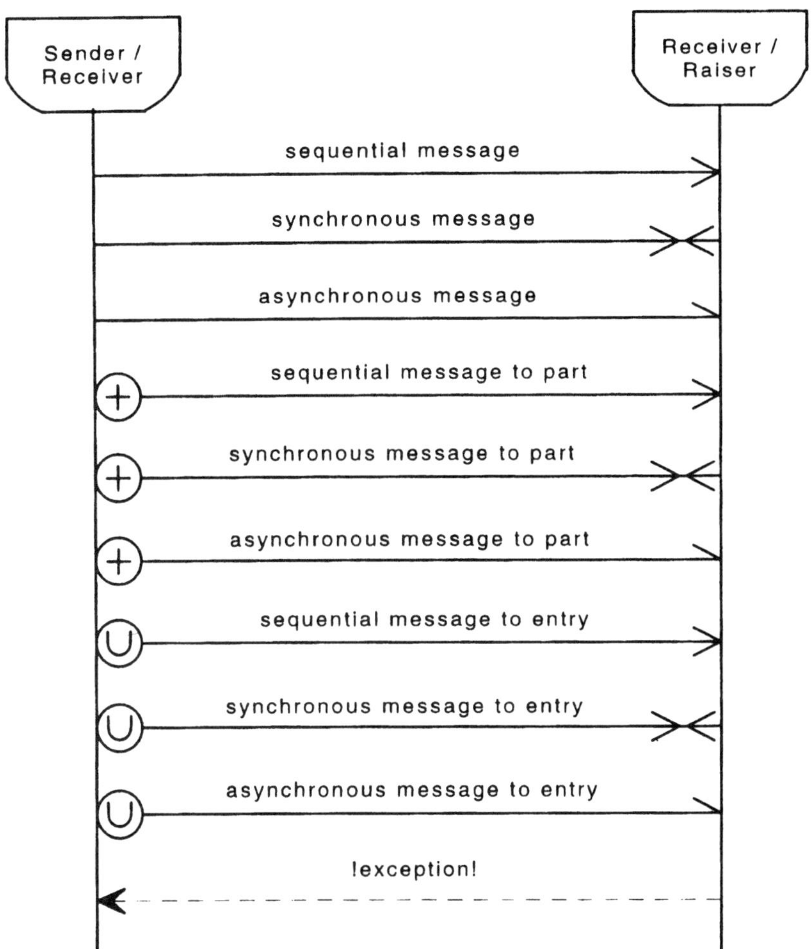

Figure 3.73. Messages and exceptions on sequence diagrams.

be viewed as emergency vehicles that go the "wrong way" on those roads. Interaction diagrams therefore use the standard association and linkage arcs, optionally including aggregation, containment, and concurrency annotations.

By listing multiple messages and exceptions on the same referential relationship arcs rather than natural language descriptions or responsibilities, the number of arcs between nodes is minimized, thereby minimizing the clutter of collaboration diagrams.

Because interaction diagrams are more design level than semantic nets, the arrowhead on interaction arcs captures the kind of message protocol:

- The arrowhead for *sequential messages* is a standard arrowhead because the most common message type is sequential. Because most messages (those supported by most current OOPLs) are sequential, we use the same icon for association/linkage as for sequential messages.

- The arrowhead for *synchronous messages* shows two arrowheads meeting at the receiver end because this implies the rendezvous of the two threads at the receiver object.

- The arrowhead for *asynchronous messages* is missing its starboard (right) half, symbolizing the lack of a return type on these 'fire and forget' messages.

Because exceptions represent exceptional situations, exceptions are emphasized by surrounding them with exclamation marks.

Because messages and exceptions can be directly implemented in code, the standard naming conventions of the implementation language are used when dealing with internal message passing and exception raising. If it is important to show the return type and potential exceptions, they can be listed with each message.

Examples

Figure 3.74 illustrates the use of a software collaboration diagram to document a mechanism in a vending machine application. Pushing a button results in a series of interactions that causes a string to be displayed on the Display. Classes and Smalltalk naming conventions are used.

Figure 3.75 illustrates the use of a whitebox sequence diagram to document the same mechanism. Instances and Java naming conventions are used.

3.2.2.5 NOTES AND ATTRIBUTION

Definitions

The following definitions provide semantics to the partial metamodel documented in Figure 3.76:

note *n.* any developer-defined text providing a comment or listing a constraint about a specific modeling element.

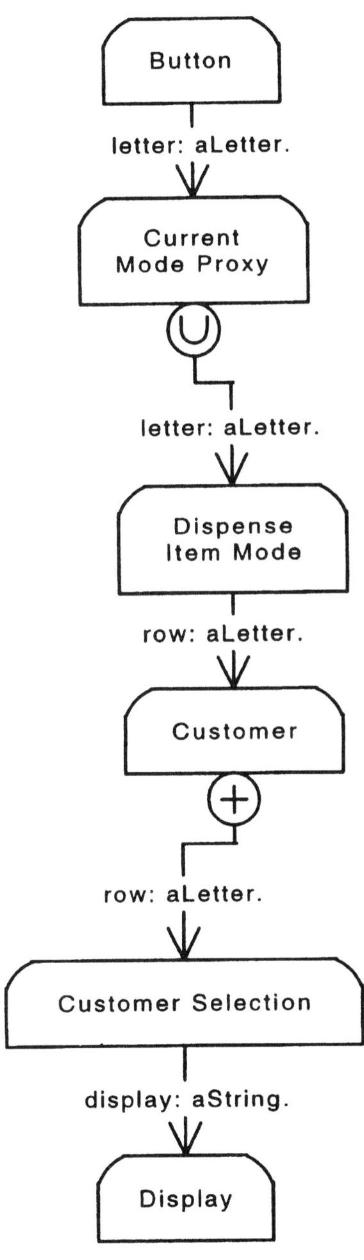

Figure 3.74. Example software collaboration diagram.

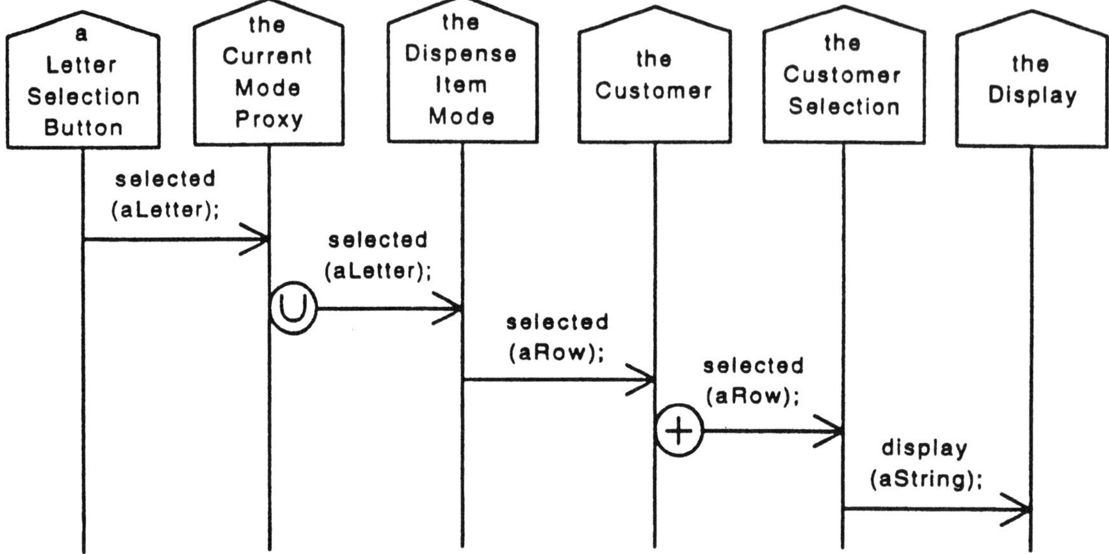

Figure 3.75. Example whitebox sequence diagram.

attributed to *n.* the referential relationship connecting a note to the modeling element(s) being described by the note.

OML Metamodel

Figure 3.76 illustrates a partial metamodel for notes and attribution relationships and captures the following information:

- Attribution relationships are a kind of referential relationship.
- Attribution relationships connect one note to one modeling element.
- Each note is a kind of thing.
- Each note is connected by one or more attribution relationships to the modeling elements that it describes.
- Each modeling element is connected by zero or more attribution relationships to note(s) that describe it.

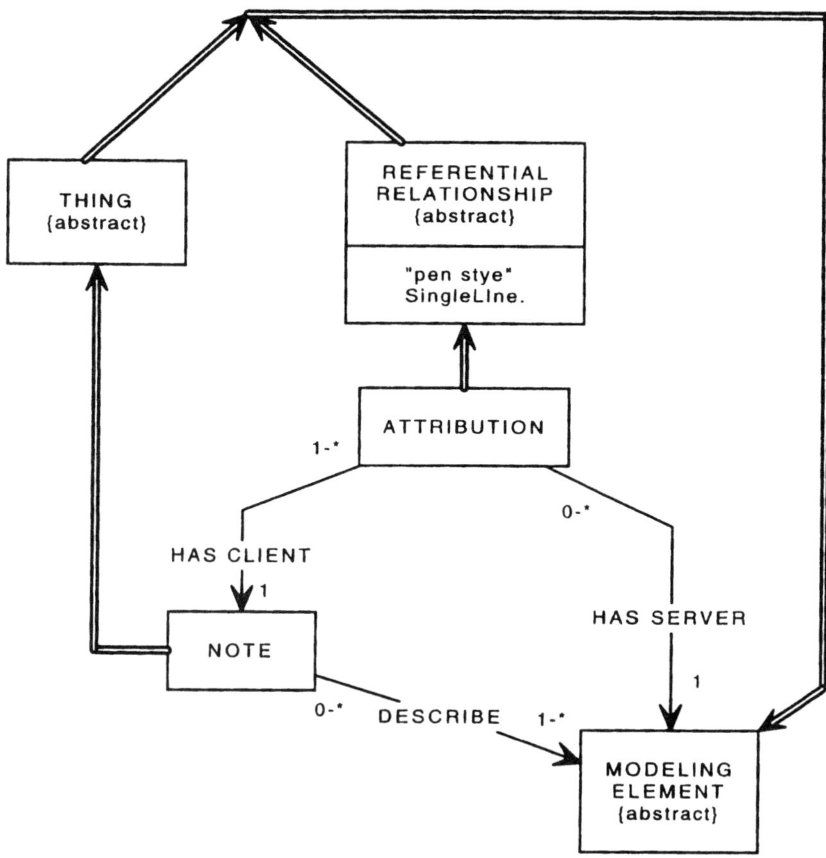

Figure 3.76. Partial metamodel for notes and attribution.

COMN Notation

note. A note is represented by a rectangle with the upper left corner turned over. The label of a note is any character string.

attribution. Each attribution relationship is represented by a dotted line connecting a note to a modeling element.

Applicable Diagrams

Notes and attribution relationships can be used on any diagram.

Usage Guidelines

1. Only use notes to provide information that is not presentable using other OML COMN notation.
2. Avoid the excessive use of notes that would clutter up the diagrams; instead consider using accompanying text.

Examples

Figure 3.51 uses notes to point out the different kinds of inheritance on an inheritance diagram.

3.3 Multiplicity

Definitions

The following definitions provide semantics for multiplicities:

multiplicity n. the potential number of things.[28]

- **multiplicity of an aggregate** n. the potential number of the aggregate's component parts.
- **multiplicity of a class** n. the potential number of the class's instances.
- **multiplicity of a container** n. the potential number of entries in the associated container.
- **multiplicity of a multiobject** n. the potential number of objects in the associated collection.
- **multiplicity of a cluster** n. the potential total number of cluster characteristics (e.g., objects, classes, clusters) in the cluster.
- **multiplicity of a cluster class** n. the potential total number of cluster class characteristics (e.g., object classes, types, cluster classes, roles) in the cluster class.
- **multiplicity of an association** n. the potential number of objects that are involved at each end of the association.

---

[28]Multiplicity is often confused with cardinality, which is defined as the *actual* number of things.

COMN Notation

Multiplicity is indicated by a character string consisting of one or more comma-separated ranges.

A range is indicated by a non-negative integer lower value followed by a hyphen followed by a upper value. A single positive integer is considered a valid range. The symbol '*' indicates an arbitrarily large upper value.

As illustrated in Figure 3.77, the multiplicity of an aggregate, container, class, multiobject, cluster, or cluster class is optionally shown in the corresponding icon above the name.

Because of its importance, the multiplicity of a singleton class is surrounded by hyphens (i.e., '-1-').

The client multiplicity of an association is shown at the port (i.e., left) side of the client end of the association arc, and the server multiplicity is shown at the starboard side of the server end of the association arc.

An upside-down capital A (i.e., "∀") at the port (left) client end of an association can be used to indicate that all instances of the client are mapped to some instance of the server.

Applicable Diagrams

Multiplicity expressions can be used on any diagram in which the corresponding modeling element (e.g., aggregate, container, class, multiobject, cluster, cluster class, association) can occur.

Usage Guidelines

1. It is typically more important to label the multiplicities of multiobjects (i.e., collections) than classes, unless they are singleton classes.

2. Use the multiplicity notation only on clusters that have not been expanded to show their contents explicitly.

3. Because the multiplicities of associations often take several iterations to get right, postpone difficult decisions until later; do not feel that you have to add multiplicities to associations immediately as the associations are identified and drawn on the diagram.

4. The multiplicities of associations are optional, but recommended.

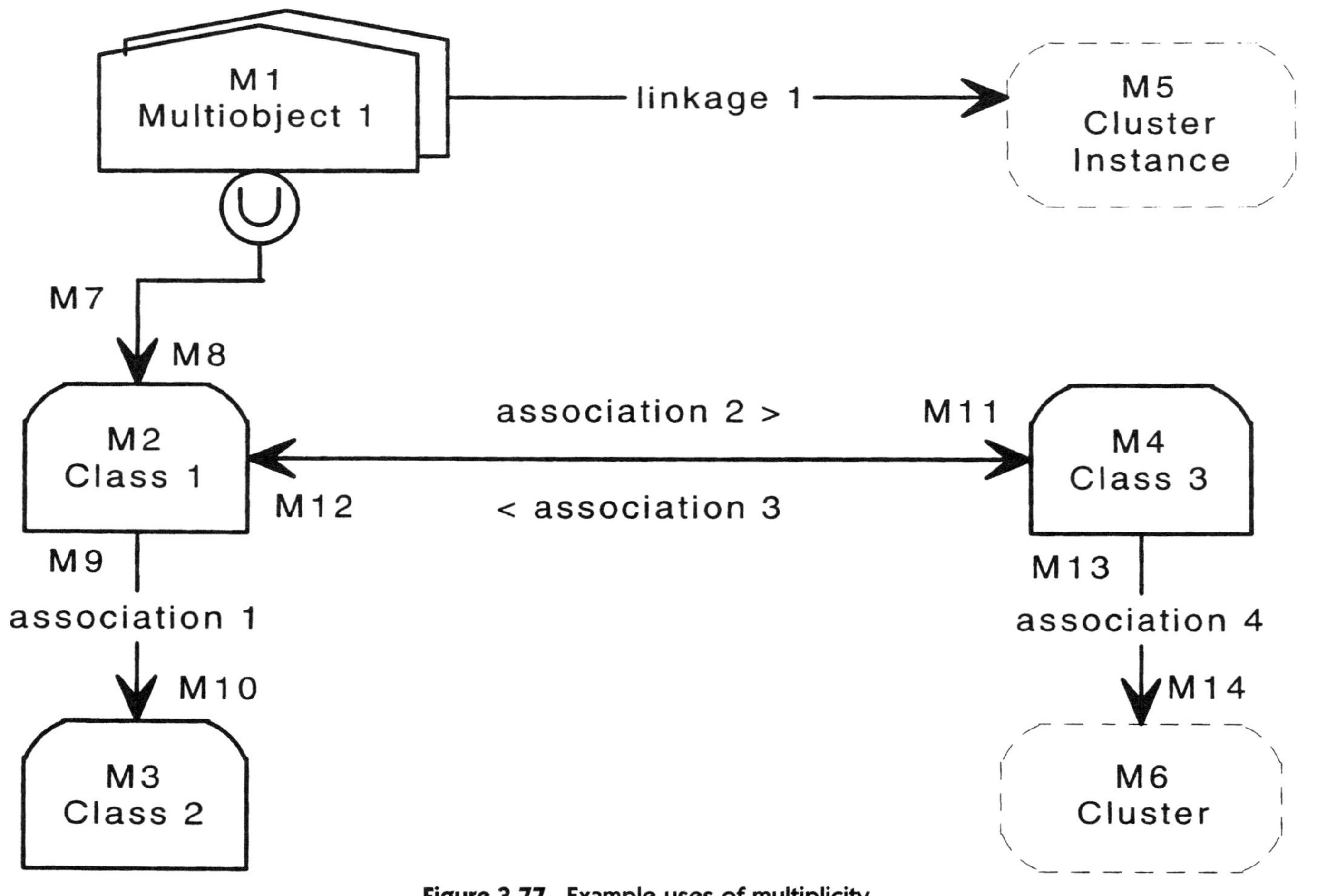

Figure 3.77. Example uses of multiplicity.

Rationale

This approach was chosen for the multiplicity of relationships over the traditional "crow's feet" notation because (1) it is more explicit and flexible and (2) the use of crows feet would prohibit the use of arrowheads on the ends of arcs, which is the optimum way to show directionality. This approach was also chosen over the use of hollow and filled multiplicity balls (e.g., OMT notation) not only because this approach is more intuitive, explicit, and flexible but also because the use of multiplicity balls would prohibit the use of arrowheads on the ends of arcs.

The use of hyphens rather than a pair of dots (e.g., UML notation) was chosen because it is more intuitive, eliminates the necessity to remember the number of dots.

Examples

1	one (on relationship arcs)
-1-	one on singleton classes
0-1	zero or one
0-*	zero or more
1-*	one or more
3-5,7,15	three, four, five, seven, or fifteen
0,3-*	zero, three or more

Figure 3.77 illustrates the following multiplicities:

- M1 is the potential number of entries in the multiobject.
- M2 is the potential number of instances of class Class1.
- M3 is the potential number of instances of class Class2.
- M4 is the potential number of instances of class Class3.
- M5 is the potential number of characteristics of Cluster1.
- M6 is the potential number of characteristics of ClusterClass1.
- M7 is the potential number of multiobjects in which an instance of Class1 can be an entry.
- M8 is the potential number of instances of Class 1 that can be entries in the multiobject. Note that this is another way of expressing the same information as expressed by M1.

- M9 is the potential number of instances of Class1 associated by association 1 with each instance of Class2.

- M10 is the potential number of instances of Class2 associated by association 1 with each instance of Class1. Note that all instances of Class1 are mapped to some instance of Class2.

- M11 is the potential number of instances of Class3 associated by association 2 with each instance of Class1.

- M12 is the potential number of instances of Class1 associated by association 3 with each instance of Class3.

- M13 is the potential number of instances of Class3 associated by association 4 with each instance of ClusterClass1.

- M14 is the potential number of instances of ClusterClass1 associated by association4 with each instance of Class3.

3.4 Naming Conventions

In order to promote uniformity and traceability to the software, OML recommends that the naming conventions (e.g., capitalization, message signatures, multiword names, special characters) of the implementation language be used in the diagrams.

For example, if Smalltalk is the implementation language:

- Classes will begin with an uppercase letter (e.g., Customer, Order).
- Where practical, instances will be named after their class, beginning with either a lowercase "a" or "an" (e.g., aCustomer).
- Operation names will begin with a lowercase letter.
- Message names on interaction diagrams will include the signature and optionally the return type (e.g., valid: aCoin ^self).
- Multiword names will be written together without spaces with subsequent words starting with uppercase letters (e.g., OrderItem).

For example, if Java is the implementation language:

- Classes will begin with an uppercase letter (e.g., Customer, Order).
- Where practical, instances will be named after their class, beginning with either a lowercase "a" or "an"(e.g., aCustomer).

- Operation names will begin with a lowercase letter.
- Message names on interaction diagrams will include the signature and optionally the return type. For example, void valid (Coin aCoin);
- Multiword names will be written together without spaces with subsequent words starting with uppercase letters (e.g., OrderItem).

For example, if Eiffel is the implementation language:

- Classes will be written fully in uppercase (e.g., CUSTOMER, ORDER).
- Instances will be written fully in lowercase and typically the name is followed by the type name in uppercase (e.g., favorite_book : BOOK).
- Operation names will written fully in lowercase.
- Message names will be written fully in lowercase.
- Multiword names will be separated by underscores (e.g., ORDER_ITEM).

In applications using multiple implementation languages, an organizational naming convention should be created.

If no implementation languages is to be used (e.g., during domain analysis), an organizational or project naming convention is still highly recommended.

COMN does not specify the font, font size, or the use of bold face, italics, underlining, and color.

4   Diagrams

A COMPLETE object model can describe a software application or an entire system including hardware, software, wetware (personnel), and paperware (documentation). Any non-trivial system or application is so complex that depicting all of its relevant requirements and design on a single diagram is impossible. It is thus necessary to document multiple views of the *single underlying object model*, with these views being of different kinds (e.g., static architecture, dynamic behavior) and at different level of abstractions (e.g., application, cluster, class). Each view is captured by a diagram: either a semantic net, use case diagram, interaction diagram, or state transition diagram. Each of these diagram types is described in one of the next four major sections. Because they all describe different aspects of the same underlying object model, it is therefore critical that changes made to one diagram are synchronized across and reflected in appropriate changes being made to other diagrams, hopefully automatically by a CASE tool.

Kinds

The rest of this section will document the following four major kinds of diagrams, many of which come in multiple varieties serving different purposes:

1. Semantic Nets:
   - Context Diagrams:
     — System Context Diagrams
     — Software Context Diagrams
   - Layer Diagrams

- Configuration Diagrams
- Cluster Diagrams
- Inheritance Diagrams
- Deployment Diagrams

2. Scenario Class Diagrams:

- Mechanism Diagrams
- Task Script Diagrams
- Use Case Diagrams

3. Interaction Diagrams:

- Collaboration Diagrams:
    — Cluster Collaboration Diagrams
    — Scenario Collaboration Diagrams
    — Internal Collaboration Diagrams
- Sequence Diagrams:
    — Blackbox Sequence Diagrams
    — Whitebox Sequence Diagrams

4. State Transition Diagrams

4.1   Semantic Nets

Definition

semantic net (SN) *n.* any directed graph documenting the static structure of a cohesive collection of related things (e.g., objects including externals, classes, clusters) connected by the semantically-meaningful relationships (e.g., association, aggregation, inheritance) between them.

Kinds

COMN recognizes the following six kinds of semantic nets:

1. Context Diagrams:

- System Context Diagrams
- Software Context Diagrams

2. Layer Diagrams

3. Configuration Diagrams

4. Cluster Diagrams

5. Inheritance Diagrams

6. Deployment Diagrams

Rationale

The semantic net is the most important and most widely-used diagram type in the OPEN method. OPEN uses semantic nets instead of extended entity relationship diagrams because:

- Semantic nets from the artificial intelligence community are designed to document static architecture in terms of modeling elements and the semantically important relationships among them.

- Semantic nets naturally capture classification (is a), specialization (a kind of),[1] and aggregation (has part) relationships.

- These diagrams primarily document objects and classes, rather than relational database tables. Entity relationship diagrams from data models are therefore misleading.

- These diagrams should not be called class diagrams (as they are by UML) because they document objects, externals, and clusters as well as classes.

Guidelines

1. If CASE tool vendors use a single diagram editor for all semantic nets, they should allow the user to select the specific subkind and then disable the inappropriate icons.

4.1.1 Context Diagrams

Definitions

context diagram *n.* any specialized semantic net, the purpose of which is to docu-

---

[1]The AI community also do not confuse is-a and a-kind-of relationships, which is, unfortunately, common in the object community.

ment the scope and environment of an application, layer, or subdomain treated as a blackbox in terms of itself, its externals and the semantically-meaningful relationships between them (e.g., association, aggregation, inheritance).

- **system context diagram** *n.* any context diagram used to document the context of an entire system potentially consisting of hardware, software, wetware (people), and paperware (documentation).

- **software context diagram** *n.* any context diagram used to document the context of a cohesive collection of software (e.g., an entire software application, a layer, or a subdomain within an application).

Audience

The primary intended audience for a context diagram consists of domain experts, business analysts, customers, managers, architects, and modelers.

Permitted Icons

The following nodes and arcs are permitted on context diagrams:

- Nodes:
  - The single primary node representing the scope of the diagram, either a system or a software application, layer, or subsystem.
  - Externals
    These nodes include both direct and (where appropriate) indirect externals of the system or software application.
- Arcs:
  - Linkage arcs
    These are the primary arcs on the diagram. They are primarily used to document the important relationships between the system or application node and its externals, but they may also be optionally used to show important relationships between externals.
  - Aggregation arcs
    These arcs are optional, are used to link related externals, and are typically only used if they simplify the diagram or make it easier to understand.

— Inheritance arcs
These arcs are optional, are used to connect externals related by inheritance, and are typically only used if they simplify the diagram or make it easier to understand. For example, because children should inherit the associations and aggregation relationships of their ancestors, the use of inheritance arcs may minimize the number of associations/links connecting the scope of the diagram to its externals.

Guidelines

1. A context diagram is typically one of the first diagrams developed using the OPEN method.

2. Start with the single primary icon representing the system or the software application. Add externals and connect them with the primary icon with linkage arcs. Add other relationships between the externals are appropriate.

3. If the number of externals is so large that the diagram would be too big and complex to fit on a single page, then the diagram may be broken into multiple subdiagrams.

Rationale

Using context diagrams to document the scope of an application has long been a good idea, and the term context diagram has traditionally been used for diagrams having this purpose.

The use of linkage relationships labeled with narrative language verb phrases is at the right level of abstraction for when context diagrams are developed and for communication with the intended audience for context diagrams.

However, traditional context diagrams were based on data flow, which is both inappropriate for object-oriented development and at too low of a level of abstraction for initial work.

Context diagrams based on message passing are also inappropriate because:

- the level of abstraction is too low,

- context diagrams are requirements-level diagrams and message signatures would be design information,

- messages are harder for the intended audience to read than narrative language phrases, and

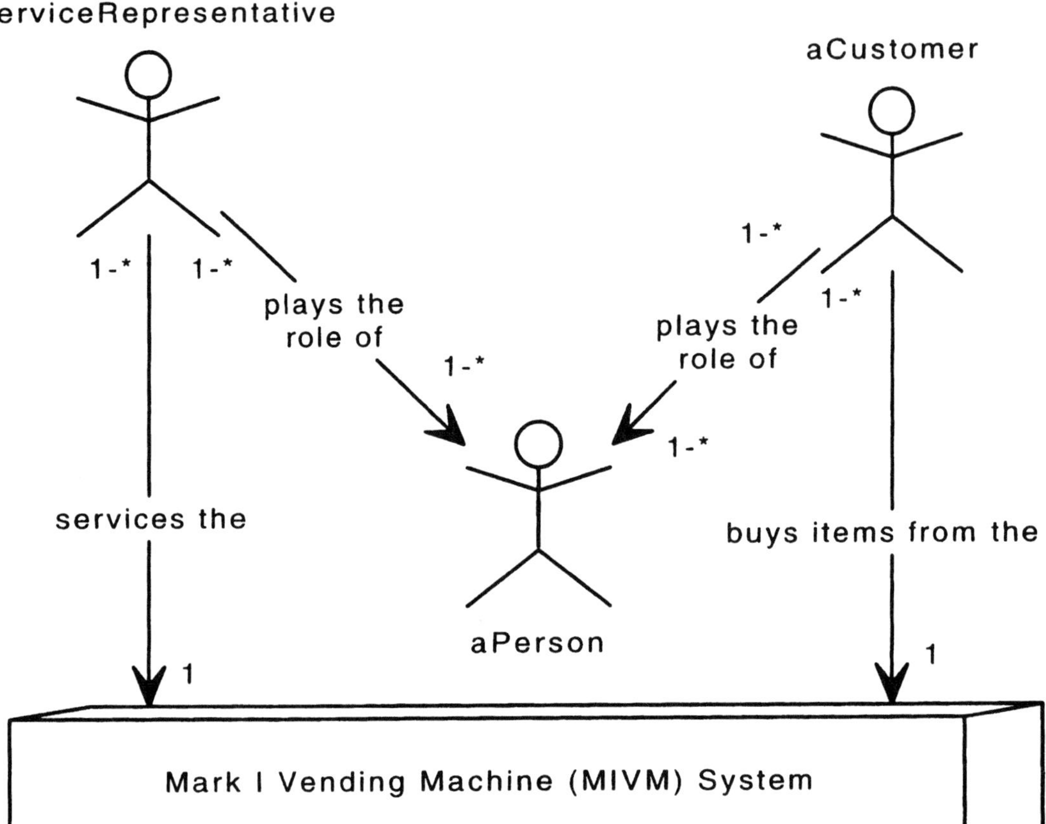

Figure 4.1. System-level context diagram for a vending machine application.

- many externals do not consist of object-oriented software and therefore do not send or respond to messages in the object-oriented sense.

Examples

Figure 4.1 is an example system context diagram for a vending machine applica tion. Note that the application has two actors, which are roles played by persons.

Figure 4.2 is an example software context diagram for the same application. Notice that this software context diagram contains many more externals than the corresponding system context diagram.

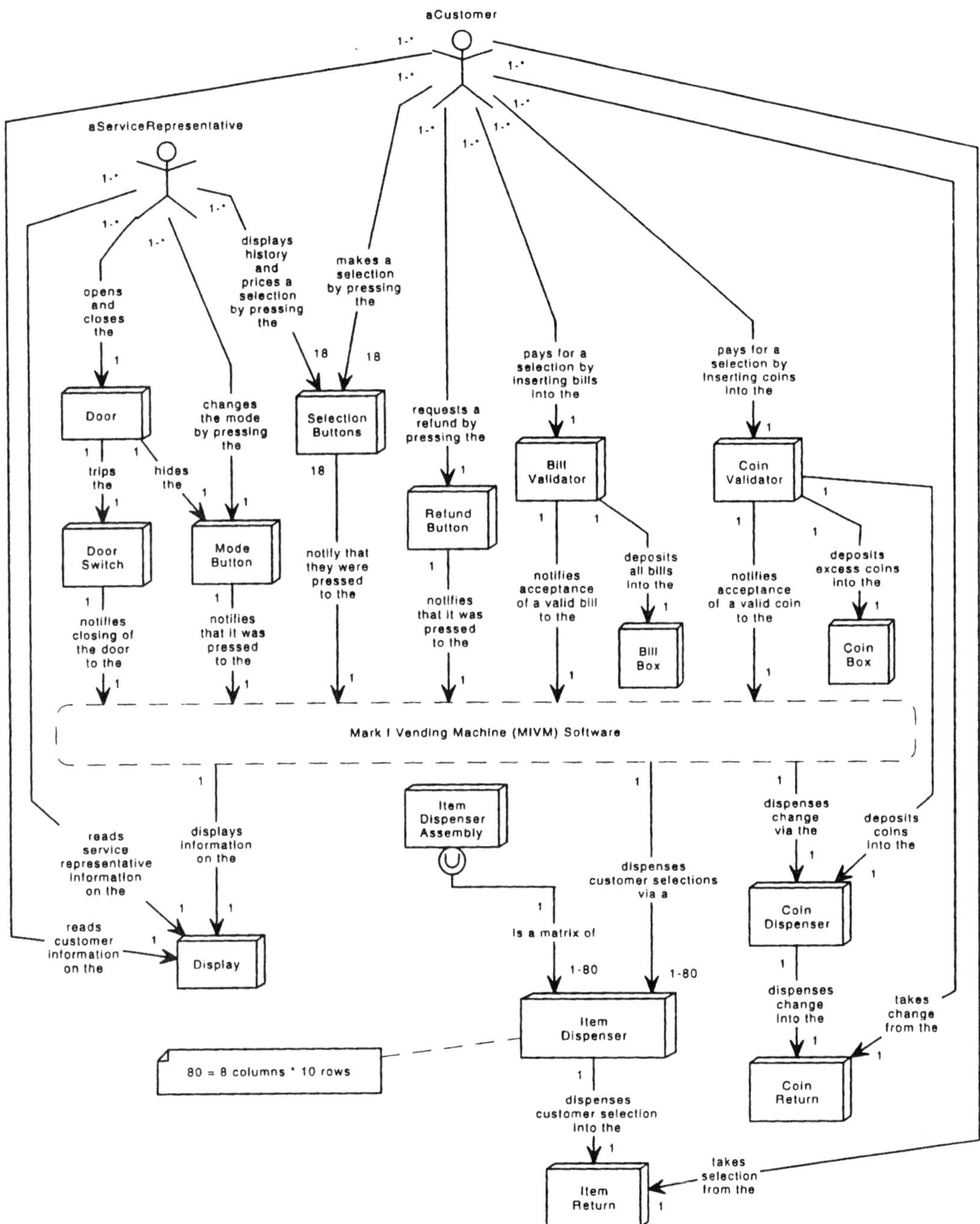

Figure 4.2. Software context diagram for a vending machine application.

4.1.2 Layer Diagrams

Definition

layer diagram *n.* any specialized semantic net, the purpose of which is to document the software architecture of an application and the software allocation to the resulting processors.

Audience

The primary intended audience for a layer diagram consists of domain experts, business analysts, customers, managers, architects, and modelers.

Permitted Icons

The following nodes and arcs are permitted on layer diagrams:

- Nodes:
    - Cluster icons
- Arcs:
    - Association and linkage arcs
      These are the primary arcs on the diagram. They are used to connect the primary node with the externals.

Guidelines

1. A layer diagram is typically one of the first diagrams developed using the OPEN method.
2. Use a separate layer diagram for the software on each processor in a distributed system.

Rationale

A layer diagram is useful for capturing the overall layered architecture of an application or a major part of an application.

Examples

Figure 4.3 documents the layer diagram for a typical two-tier client/server application. Each main cluster represents the software allocated to the associated hardware and contains internal clusters representing the layers making up that software. Notice that the lowest layer in the client software is connected to the top layer in the server software by an observer linkage.

4.1.3 Configuration Diagrams

Definitions

configuration diagram *n.* any specialized semantic net, the purpose of which is to document the overall structure of an application, layer, or subdomain in terms of its component layers, subdomains, and clusters respectively, their visibility (i.e., encapsulation), and the semantically important relationships among the component parts.

Aggregation is documented by nesting if the number of components is small and by using aggregation arcs if the number of components is large. Another option for large systems is to use abstraction and layering techniques. At a high level of abstraction (coarse granularity), the aggregate is shown as a blackbox; if more detail (of its components) is required, a "lower layer" diagrams may be added. This is equivalent to CASE tools that reveal internal details when you double click on an item.

- **system configuration diagram** *n.* any configuration diagram that is used to document an entire system consisting of hardware, software, and possibly wetware (people) and paperware (documentation)
- **software configuration diagram** *n.* any configuration diagram that is used to document a software application, layer, or subdomain.

Audience

The primary intended audience for configuration diagrams consists of domain experts, business analysts, customers, managers, architects, and modelers.

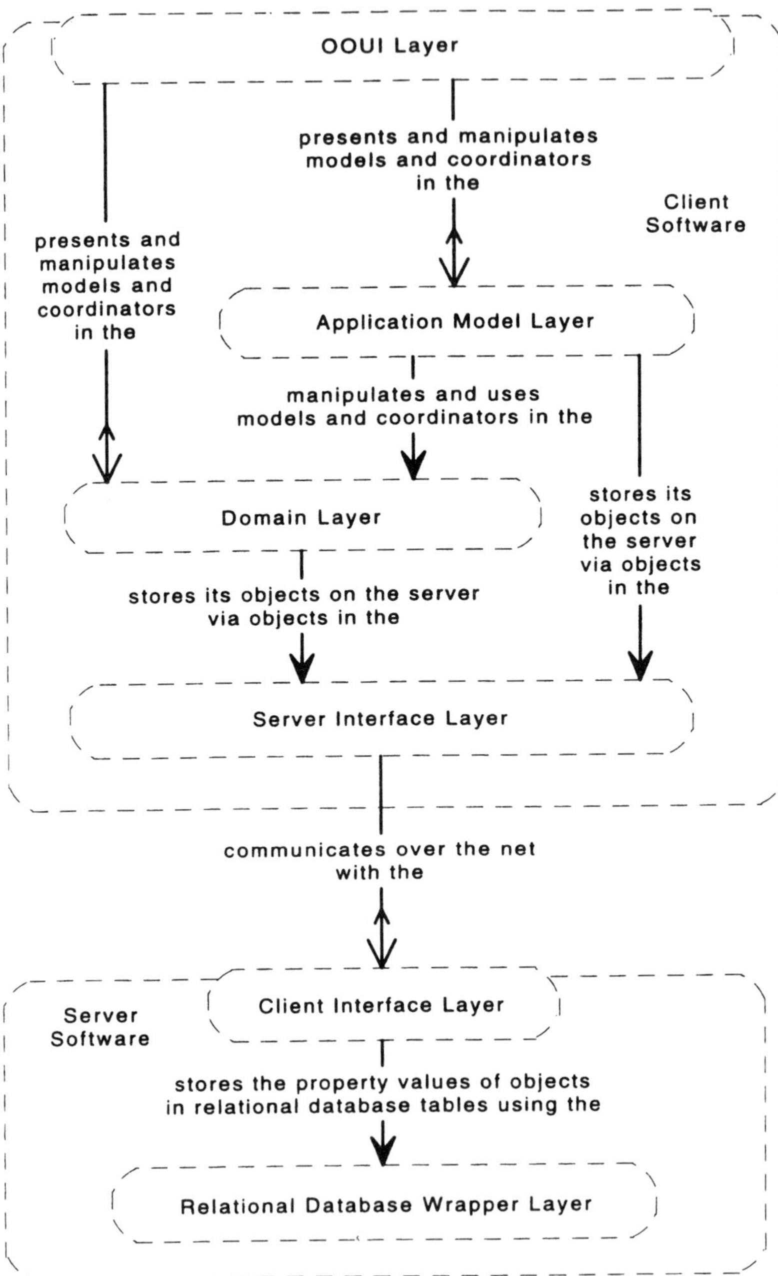

Figure 4.3. Layer diagram for a two-tier client server application.

Permitted Icons

The following nodes and arcs are permitted on configuration diagrams:

- Nodes:
  - Cluster icons
  - Cluster instance icons
- Arcs:
  - Association and linkage arcs
    These arcs document the dependencies among clusters and cluster instances.

  - Aggregation arcs
    These arcs are used when too many nodes exist for nesting to be practical.

Guidelines

1. Incrementally and iteratively develop the configuration diagram as new clusters are identified and developed.
2. Label the association arcs between clusters and the linkage arcs between cluster instances.
3. Ensure that the narrative language association and linkage arc labels remain at a high level of abstraction and do not merely attempt to summarize the messages on the collaboration diagrams that will flow along them.
4. Use aggregation arcs rather than nesting if the number of clusters is too great to make nesting practical.
5. Although this is typically one of the first diagrams to be started when using the OPEN method, it is also one of the last to be completed because of the iterative and incremental nature of the object-oriented development cycle.

Rationale

A small application consists of dozens of classes, and typical applications consist of hundreds or even thousands of classes. These classes are typically organized into layers, subdomains, and clusters for the sake of human understandability, team management, configuration management, and the organization of documentation. One or more diagrams are needed to indicate these divisions and provide a summary of the overall architecture of the application.

Examples

Figure 4.4 documents the software configuration diagram of a vending machine application.

4.1.4 Cluster Diagrams

Definition

cluster diagram *n.* any specialized semantic net, the purpose of which is to document the static structure of a cluster or mechanism of collaborating objects or roles respectively in terms of the semantically meaningful relationships between them and possibly any relevant externals.

Audience

The primary intended audience for the cluster diagrams consists of domain experts, architects, modelers and programmers.

Permitted Icons

The following icons are permitted on cluster diagrams:

- Primary Nodes:
    - Object icons (on engineering applications)
    - Multiobject icons (on engineering applications)
    - Class icons (on MIS applications)
    - Role icons (during requirements analysis)
    - Cluster instance icons
    - Cluster icons
- Secondary Nodes:
    - External icons
    - Mechanism icons
    - Non-OO modeling icons (if necessary)

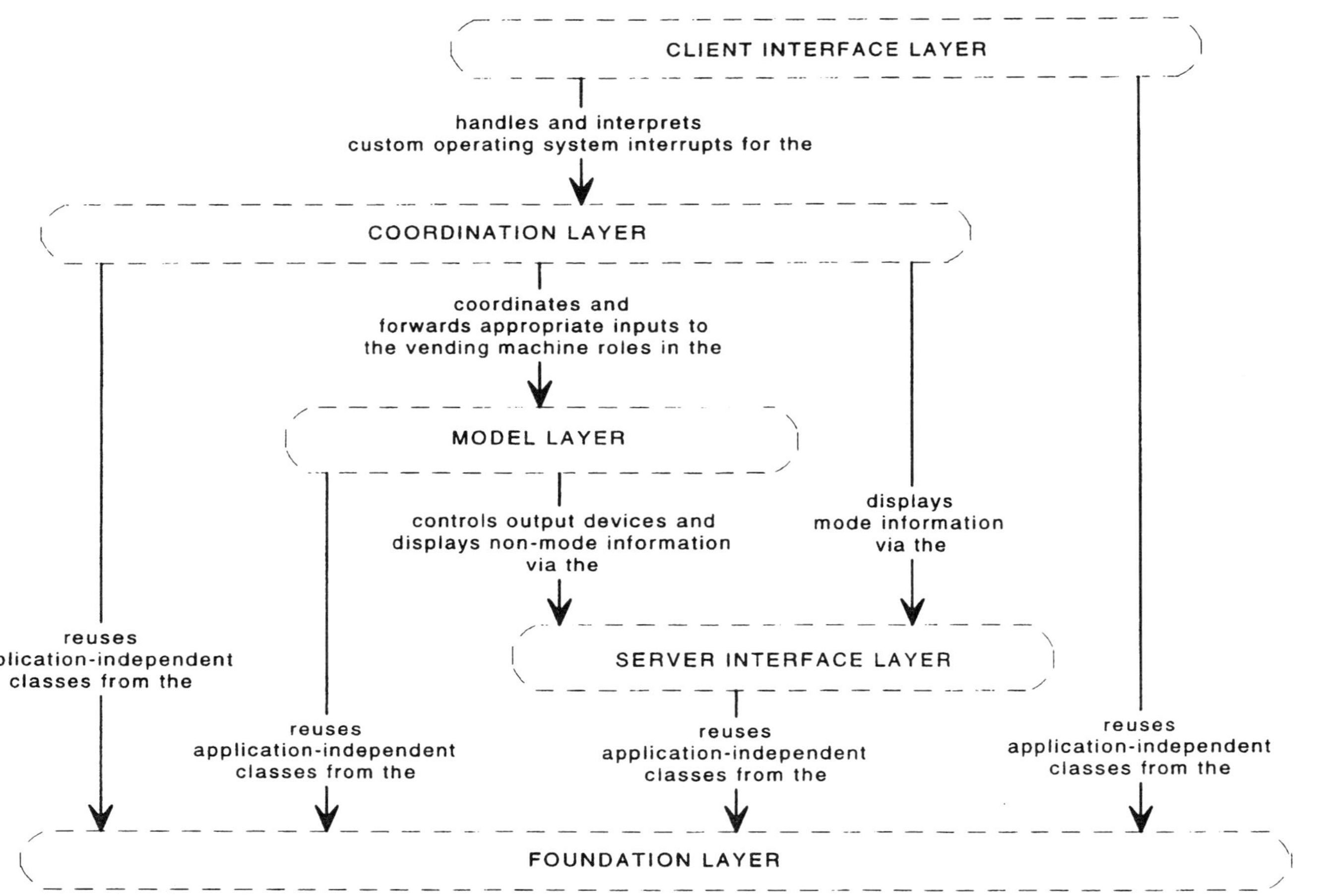

Figure 4.4. Configuration diagram for a vending machine application.

- Primary Arcs:
  - — Association and linkage arcs
  - — Aggregation arcs
- Secondary Arcs (to simplify and clarify diagrams):
  - — Inheritance arcs
  - — Classification arcs
  - — Implementation arcs

Guidelines

1. Emphasize association/linkage (collaboration) over inheritance.
2. It is typically useful to label the association/linkage arcs with meaningful verb phrases that remain at a high level of abstraction.
3. Where feasible, place clients above servers so that the overall control flow and dependency structure is obvious.
4. Emphasize objects and linkage if classes can or will have only one instance or if instances are not treated identically (e.g., many embedded applications—Figure 3.68).
5. Emphasize classes and association if classes have multiple instances, all of which are treated identically (e.g., typical MIS applications—Figure 3.69).
6. Show visibility within a cluster. Show cluster-external modeling elements where appropriate. Show inheritance and classification arcs if it simplifies the diagram or makes it more understandable.
7. Do not use non-OO modeling elements unless necessary (e.g., for the reverse engineering of hybrid software).

Rationale

Cluster diagrams are best used to show collaborating objects, classes, and roles; primarily use inheritance diagrams to document inheritance structures.

By providing a summary of the static architecture of a cluster at a high-level of abstraction, cluster diagrams act as blueprints to the cluster architecture for discussions with domain experts.

The visibility of cluster components is important during design, even though most languages do not adequately support it when it comes to implementation.

Examples

Figure 4.5 documents a cluster diagram showing objects in the role cluster, the external objects and clusters with which they relate, and the semantically important relationships between them. When setting the price of a service representative selection, the corresponding object must ask the coin dispenser assembly object if the price is practical given the kinds of coins the coin dispenser assembly can dispense when making change. When coins are inserted, the customer credit object notifies the coin dispenser because real coins are stored in the hardware coin dispenser assembly (if there is room) and the software coin dispenser assembly must know if such an event changes its state (e.g., from not being able to make change to being able to make change).

Figure 4.6 documents the cluster diagram for four clusters of classes for a food delivery order entry application. Note that while internal objects may send messages to other objects both inside and outside of its cluster, only exported objects on the cluster boundary may be the target of a message from outside the cluster.

4.1.5 Inheritance Diagrams

Definition

inheritance diagram *n.* any specialized semantic net, the purpose of which is to document the static structure of all or part (e.g., branch) of an inheritance graph.

Audience

The primary intended audience for the inheritance diagrams consists of architects, modelers and programmers.

Scope

The scope of an inheritance diagram is a contiguous graph of classes related by inheritance. This can include anything from an entire tree to a small branch.

Permitted Icons

The following icons are permitted on inheritance nets:

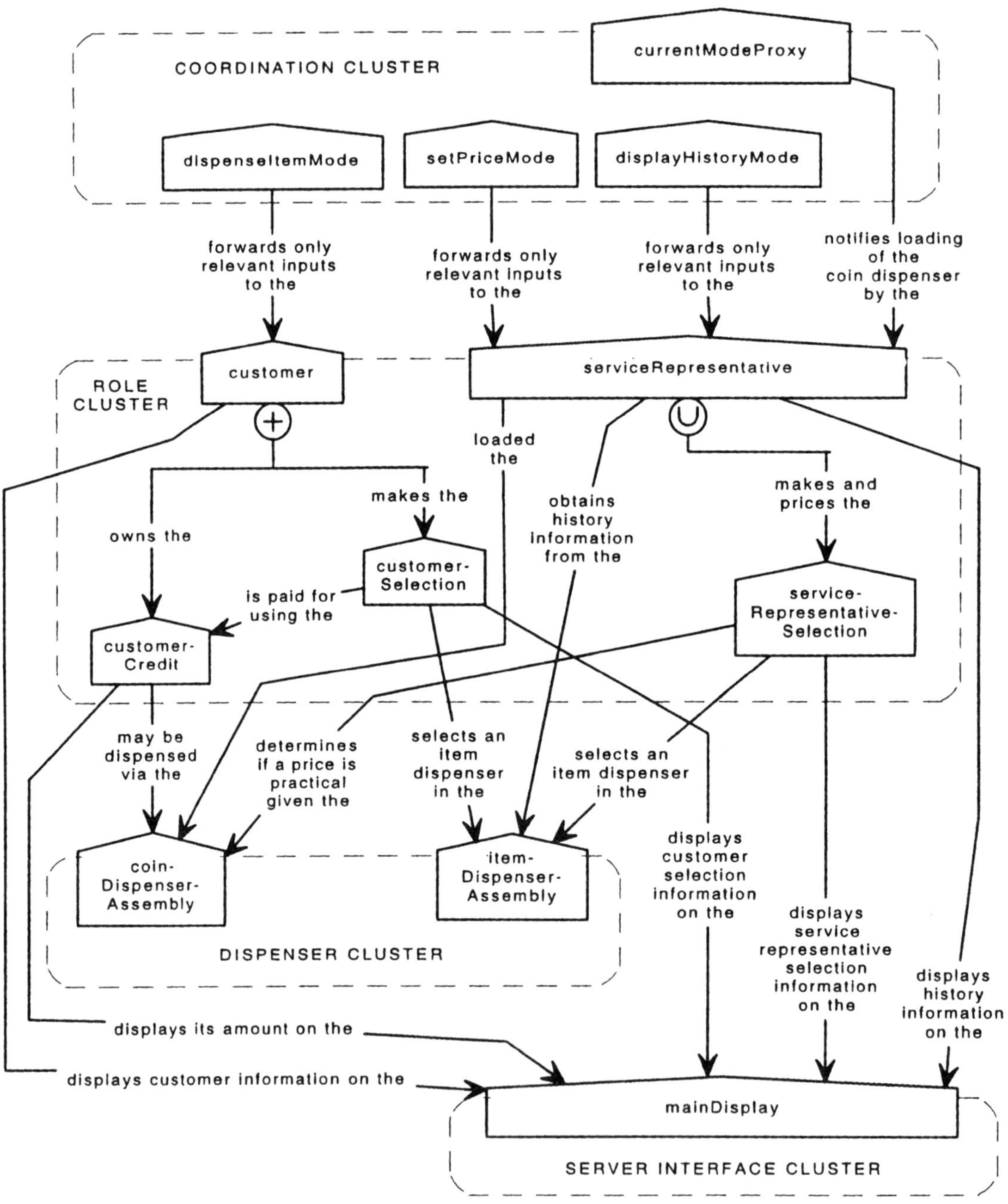

Figure 4.5. Cluster diagram for the customer cluster of a vending machine application.

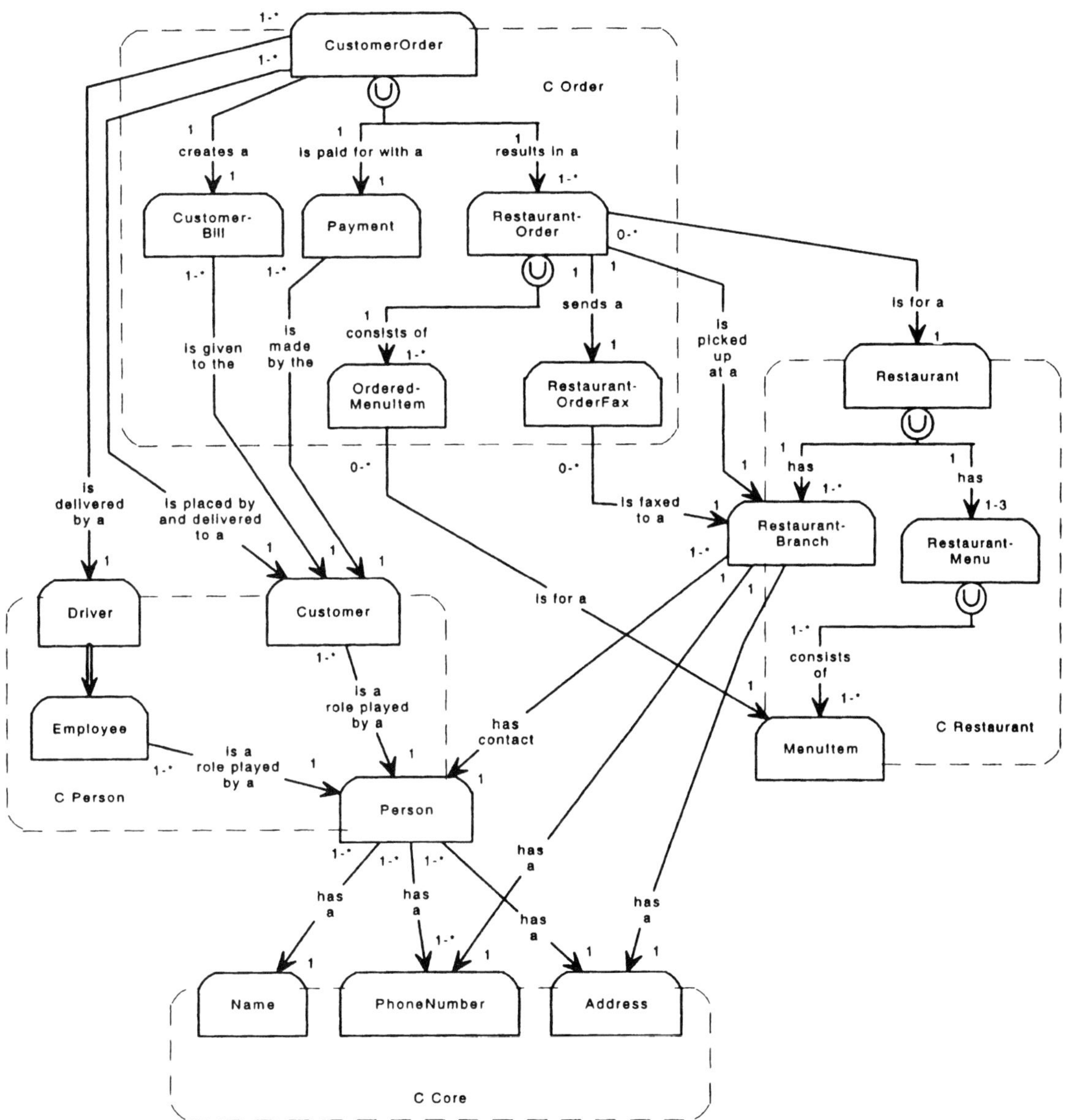

Figure 4.6. Cluster diagram showing classes for a food delivery order entry application.

- Primary Nodes:

  — Class icons
  — Type icons
  — Class implementation icons

- Primary Arcs:

  — Specialization arcs
  — Inheritance arcs

- Secondary Arcs:

  — Association/Link arcs
  — Aggregation arcs

Guidelines

1. Merge inheritance arcs from multiple children if they belong to the same partition. Line up all members of the same partition.

2. There is no semantic meaning to the placement of children relative to their parents. Organize the nodes to best fit the diagram and minimize the crossing of relationship arcs. However, where practical, consistently use one of following approaches:

   - Place parents above children. This is the traditional placement in both computer science and, for example, genealogical trees. It has the advantage of familiarity, especially for experienced software professionals. It is also easy to add new subclasses at the base since most people begin to draw on paper from the top downwards.

   - Place parents to the left of children. This mirrors the use of indentation found in single-inheritance browsers.

   - Place children above their parents. Advantages of this approach include:

     — All arcs (linkages, association, aggregation, classification, inheritance) run downhill from client to server (in the direction of dependency), making it easier to determine the overall dependency structure of the nodes so that dependency-based development and testing can be used.

     — It is more intuitive because reuse has traditionally been considered to be bottom-up, and inheritance supports reuse. Children classes are built on the foundation of parent (a.k.a., base) classes. Inheritance trees grow like normal trees with their roots in the ground and leaves in the air.

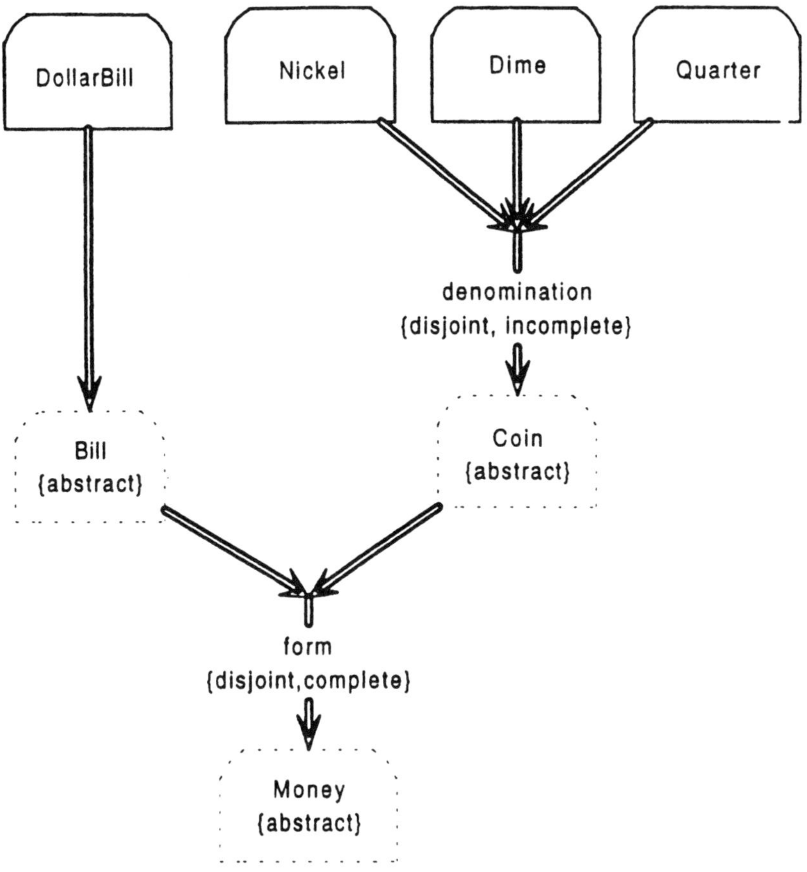

Figure 4.7. Example inheritance diagram for a money hierarchy.

Rationale

Whereas documenting delegation (via association/linkage, aggregation, and containment) and specialization/inheritance relationships on the same diagram can often be useful, such diagrams are often cluttered and confusing because they mix different abstractions with different scopes (e.g., cluster vs. inheritance branch). Use cluster diagrams to document delegation and inheritance diagrams to document inheritance.

Examples

Figure 4.7 is an inheritance diagram for a money hierarchy. While the default is

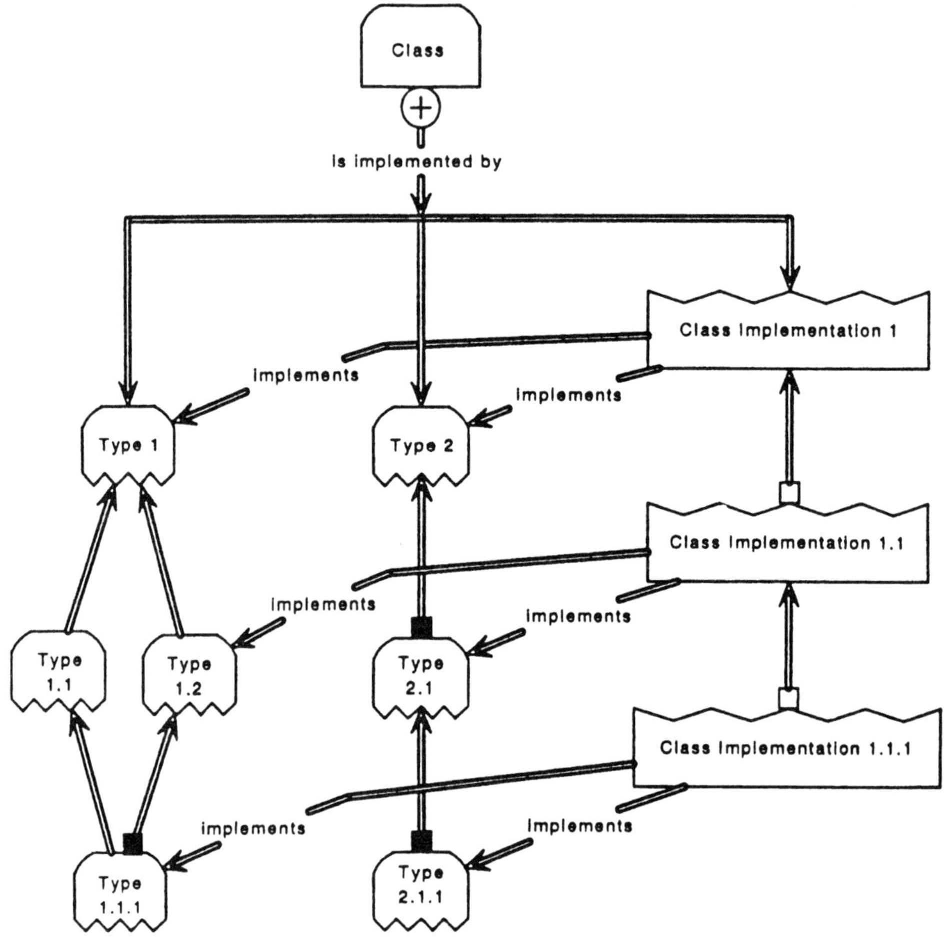

Figure 4.8. Inheritance diagram showing Java types and class implementations.

stereotypes on partitions are disjoint and incomplete, the top partition was annotated as a reminder. This diagram can supplement a cluster diagram in which only the abstract Money class appears. What might be diversionary details on a GSN are thus reserved for this adjunct inheritance diagram.

Figure 4.8 documents the inheritance structures common in Java designs. As noted before, the separation of the class implementation hierarchy and type hierarchy in Java permits the mixture of a variety of different kinds of inheritance on a single diagram.

Figure 4.9 is an inheritance diagram from a vending machine application written in Smalltalk that uses drop-down boxes to document which characteristics are inherited and overridden. On a Smalltalk project, the general trait kind "interface" may be replaced with the more popular term "public methods."

4.1.6 Deployment Diagrams

Definition

deployment diagram *n.* any specialized semantic net, the purpose of which is to document the structure of hardware on which an application runs and the [static] allocation of the software to that hardware in a distributed application.

Audience

The primary intended audience for the deployment diagrams consists of domain experts, architects, and modelers.

Scope

The typical scope of a deployment diagram includes all hardware used in the application.

Permitted Icons

The following icons are permitted on deployment diagrams:

- Primary Nodes:
  - Hardware externals (including systems)
  - Persistent memory externals
- Secondary Nodes:
  - Drop-down boxes documenting allocation of software to hardware
- Primary Arcs:
  - Association/Link arcs
- Secondary Arcs:
  - Aggregation arcs
  - Inheritance arcs

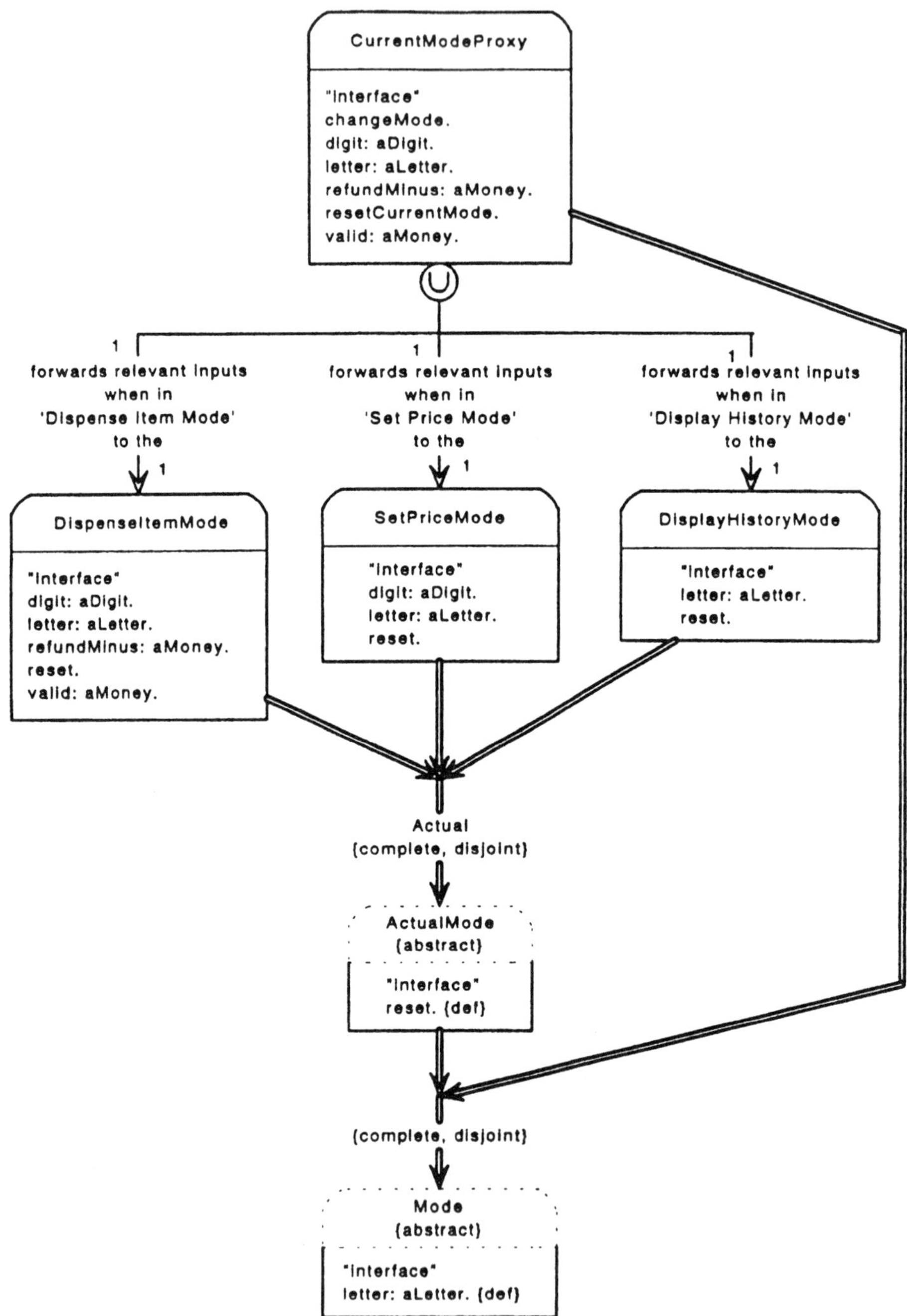

Figure 4.9. Example inheritance diagram showing inherited characteristics.

Guidelines

1. Use deployment diagrams to capture devices as well as hardware which has significant computational resources.

Rationale

More and more applications (e.g., client/server) are distributed across multiple processors, making it important to capture the allocation of software and processes to processors.

Examples

Figure 4.10 documents the hardware architecture and software allocation for a rental company's order entry and processing application. Note that the diagram documents four kinds of internal computers (the server and three PCs), six internal devices (readers, printers, and modem), an internal database, and the external credit verification system.

4.2   Scenario Class Diagrams

Definitions

scenario class diagram *n.* any diagram that documents a set of collaborating scenario classes and the invocation and precedes relationships between them.

- **mechanism diagram** *n.* any scenario class diagram, the purpose of which is to document one or more mechanisms, any associated objects or classes, and the semantically important relationships between them.
- **task script diagram** *n.* any scenario class diagram, the purpose of which is to document one or more task scripts, any associated externals, and the semantically important relationships between them.
- **use case diagram** *n.* any scenario class diagram, the purpose of which is to document one or more use cases, any associated externals that either use or are used by them, and the semantically important relationships between them.

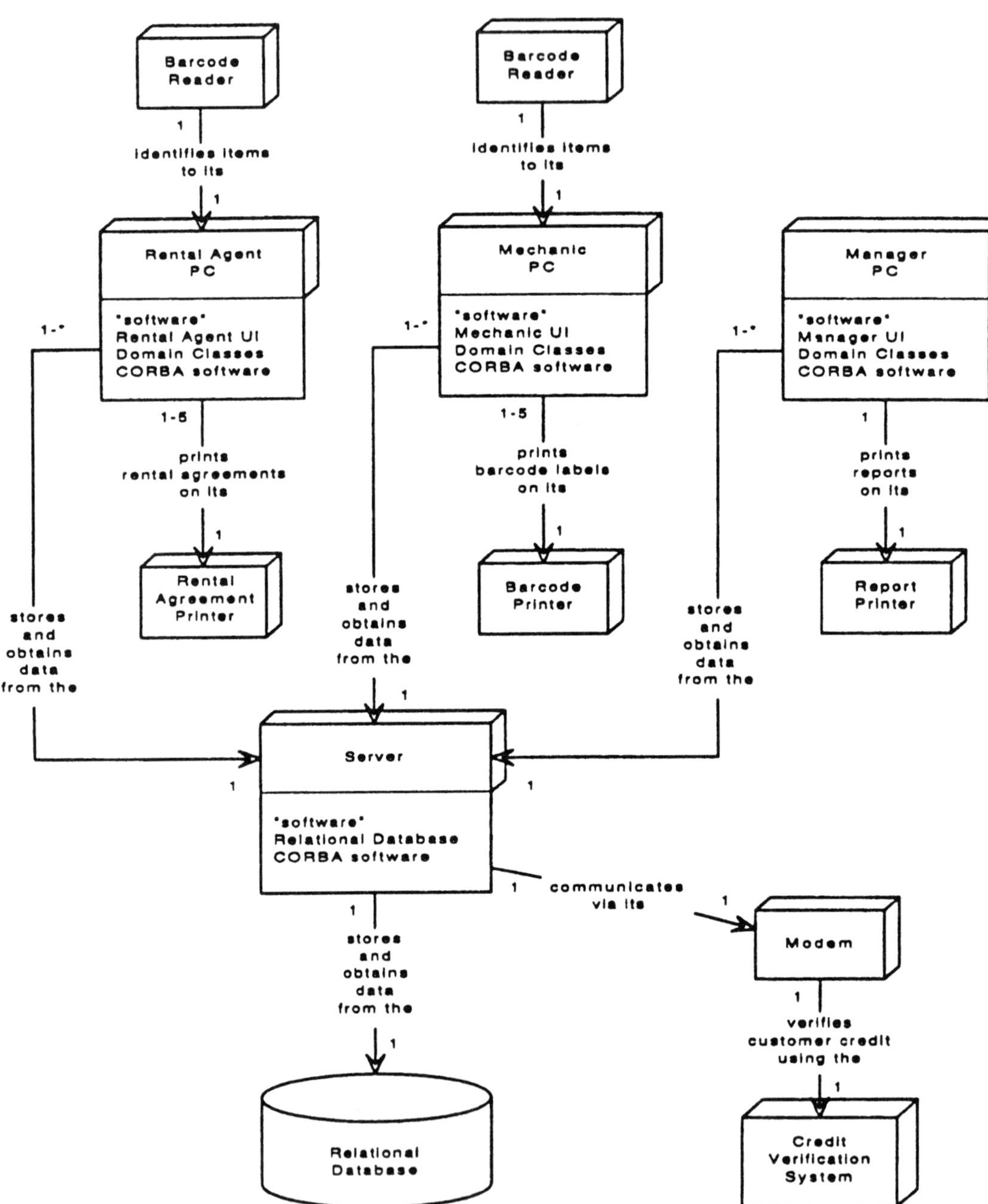

Figure 4.10. Deployment diagram for an order entry and processing application.

application *n.* the scope of development, being either a system or a cohesive amount of software.

uses relationship *n.* the binary dependency relationship between a external and a scenario class.

invokes relationship *n.* the binary dependency relationship between two scenario classes whereby the server scenario class is invoked at a specific point in the execution of the client scenario class.

precedes relationship *n.* the binary dependency relationship between two scenario class whereby the client scenario class must complete execution before the server scenario class is permitted to begin execution.

Metamodel

Figure 4.11 illustrates a partial metamodel for scenario relationships that captures the following information:

- All scenario relationships are completely and disjointedly partitioned into precedes relationships, invokes relationships, and uses relationships.
- Each precedes relationship connects one predecessor to one follower, whereby the execution of the predecessor must precede the execution of the follower in time and the predecessor and follower are roles that can be played by either two scenarios or two scenario classes.
- Each invokes relationship connects one invoker to one invokee, whereby the invoker causes the execution of the follower and the invoker and invokee are roles that can be played by either two scenarios or two scenario classes.
- Each uses relationship connects one user to one usee, whereby the user uses the usee and the user and usee roles can be played by either an external and a use case or a use case and an external.

Audience

The primary intended audience for the scenario class diagrams includes domain experts, users, customers, architects, and modelers

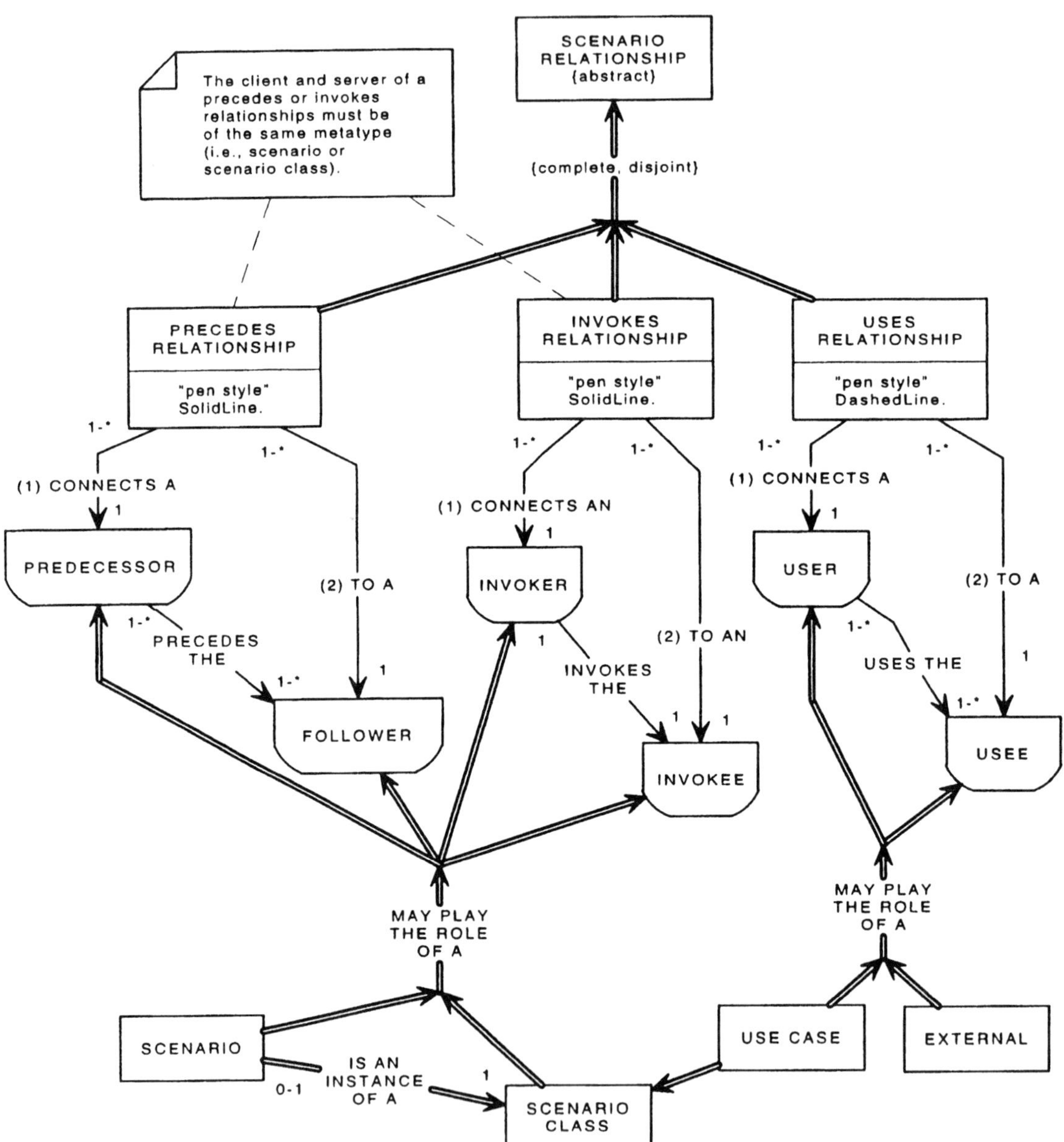

Figure 4.11. Partial metamodel for scenario class relationships.

Permitted Icons

The following icons are permitted on mechanism diagrams:

- Nodes:
    - Cluster icon
    - Mechanism icons
- Arcs:
    - Uses arcs
    - Invokes arcs
    - Precedes arcs

The following icons are permitted on task script diagrams:

- Nodes:
    - Task script icons
- Arcs:
    - Uses arcs
    - Invokes arcs
    - Precedes arcs

The following icons are permitted on use case diagrams:

- Nodes:
    - External icons
    - Use Case icons
    - Application icon
- Arcs:
    - Uses arcs
    - Invokes arcs
    - Precedes arcs

Notation

uses relationship. The uses relationship is represented by a dotted line with an
arrowhead on one or both ends showing the direction(s) of dependency.

invokes relationship. The invokes relationship is represented as a solid line with an arrowhead on the end pointing at the invoked (i.e., server) scenario or scenario class and labeled with the word "invokes."

precedes relationship. The precedes relationship is represented as a solid line with an arrowhead on the end pointing at the following (i.e., server) scenario or scenario class and labeled with the word "precedes."

application. An application is represented by a three dimensional box if it is a system and a dashed rounded rectangle if it is a software application.

Guidelines

1. Remember that scenario classes are functional rather than object-oriented and should therefore be used with great care in order to avoid creating and implementing an implicit functional design.
2. Avoid functionally decomposing the scenario classes too far or without adequate reason. Too many levels of decomposition promote a functional decomposition mindset that is inconsistent with the object paradigm.
3. Remember that a single scenario class may involve multiple externals.
4. Because use cases are all visible, do not attach them to the boundaries of the application icon.

Rationale

As illustrated in Figure 4.12, scenario class diagrams help organize use cases and their relationships: both uses relationships involving externals and invokes and precedes relationships with other use cases.

Because an "invokes" relationship is a referential relationship between modeling entities (use cases) of the same metatype, it is represented by a solid single line arrow.

Because a "precedes" relationship is a referential relationship between modeling entities (use cases) of the same metatype, it is represented by a solid single line arrow.

Because a "uses" relationship is a referential relationship between modeling entities (external, use case) of different metatype, it is represented by a dotted single-line arrow.

For consistency sake, system and software applications are represented by the same icons as the corresponding externals.

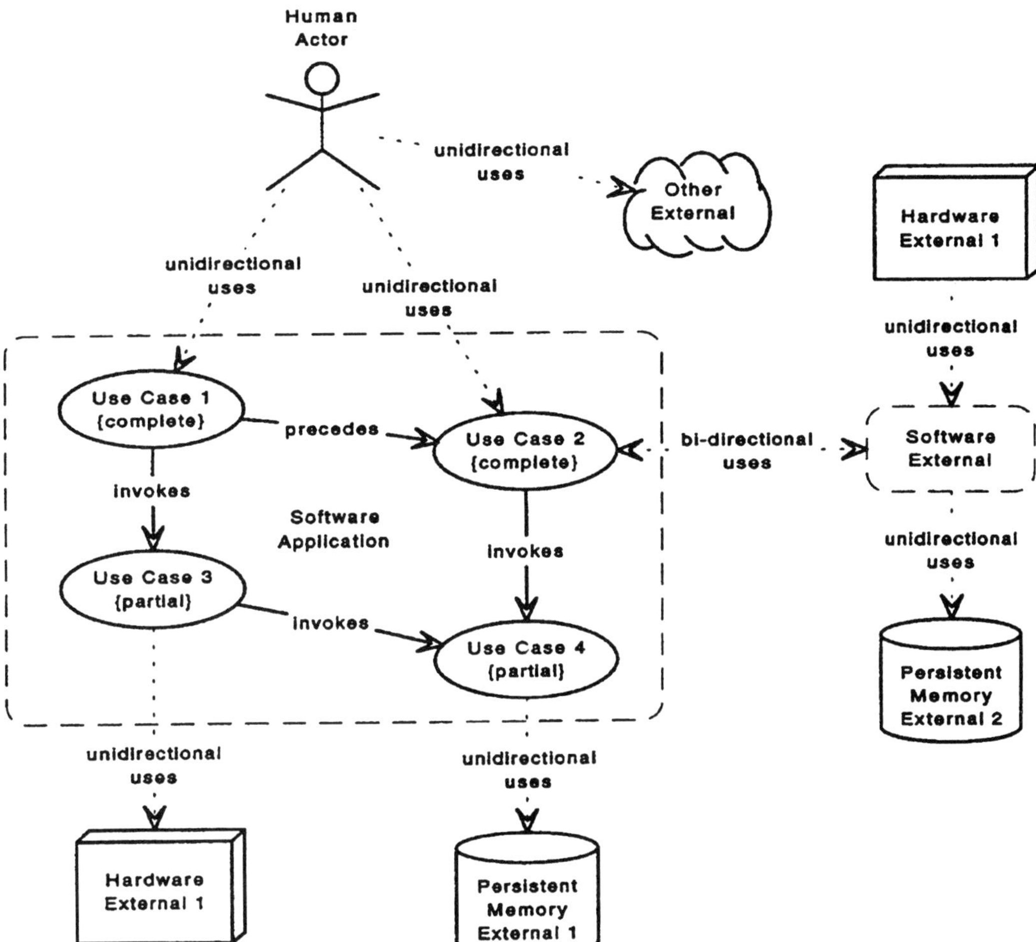

Figure 4.12. Scenario class diagram icons.

Example

Figure 4.13 is a mechanism diagram that illustrates the use of scenario classes on cluster diagrams to capture the behavior of clusters.

Figure 4.14 is a task script diagram that illustrates the use of task scripts to record behavior during business process modeling.

Figure 4.15 is a use case diagram that illustrates the use cases for a rental management application, the invokes and precedes relationships between the use cases,

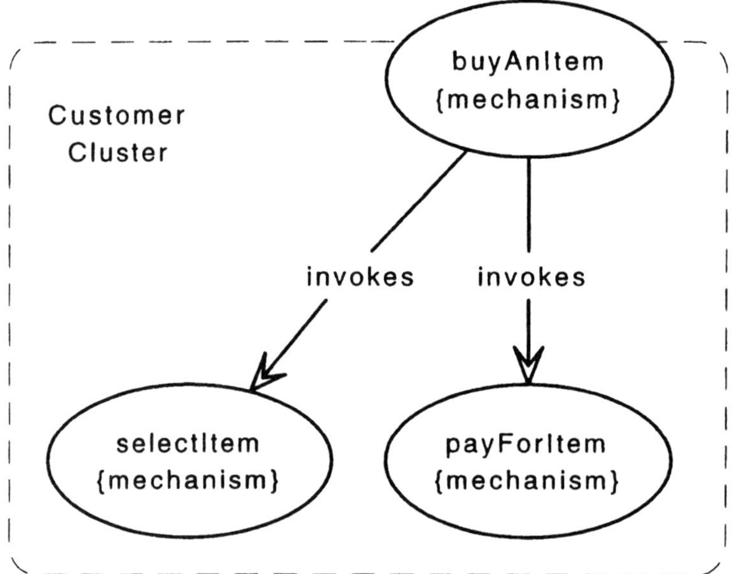

Figure 4.13. Example mechanism diagram.

the human client actors that use the system, the device and database externals used by the system, and the uses relationships between the externals and the use cases.

4.3   Interaction Diagrams

Definition

interaction diagram *n.* any diagram, the purpose of which is to document the interactions either among externals and the application or among objects and classes within [part of] the application. The nodes of an interaction diagram represent either things or their time lines, and the arcs of the graph represent the interactions between nodes.

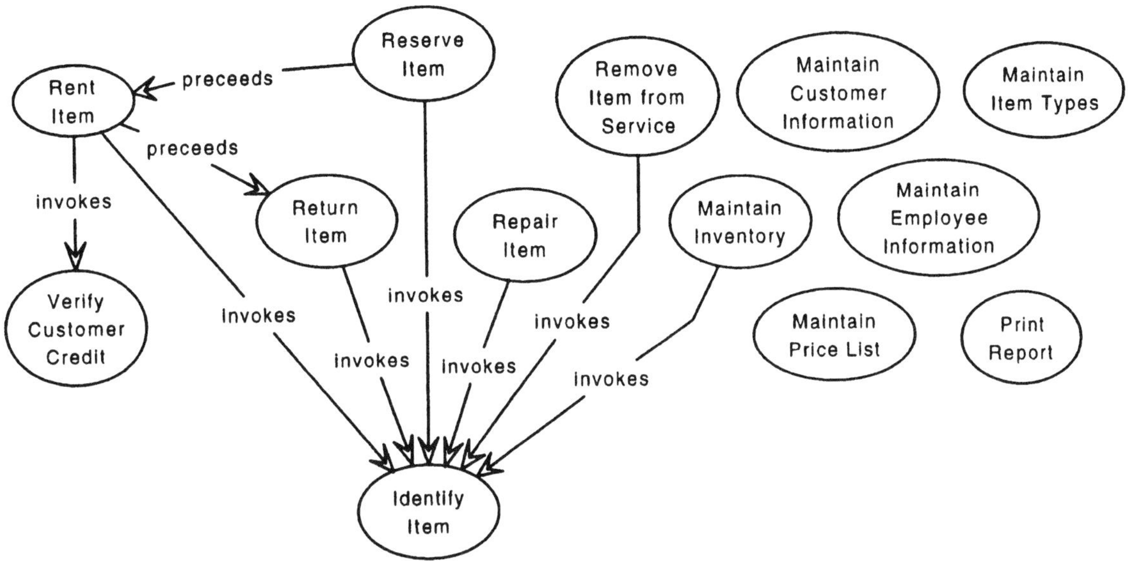

Figure 4.14. Example task script diagram.

Kinds

Interaction diagrams come in the following two forms:

1. Collaboration Diagrams:

- Cluster Collaboration Diagrams
- Scenario Collaboration Diagrams
- Internal Collaboration Diagrams

2. Sequence Diagrams:

- Blackbox Sequence Diagrams
- Whitebox Sequence Diagrams

Rationale

Interaction diagram was the original term used by Ed Colbert for collaboration diagrams, before the term was popularized by Ivar Jacobson to mean sequence diagram.

Collaboration diagram is the term used by Rebecca Wirfs-Brock.

The term interaction diagram is more general than the term "object diagram" because the diagrams have more than just objects as nodes.

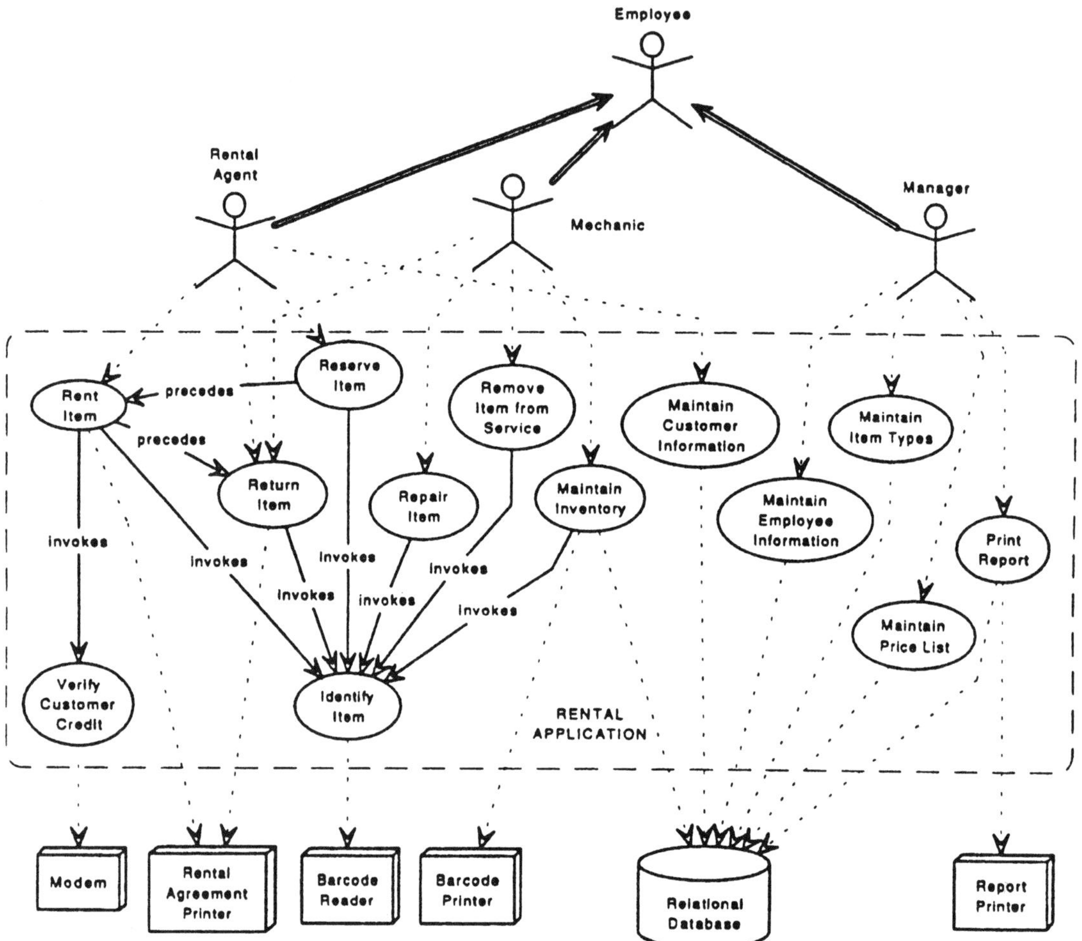

Figure 4.15. Example use case diagram for a rental management application.

The term "sequence diagram" is more intuitive and inclusive that the term "message flow diagram," especially because it displays exception raising as well as message passing.

4.3.1 Collaboration Diagrams

Definitions

collaboration diagram *n.* any interaction diagram in the form of a graph, the purpose of which is to document the potential collaboration of a cluster of classes and objects in terms of the messages and exceptions they may send and raise.

If the associations, linkages, aggregation arcs, and containment arcs on cluster diagrams are viewed as roads connecting the classes and objects, then the messages and exceptions on the collaboration diagrams can be viewed as the traffic on those roads. Collaboration diagrams typically have the same nodes and topology as the corresponding cluster diagrams, but the arcs are labeled with messages and exceptions rather than with static relationships.

In many cases, especially in concurrent situations, the ordering of this message and exception "traffic" is important. Thus, the arcs on collaboration diagrams can be optionally labeled with sequence numbers.[2]

- **cluster collaboration diagram** *n.* any specialized collaboration diagram, the purpose of which is to document the potential collaboration of a cluster or cluster instance of blackbox classes and objects in terms of the messages and exceptions they may send and raise.

  A cluster collaboration diagram can be used to summarize all of the interactions on all sequence diagrams involving the scope of the collaboration diagram.

- **scenario collaboration diagram** *n.* any specialized collaboration diagram, the purpose of which is to document the collaboration of blackbox classes and objects in involved in a scenario in terms of the messages and exceptions they may send and raise.

- **internal collaboration diagram** *n.* any specialized collaboration diagram, the purpose of which is to document the potential collaboration of operations within an individual class or object, in terms of control flow (i.e., message passing, exception raising) and object flow (the reading and writing of properties within the class or object).

---

[2]If the sequence of interactions is important, sequence diagrams are often used instead of collaboration diagrams.

object flow *n.* the shorthand way of representing on a class-internal collaboration diagram the sending of read or write accessor messages (typically to self) referencing the associated property, thereby resulting in the flow of the object represented by that property. Analogous to the term 'data flow' on a traditional data flow diagram.

Audience

The primary intended audience for *software collaboration diagrams* are modelers, architects, domain experts, and programmers.

The primary intended audience for *internal collaboration diagrams* are modelers and programmers.

Scope

The scope of a typical *software collaboration diagram* is a single cluster of collaborating classes and objects, and optionally its direct externals.

The scope of a typical *internal collaboration diagram* is an individual class and/or a typical instance of the class optionally including its externals.

Permitted Icons

The permitted icons for a *cluster or scenario collaboration diagram* include:

- Primary Nodes:
    - Object icons
    - Multiobject icons
    - Class icons
    - Type icons
    - Role icons
- Secondary Nodes:
    - Cluster icons
    - External icons
    - Non-OO software icons
- Primary Arcs:
    - Association/Link arcs (labeled with messages and exceptions)
    - Aggregation arcs (labeled with messages and exceptions)
    - Containment arcs (labeled with messages and exceptions)

- Secondary Arcs:
  - Inheritance arcs
  - Classification arcs

The permitted icons for an *internal collaboration diagram* include:

- Primary Nodes:
  - Object icons
  - Multiobject icons
  - Class icons
  - Operation icons
  - Link and Part reference icons
- Secondary Nodes:
  - Cluster icons
  - External icons
- Primary Arcs:
  - Association/Link arcs (labeled with messages and exceptions)
  - Aggregation arcs (labeled with messages and exceptions)
  - Containment arcs (labeled with messages and exceptions)
  - Object flow arcs (unidirectional and bi-directional)
- Secondary Arcs:
  - Inheritance arcs
  - Classification arcs

Notation

object flow Object flow is represented by a dotted arc connecting an operation and a property. A unidirectional object flow has a single arrowhead representing the direction of the flow. A bi-directional object flow has an arrowhead on both ends.

sequence. If the collaboration diagram is used instead of a sequence diagram to represent a specific sequence of interactions, then the messages and exceptions can be labeled with a layered decimal notation based on the ideas of the Decimal Dewey classification system used in many libraries. In a single thread, the order of the interaction can optionally be represented by a positive integer surrounded by parentheses preceding the interaction. Multiple threads can be indicated by preceding the number with a lower-case letter representing the thread.

Guidelines

1. For each cluster diagram, consider creating a corresponding software collaboration diagram having the same topology, but with the association/linkage arcs labeled with messages and exceptions. Rather than trying to automatically generate the collaboration for a set of relevant sequence diagrams, a good order of development is to rapidly generate an initial cluster collaboration diagram from the associated cluster diagram, and then augment the collaboration diagram with information derived from associated sequence diagrams.

2. Show cluster boundaries so that cluster encapsulation can be documented.

3. Show interactions between objects and classes within the cluster and those objects and classes outside the cluster with which they interact.

4. Use internal collaboration diagrams (e.g., Figure 4.18) only if the class or its instances is relatively complex and the diagram is a cost-effective way to analyze and document the internal interactions between operations and properties. Note that an internal collaboration diagram can provide a global view of the object that is difficult to obtain with a browser that only shows local dependencies.

5. Remember to document exception raising as well as message passing.

6. Use object flow arcs on internal collaboration diagrams to implicitly represent the read and write accessor operations, which would clutter up the diagram.

7. On collaboration diagrams, draw senders above receivers so that the overall control flow of the diagram is clear.

8. Use collaboration diagrams instead of sequence diagrams if:
   - the scope is an entire cluster,
   - a cluster collaboration diagram is needed to provide a summary of multiple sequence diagrams is desired,
   - structure is more important than sequence,
   - an internal collaboration diagram is needed to document the internals of a complex object or class, or
   - the starting point is a cluster diagram.

Rationale

Encapsulation and interfaces are important to the design of clusters for the same reasons that they are important in the design of objects and classes. It is therefore important to show cluster boundaries and the visibility of cluster components on collaboration diagrams, especially since most implementation languages do not enforce it.

Objects and classes interact by raising exceptions as well as by sending messages. If exception traffic is not documented on the diagram, developers are not as likely to provide exception handlers and the application will crash when exceptions are raised. Out of sight, out of mind and what you don't know can indeed hurt you.

Classes should be documented on collaboration diagrams because they are objects too. They send and receive messages, as well as raise and handle exceptions.

Because both objects and classes encapsulate both operations and properties, they can have a complex internal structure that may be difficult to grasp merely by using browsers at the code level. Thus, internal collaboration diagrams can be quite useful.

Some way is required to differentiate class-level characteristics from instance-level characteristics. It is intuitive to place class-level characteristics in class icons and instance-level characteristics in object icons. See Figure 4.18 for an example of this.

Properties are *not* objects, even in pure languages such as Smalltalk. Instead, properties are merely data (e.g., a memory address in C++) that are used as references or pointers to objects. Nevertheless, it is still intuitive to use the icon for the object referenced to represent a property referencing an *encapsulated* object because (1) the distinction between the reference and the object referenced is not important except for pedagogical reasons and (2) this greatly minimizes the clutter of internal collaboration diagrams. However, a traditional datastore icon (i.e., two parallel lines) was chosen to represent the reference to an *external* object because (1) the distinction between the internal reference and the referenced external object is important in this case and (2) the datastore icon is the traditional icon for representing data.

The use of object flow arcs simplifies the internal diagram by ignoring (eliminating the need to show) read and write accessor operations, the use of which is assumed.

Examples

Figure 4.16 documents the cluster collaboration diagram for the Role Cluster from a vending machine application. In addition to showing the messages and

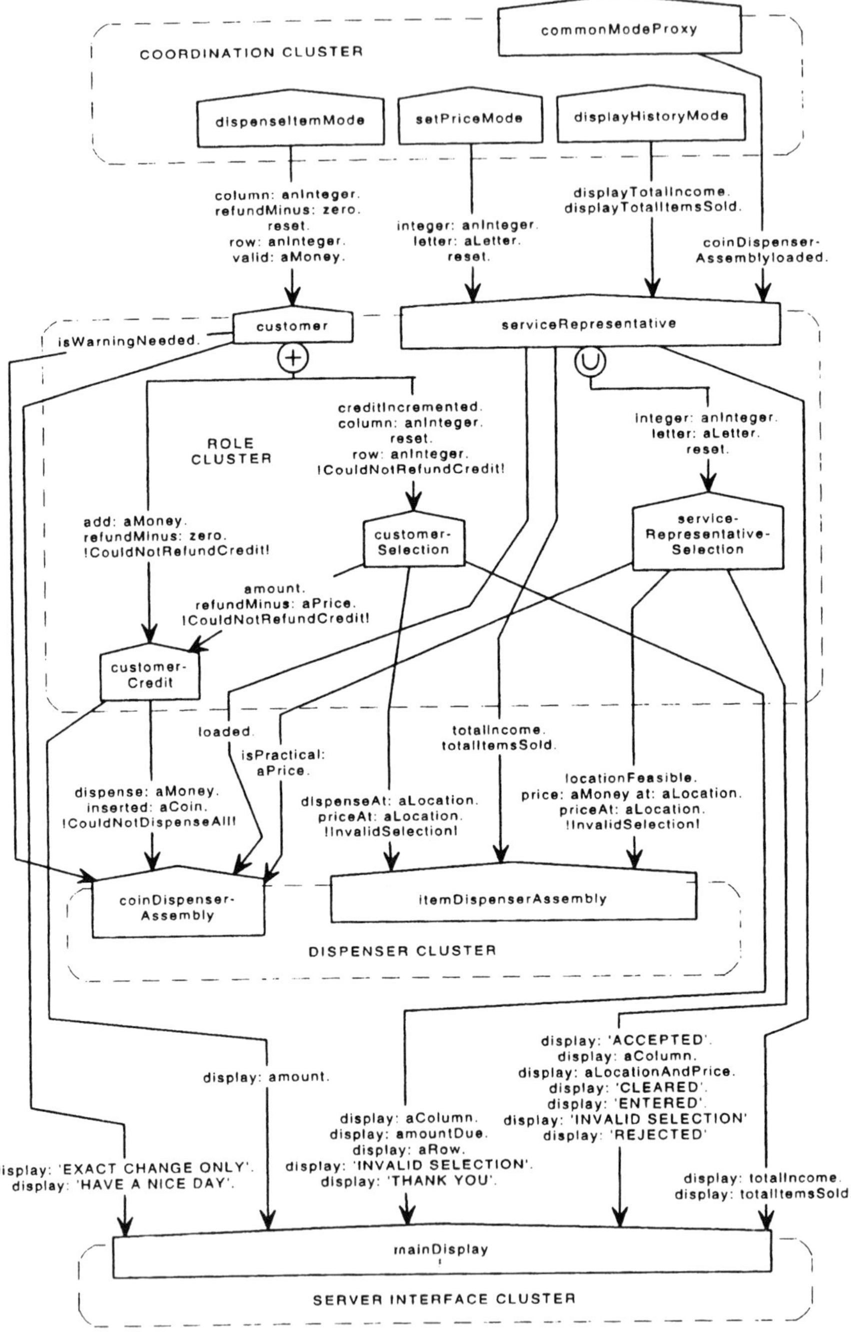

Figure 4.16. Cluster collaboration diagram for the customer cluster of a vending machine application.

exceptions that flow between blackbox objects within the cluster, it also shows message and exception traffic across the cluster boundaries.

Figure 4.17 is a scenario collaboration diagram for a vending machine that documents what may happen when a customer makes a selection, pays for it, and the vending machine cannot make change. Although the interactions in a scenario collaboration diagram are numbered to show their order, a sequence diagram will usually make the order more obvious. Although messages 19 and 28 appear to display the wrong information (i.e., customerFunds amount) on the display, this information is immediately overridden by messages 22 and 37; this apparently redundant design was chosen in order to handle the situation where money is inserted before a selection is made.

Figure 4.18 documents the icons for characteristics of objects and classes on internal collaboration diagrams.

Figure 4.19 provides an example internal collaboration diagram for a customer selection object from a vending machine application.

4.3.2 Sequence Diagrams

Definitions

sequence diagram *n.* any interaction diagram in the form of a "fence" diagram, the purpose of which is to document the sequence of interactions among either externals and the application or among objects within [part of] the application.

- **blackbox sequence diagram** *n.* any specialized kind of sequence diagram, the purpose of which is to document the sequence of interactions between externals and the blackbox system or software application involved in a single path of a use case.

  A blackbox sequence diagram treats the application as a blackbox and is used to capture user-oriented requirements, verify the context diagram, and document an acceptance test case.

- **whitebox sequence diagram** *n.* any specialized kind of sequence diagram, the purpose of which is to document the sequence of interactions among objects and classes involved in a single mechanism, design pattern, or [partial] path of a use case.

  A whitebox sequence diagram treats the application as a whitebox, showing the interactions among its internal objects. It is used to capture user-oriented requirements, verify the context diagram, and document an acceptance test case.

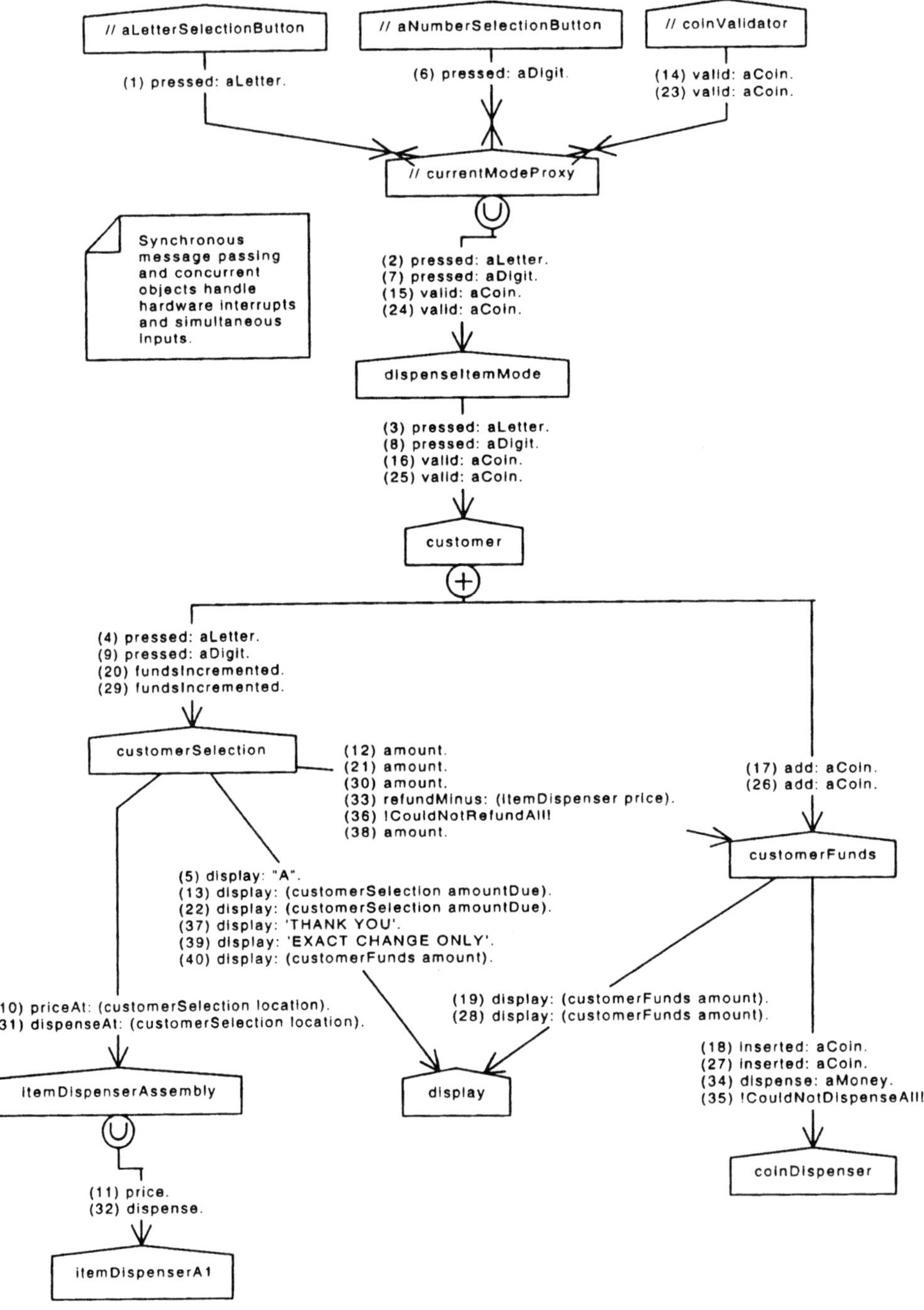

Figure 4.17. Scenario collaboration diagram for a vending machine application.

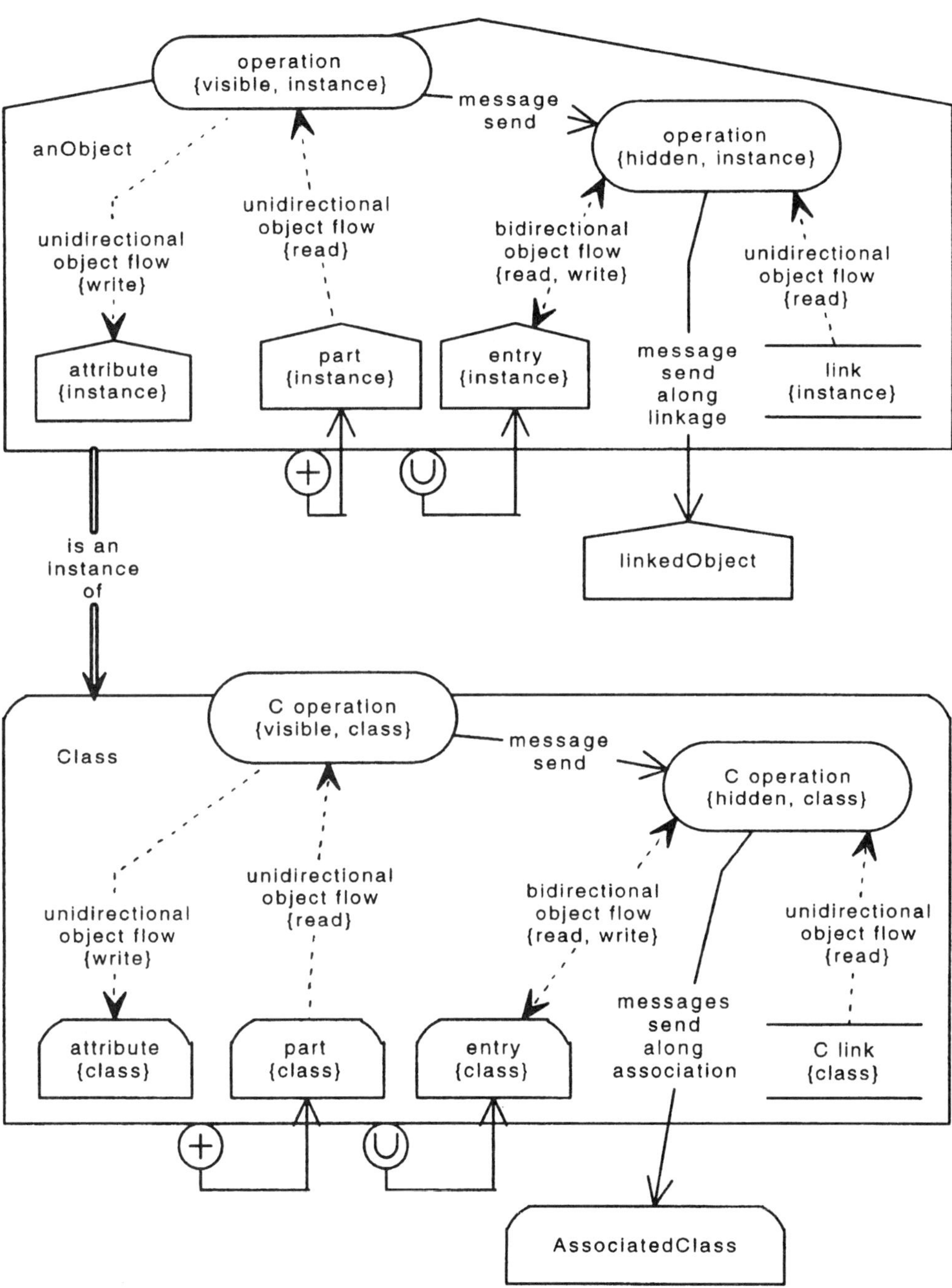

Figure 4.18. Icons for characteristics on internal collaboration diagrams.

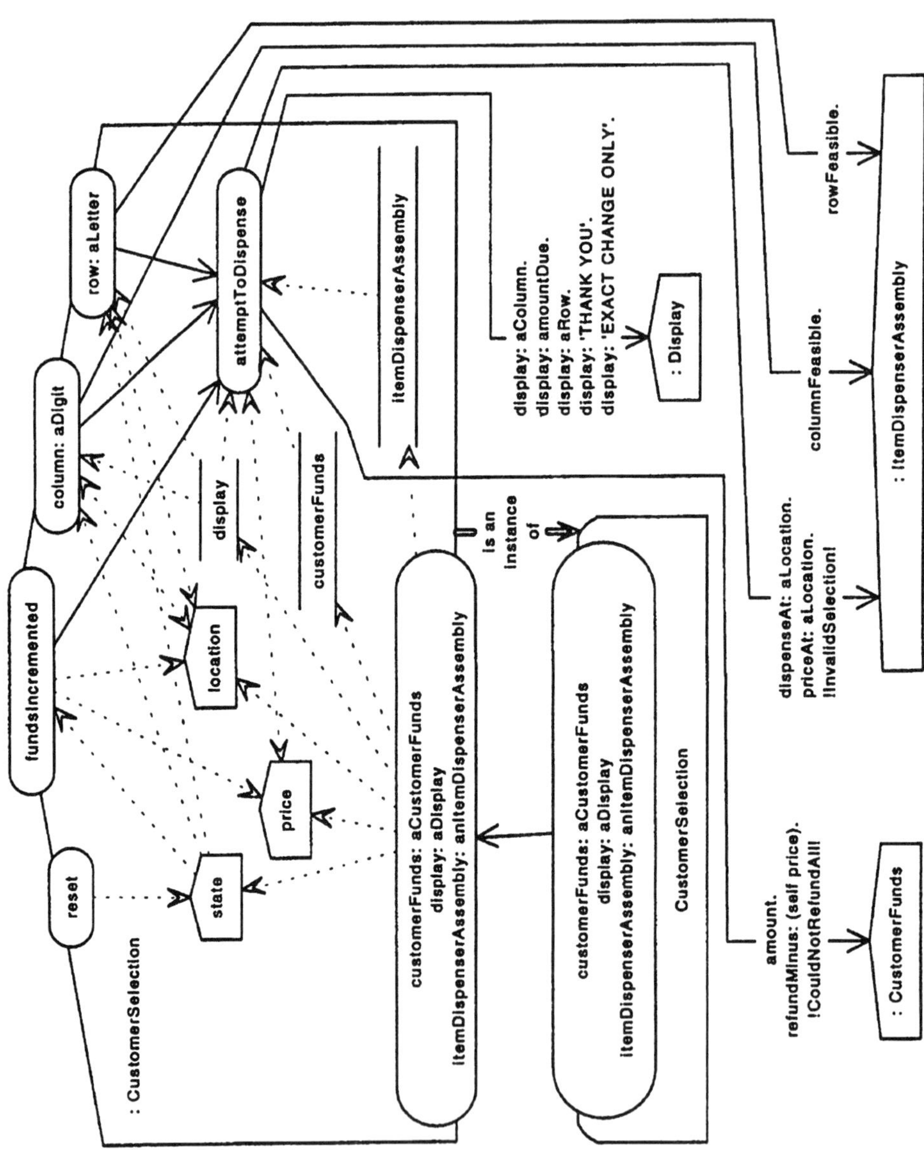

Figure 4.19. Internal collaboration diagram from a vending machine application.

timeline *n.* any vertical line, topped with the icon of a node, representing that node over time.

- **application timeline** *n.* any timeline representing an application over time.
- **object timeline** *n.* any timeline representing an object over time.
  - **class timeline** *n.* any timeline representing a class over time.
  - **external timeline** *n.* any timeline representing an external over time.
  - **multiobject timeline** *n.* any timeline representing a multiobject over time.
- **role timeline** *n.* any timeline representing a role over time.

logic box *n.* any rectangle spanning one or more timelines and containing text that together with other such boxes represents a logic construct (e.g., branch, loop).

Audience

The primary intended audience for the blackbox sequence diagrams consists of domain experts, users, architects, and modelers.

The primary intended audience for the whitebox sequence diagrams consists of architects, modelers, and programmers.

Scope

The scope of a typical *blackbox sequence diagram* is a single path of a use case.

The scope of a typical *whitebox sequence diagram* is a single mechanism, design pattern, or [partial] path through a use case. Larger sequences may cut across cluster and layer boundaries.

Permitted Icons

The permitted icons for *blackbox sequence diagrams* are:

- Primary Nodes:
  - Application timeline
  - External timelines
  - Role timeline
- Secondary Nodes:
  - Branch logic boxes
  - Loop logic boxes

- — Concurrency logic boxes
- — Timing logic boxes
- Arcs:
  - — Linkage arcs:
    - Sequential message arcs
    - Synchronous message arcs
    - Asynchronous message arcs
  - — Exception arcs

The permitted icons for *whitebox sequence diagrams* are:

- Primary Nodes:
  - — Object timelines
  - — Multiobject timelines
  - — Class timelines
  - — Role timeline
- Secondary Nodes:
  - — External time lines
  - — Branch logic boxes
  - — Loop logic boxes
  - — Concurrency logic boxes
  - — Timing logic boxes
- Arcs:
  - — Message arcs:
    - Sequential message arcs
    - Synchronous message arcs
    - Asynchronous message arcs
  - — Exception arcs

Notation

message. A message is represented by a horizontal solid single-line arrow pointing from the time line of the sender to the time line of the receiver.

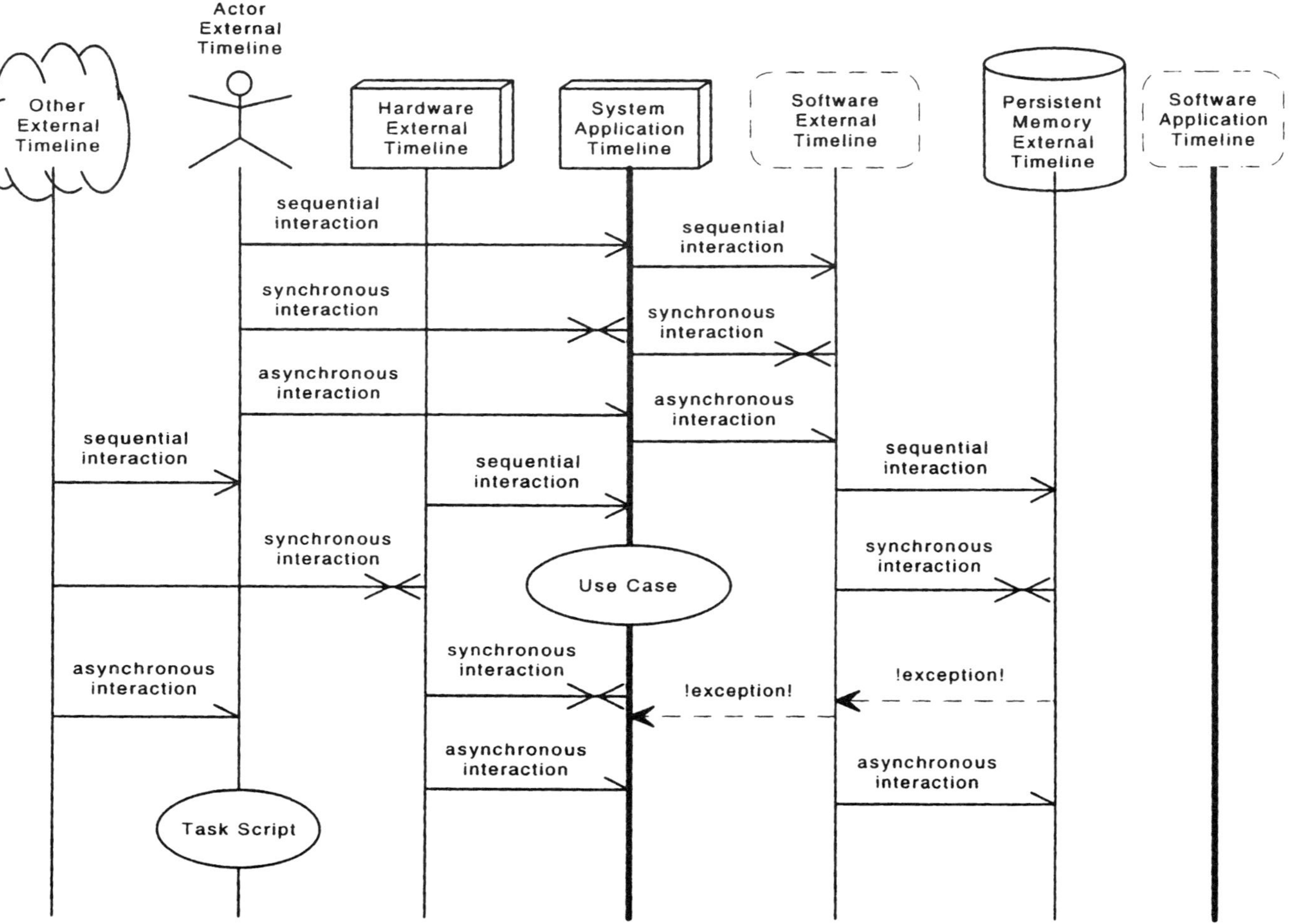

Figure 4.20. Notation for blackbox sequence diagrams.

- *sequential message.* A sequential message is represented by a message with a normal arrowhead pointing at the time line of the receiver.

- *synchronous message.* A synchronous message is represented by a message arc with a two arrowheads pointing at each other near the time line of the receiver.

- *asynchronous message.* An asynchronous message is represented by a message arc with a half arrowhead pointing from the time line of the sender to the time line of the receiver.

- *aggregation message.* An aggregation message is represented by a message arc with a circle containing a plus sign at the sender end.

- *containment message.* A containment message is represented by a message arc with a circle containing a large U at the sender end.

exception. An exception is represented by a horizontal dashed single-line arrow with a normal arrowhead pointing from the time line of the raiser to the time line of the handler.

time line. A time line is represented by a vertical sold line descending from the icon of the node of which it represents the life.

- *object time line.* An object time line is represented by a time line topped by the icon of the associated object.

    — *external time line.* An external time line is represented by a time line topped by the icon of the associated external.

- *class time line.* A class time line is represented by a time line topped by the icon of the associated class.

- *application time line.* An application time line is represented by a time line drawn with a thick line and topped by the icon of the associated application.

- *role time line.* A role time line is represented by a time line topped by the icon of the associated role.

logic box. A logic box is represented by a long short rectangle, labeled with the appropriate information, drawn over the time lines and extending left and right to bound the scope of the logic box. Logic boxes are used to document branching logic, loops, concurrency, and temporal requirements.

Guidelines

1. Order the time lines from left to right so that control flow is roughly left to right.
2. On blackbox sequence diagrams, show indirect as well as direct externals if this helps capture the use case path.
3. On blackbox sequence diagrams, document interactions in narrative text.
4. On whitebox sequence diagrams, document interactions using the syntax of the implementation language.
5. Use logic boxes if this helps reduce the number of diagrams without making any diagram too cluttered or complex.
6. Use collaboration diagrams instead of sequence diagrams if:

   - the starting point is a task script or use case and the scope is therefore a task script or use case, or
   - sequence is more important than structure,

Rationale

Sequence diagrams are a natural and traditional way of showing sequencing.

The timelines increase downwards so that they may be read top-to-bottom (like most human languages).

In order to minimize confusion between objects, classes, and externals having the same name, the icon representing the object, class, or external may be optionally attached to the top of the timeline.

The timelines for system and software applications on blackbox sequence diagram are drawn with thick lines in order to (1) differentiate them from the analogous symbols for hardware and software externals and (2) symbolize the hidden internal complexity which may be viewed on a whitebox sequence diagram.

Associations/linkages are used instead of messages and exceptions (i.e., English phrases are used instead of code snippets) on *blackbox* sequence diagrams because these diagrams are used to communicate with domain experts and other, non-software people.

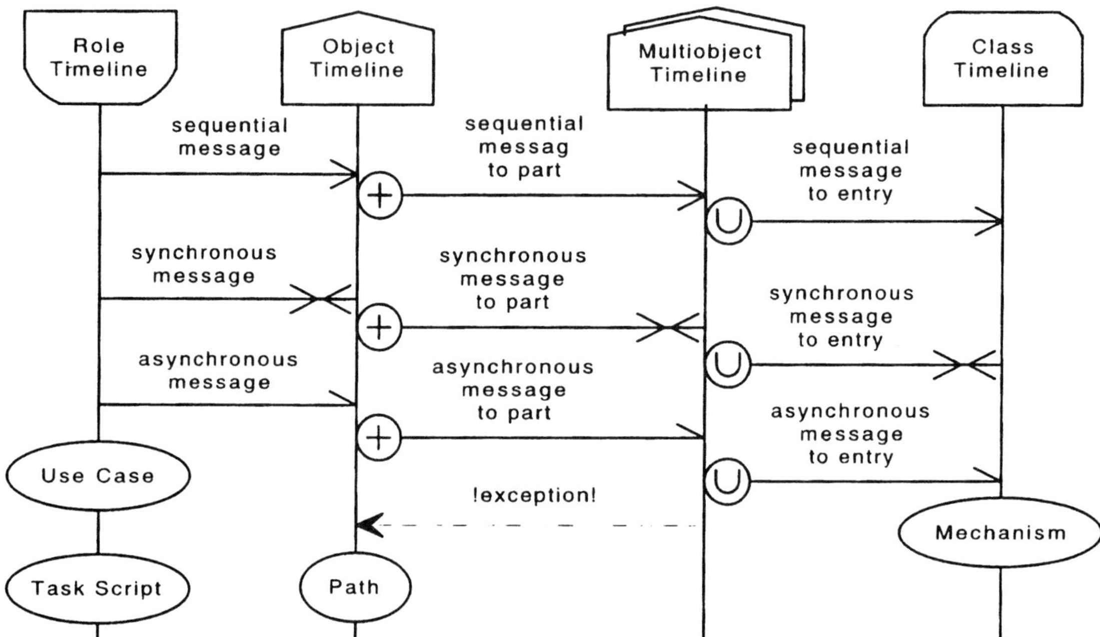

Figure 4.21. Notation for whitebox sequence diagrams.

Examples

Figure 4.22 is an example of the notation for logic boxes when used to illustrate the use of branching logic in a vending machine partial use case.

Figure 4.23 is an example of the notation for logic boxes when used to illustrate the use of loops in the same vending machine. Note that the interactions involved in the branching logic of the previous figure are now summarized as a partial use case.

Figure 4.24 is an example of the notation for logic boxes when used to illustrate the use of concurrency (in this case, the interleaving of use cases).

Figure 4.25 is an example of the notation for logic boxes when used to illustrate temporal requirements.

Figure 4.26 is an example system sequence diagram showing the interactions between externals and an application (the Mark I Vending Machine Software)

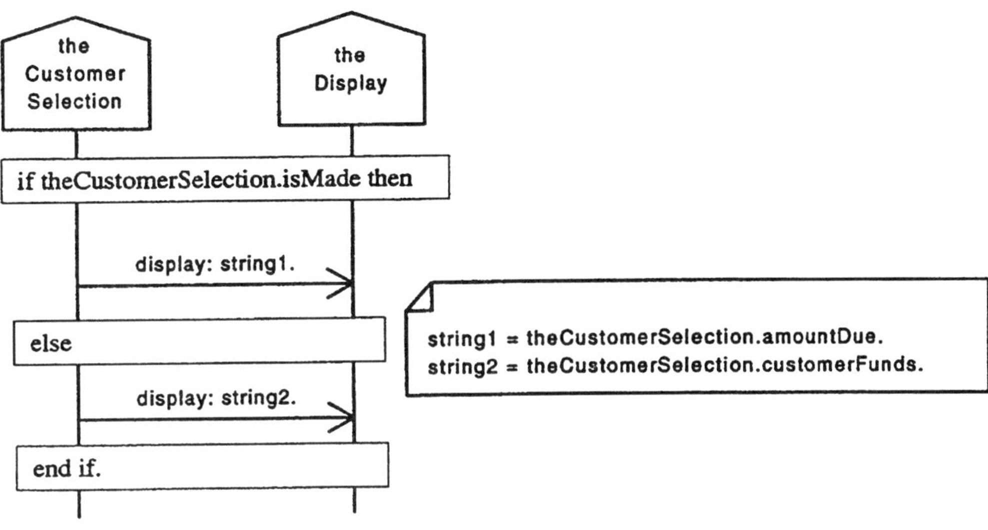

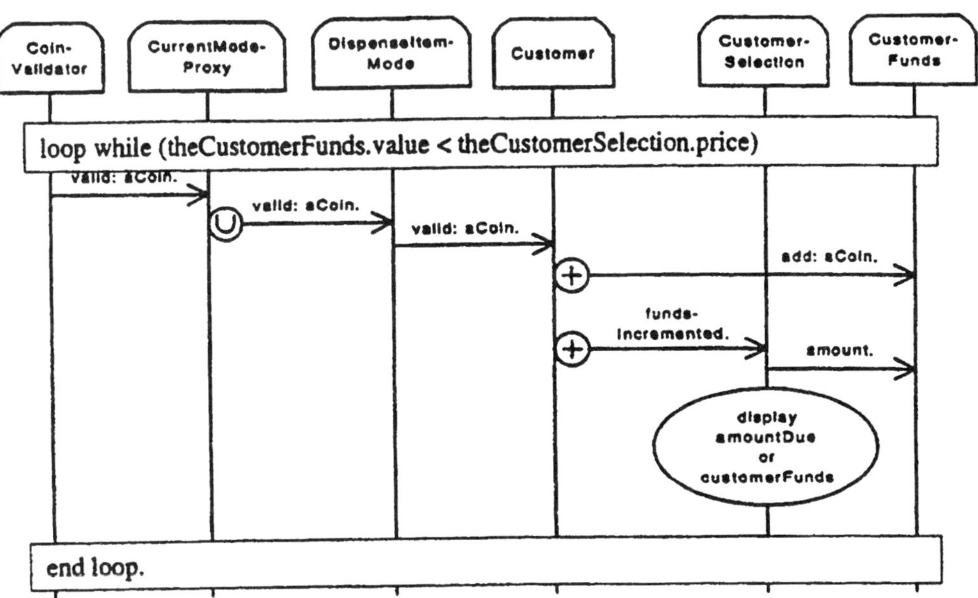

Figure 4.23. Logic boxes for loops.

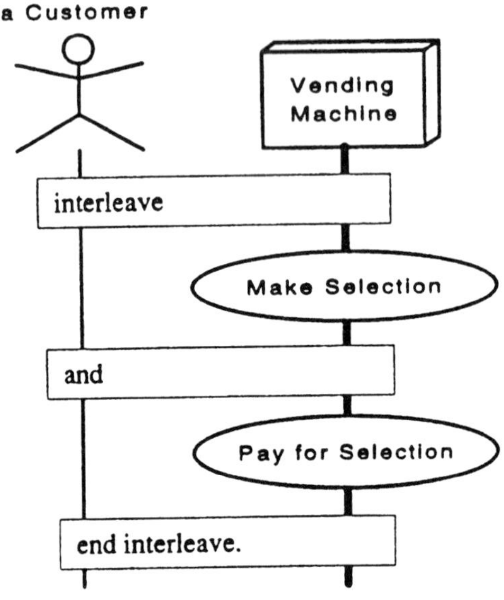

Figure 4.24. Example using notation for concurrency.

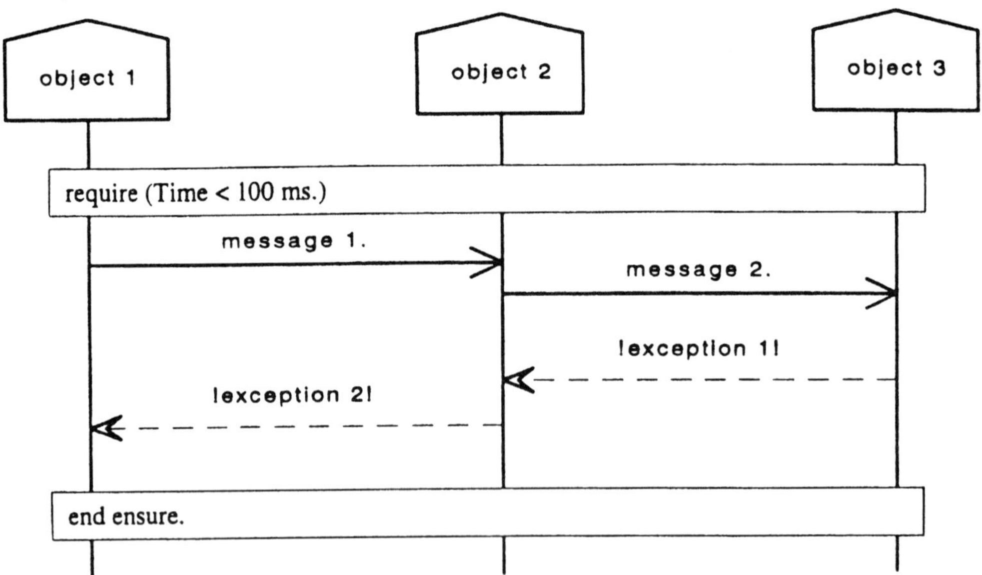

Figure 4.25. Example using notation for timing information.

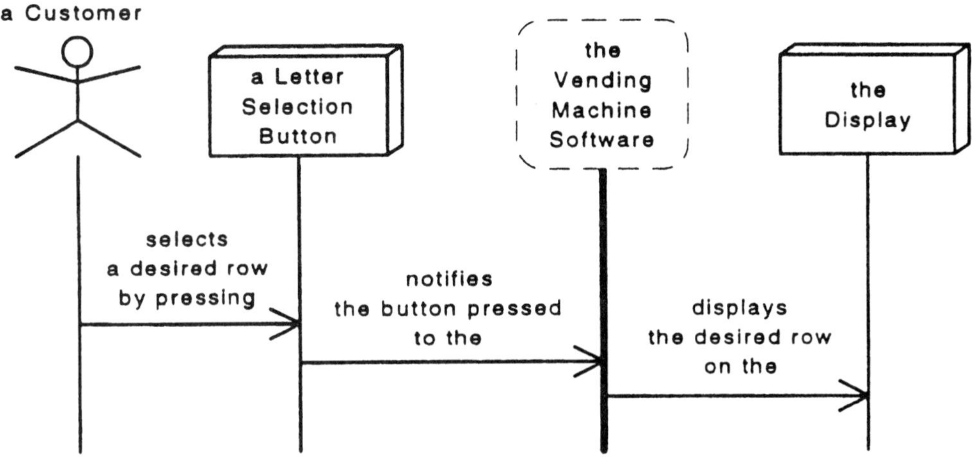

Figure 4.26. Blackbox sequence diagram for a use case path of a vending machine.

that occur when a customer selects a row by pressing a letter selection button when no column has been selected and no money has been deposited. Note that the system-level interactions with externals are labeled with English verb phrases because no software messages in the OO sense exist outside of the application.

Figure 4.26 is an example software sequence diagram showing the interactions between objects that occur when a customer selects a row by pressing a letter selection button when no column has been selected and no money has been deposited. Note that the messages use Java syntax as their naming convention.

4.4   State Transition Diagrams

Definitions

state transition diagram (STD) *n.* any directed graph of states (nodes[3]) connected by transitions (directed arcs) that is used to specify the common *qual-*

---

[3]Although graphed as nodes both in the metamodel and on model diagrams, guard conditions are better considered a part of the transition they control.

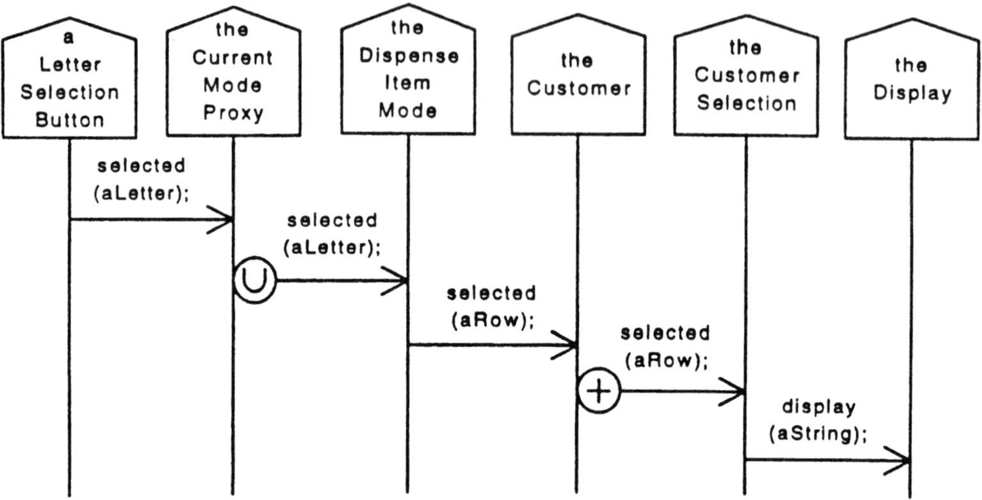

Figure 4.27. Whitebox sequence diagram for a use case path of a vending machine.

itative[4] behavior of the instances of a class. An STD describes the potential life history of objects of a given class, in terms of the ways they respond to interactions (messages from, exceptions raised by) other objects.

state *n.* any equivalence class of property values[5] used to represent a status, situation, condition, mode, or life-cycle phase of an instance during which certain rules of qualitative behavior apply. A state typically lasts for a significant period of time. OML recognizes the following kinds of state:

- **atomic state** *n.* any state that is not decomposed into substates.

- **start state** *n.* any atomic state of an object or class upon instantiation and initialization.

- **stop state** *n.* any terminal state from which the object or class cannot transition.

---

[4]By qualitative behavior, we mean whether or not an operation executes or which path of a logic branch is taken.

[5]Note that all properties need not influence the qualitative behavior of objects. In fact, many objects do not exhibit any significant state behavior at all and therefore do not need a state transition diagram.

- **substate** *n.* the role played by any state that specializes another state (its superstate). Note that the equivalence classes of property values of substates partition (i.e., form a disjoint cover of) the equivalence class of their superstates. A substate therefore inherits the outgoing group transitions of its superstate.

- **superstate** *n.* the role played by any aggregate state that is specialized by its substates. A superstate has a default starting substate to which incoming group transitions point.

- **atomic state.** any state that does not have specialized substates.

- **aggregate state.** any general state that has specialized substates.

transition *n.* any change in state. Because states are defined in terms of property values, a change in state is typically of such short duration compared to a state as to be instantaneous. OML recognizes the following kinds of state transitions:

- **normal transition** *n.* any transition caused by a message or operation.

- **exceptional transition** *n.* any transition caused by an exception or exception handler.

- **leaving transition** *n.* any transition that causes the object to leave its pre-transition state and transition to its post-transition state.

- **remaining transition** *n.* any transition that causes the object to remain in its pre-transition state while also transitioning to its post-transition state. This is equivalent to a synchronous transition from a pre-transition state to both the pre-transition state and one or more post-transition states.

- **group transition** *n.* any transition to or from an aggregate state.

- *sequential transition* *n.* any single transition from and to a single [sub]-state. A sequential transition does not increase or decrease the number of concurrent states.

- **synchronous transition** *n.* any single transition from or to multiple [sub]-states. A synchronous transition increases or decreases the number of concurrent states.

trigger *n.* anything that causes a state transition by changing the associated state property values. Most state modeling techniques refer to triggers as events, without specifying what they are in terms of object-oriented concepts. OML recognizes the following kinds of triggers:

- message received or the execution of the corresponding operation, which cause normal transitions

- exception caught or the execution of the corresponding exception handler, which cause exceptional transitions.

guard condition *n.* any condition (either Boolean or of enumeration type) that must evaluate properly in order for the trigger to cause the corresponding transition to fire.

OML Metamodel

Figure 4.28 illustrates a partial metamodel for state-related concepts and captures the following information:

- A class may optionally define one or more state machines for its instances.

- Each state machine consists of two or more states connected by 1 or more transitions.

- States can be partitioned into aggregate states containing other states as substates and an atomic state which do not.

- Any state can play the role of substate, but only aggregate states can play the role of superstates.

- Substates inherit the transitions of their superstates.

- States can also be partitioned into start states, normal states, and stop states.

- Transitions cannot leave stop states (i.e., any state can play the role of a post-transition state, but only non-stop states can play the role of pre-transition states).

- Transitions can be completely and disjointedly partitioned into remaining transitions and leaving transitions.

- All transitions change the current state(s) into the associated post-transition state(s), but only leaving transitions change the current state(s) from the pre-transition state(s).

- Transitions can also be completely and disjointedly partitioned into normal transitions and exceptional transitions, whereby operations fire normal transitions and exception handlers fire exceptional transitions. Thus, operations and exception handlers play the roles of triggers of transitions.

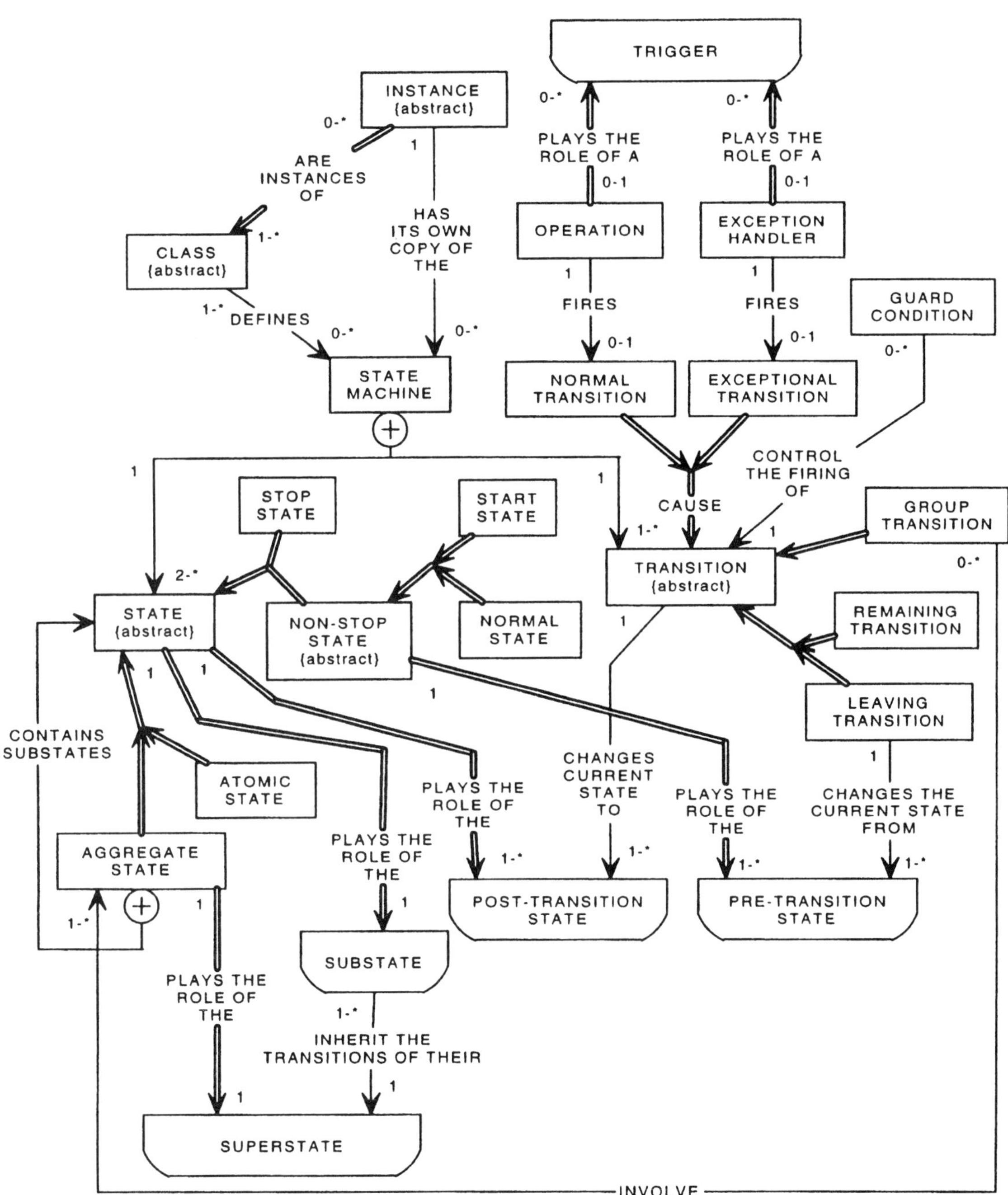

Figure 4.28. Partial metamodel for state-related concepts.

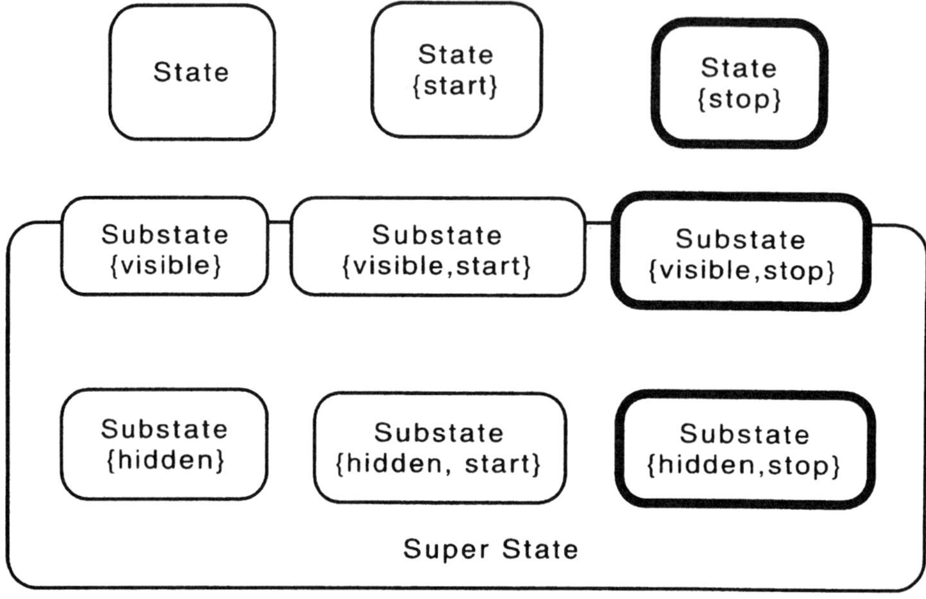

Figure 4.29. State icons.

- Group transitions are a kind of transition involving aggregate states.
- Guard conditions control the firing of the associated transitions.

COMN Notation.

state. A state is represented by a solid rounded rectangle. The label of a state icon is a character string consisting of the name of the state.

- **start state.** A start state is annotated with the stereotype {start}.
- **stop state.** A stop state is drawn with a thick solid line.
- **visible substate.** A visible substate is represented by a state icon attached to the boundary of its superstate's icon.
- **hidden substate.** A hidden substate is represented by a state icon nested within the boundary of its superstate's icon.

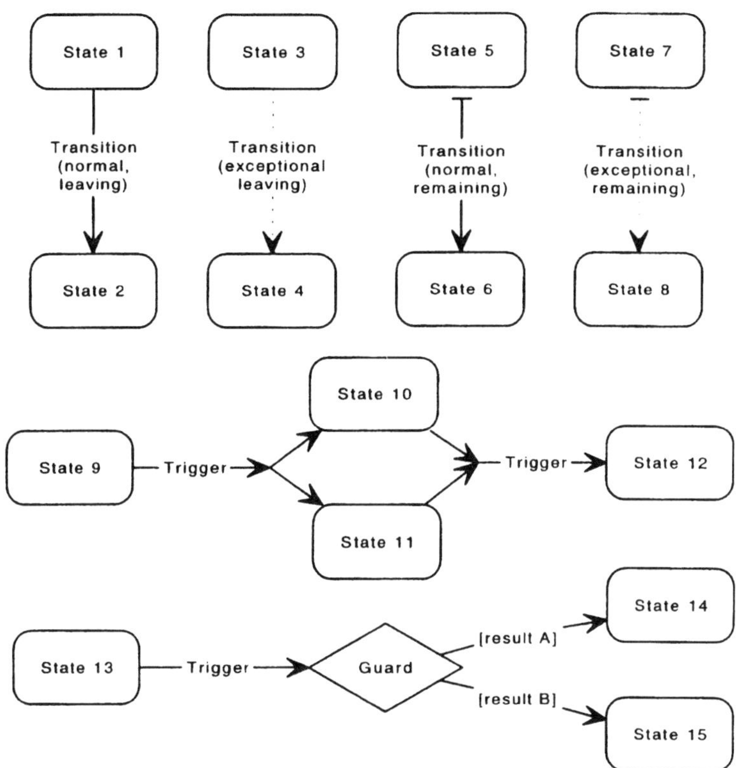

Figure 4.30. Transition icons.

transition. A transition is drawn as a line drawn from the initial state[s] to the resulting state[s] having arrowhead[s] on the resulting state[s] end.

normal transition. A normal transition is drawn as a solid line.

exceptional transition. An exceptional transition is drawn as a dashed line.

leaving transition. A leaving transition is drawn as an arrow with no annotation on the initial state end.

remaining transition. A remaining transition is drawn with a bar on the initial state end.

group transition. A group transition is drawn from any superstate.

guard condition. A guard condition is represented as a diamond. The values of the guard condition are labeled on the transition arcs leaving the guard condition.

Although Figure 4.30 does not illustrate all possible combinations of kinds of transitions (normal vs. exceptional, leaving vs. remaining, sequential vs. synchronous) recognized by OML, it does illustrate the following kinds of state transitions:

- The transition from State 1 to State 2 is the normal transition triggered by the execution of an operation (caused by a message) that causes the state machine to leave State 1 and transition to State 2.

- The transition from State 3 to State 4 is the exceptional transition triggered by the handling of an exception (caused by the raising of an exception) that causes the state machine to leave State 3 and transition to State 4.

- The transition from State 5 to State 6 is the normal transition triggered by the execution of an operation that causes the state machine to transition to State 6 while remaining in State 5. Thus the object is simultaneously in one more state after the transition than before the transition.

- The transition from State 7 to State 8 is the exceptional transition triggered by the handling of an exception that causes the state machine to transition to State 8 while remaining in State 7. Thus the object is simultaneously in one more state after the transition than before the transition.

- The transition from State 9 to State 10 and State 11 is a normal synchronous transition caused by the associated trigger operation that causes the state machine to leave State 9 and transition to State 10 and State 11. Thus the object is simultaneously in one more state after the transition than before the transition.

- The transition from State 10 and State 11 to State 12 is a normal synchronous transition caused by the associated trigger operation that causes the state machine to leave State 10 and State 11 to transition to State 12. The state machine must be in both pre-transition states for the associated trigger to fire the transition, and the object is simultaneously in one less state after the transition than before the transition.

- The normal leaving transition from State 13 to State 14 or State 15 is protected by a guard expression. The results of evaluating the guard at the time of the trigger determines whether the transition will fire and the resulting state.

Audience

The primary intended audience for the state transition diagrams consists of modelers and programmers.

Scope

The scope of a state transition diagram is a single object or class. The state behavior of all instances of the same class can be modeled by a single state transition diagram. However, if the class has class-level properties, it may require its own state transition diagram

Permitted Icons

The following icons are permitted on state transition diagrams:

- Nodes:
    — State icons
    — Guard icons
    — State machine icons
- Nodes:
    — Transition icons

Guidelines

1. Only create a state transition diagram if either the instance of a class or the class itself have a significant state model.
2. Use multiple state machines if different [collections of] state properties provide relatively independent states so that multiple, small, [possibly] communicating state machines provide a simpler model than one large complex state machine.

Rationale

Attaching the icon of a substate to the boundary of the icon of the superstate is an intuitive way of showing that the substate is part of the interface of the super-

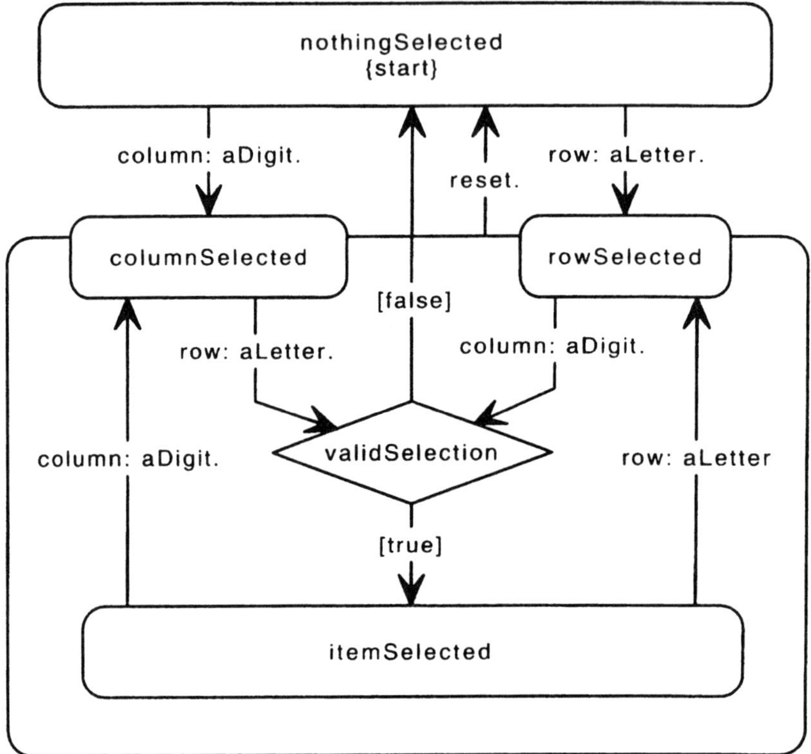

Figure 4.31. State transition diagram for a customer selection class.

state and therefore the state machine can transition from a state external to the superstate to the exported substate.

A thick border was chosen for the stop state to signify that it is like a black hole; once an object gets into this state, it cannot get out.

Because transitions are relatively instantaneous, all operations either (1) begin and end execution while the object is in a single state or else (2) begin execution in one state and complete execution in another.

Examples

Figure 4.31 illustrates the state transition diagram for the customer selection class. Notice that two transitions are protected by the same guard condition (validSelection). Notice also that the reset operation is a trigger for the group

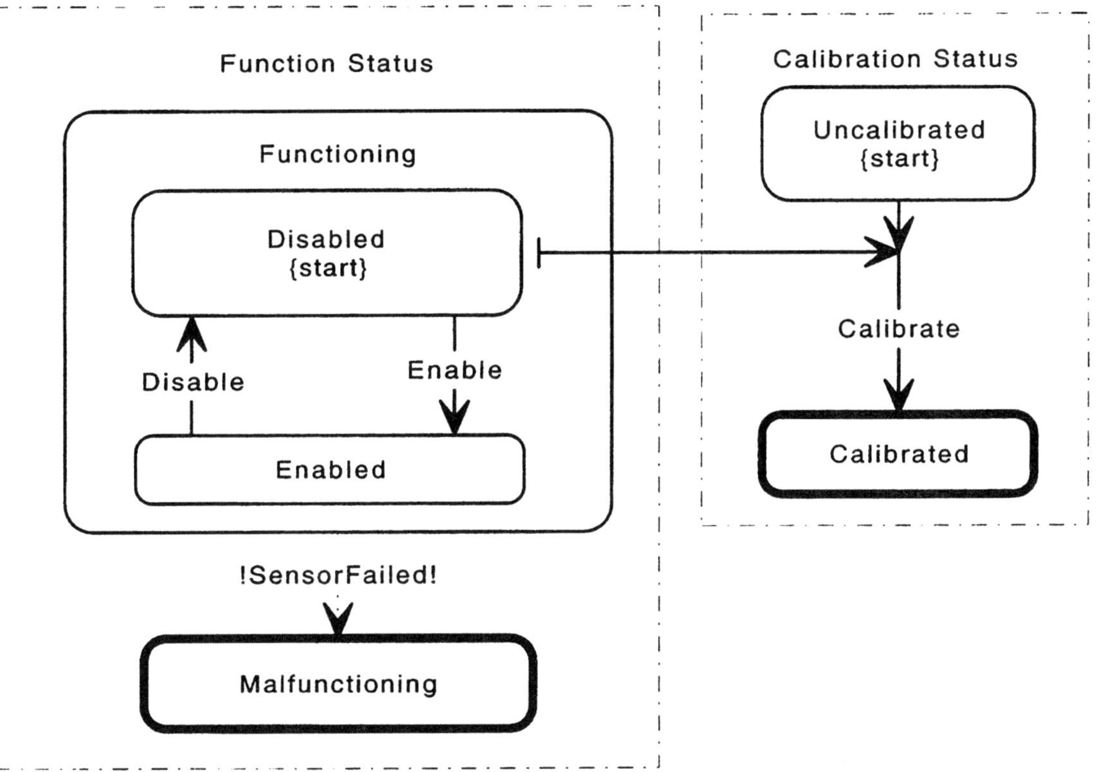

Figure 4.32. State transition diagram for a calibrated sensor.

transition from the somethingSelected state to the nothingSelected state (i.e., it does not matter in which of the three substates of the somethingSelected a customerSelection object is in, it will transition to the nothingSelected state when the reset operation executes). This example uses Smalltalk naming conventions.

Figure 4.32 documents the state transition diagram of a calibrated sensor. The state model contains two relatively independent state machines captured by two state properties: function status and calibration status. Note that the calibrate operation triggers the leaving transition from the uncalibrated state to the calibrated state only if the sensor is also in the disabled substate of the functioning state. Because the calibrate operation has no effect on the disabled substate, a remaining transition was used.

5   Class Responsibility Collaboration (CRC) Cards

Definitions

class responsibility collaborator card[1] *n.* any kind of index card used as a simple, manual upperCASE tool, the purpose of which is to document the responsibilities and associated collaborators for a class of objects, clusters, or externals.

- **object CRC card** *n.* any CRC card, the purpose of which is to document the responsibilities of a class of objects.

- **cluster CRC card** *n.* any CRC card, the purpose of which is to document the responsibilities of a class of clusters.

- **role responsibility collaborator card** *n.* any CRC card, the purpose of which is to document the responsibilities of a role.

responsibility *n.* any purpose, obligation, or required capability of the instances of a class of objects, clusters, or externals. A responsibility is typically implemented by a cohesive collection of one or more characteristics. A responsibility can be a responsibility for doing, a responsibility for knowing, or a responsibility for enforcing.

collaborator *n.* any server on which the thing documented by the responsibility collaborator card depends in order to fulfill its associated responsibility.

Guidelines

1. Expect to iterate. Fill out the CRC cards in pencil, and have a large eraser available.

2. Fill out the name and description first.

3. Use large (at least 5 by 7 inch) CRC cards so that there is adequate room to list the responsibilities and collaborators.

4. Emphasize responsibilities over collaborators. For each responsibility, list its specific collaborators opposite it.

5. Emphasize responsibilities for doing and for enforcing (e.g., business rules) over responsibilities for knowing. Document responsibilities for knowing on the back of the card under logical properties.

6. Unless obvious, ignore abstract superclasses until concrete subclasses are captured.

7. Develop responsibility collaborator cards in conjunction with the drawing of semantic nets. Use the semantic net and the direction of the relationships to help distribute the responsibilities.

8. Verify the CRC cards by role playing scenarios and mechanisms.

Rationale

Responsibility-driven approaches to object-oriented modeling have been shown to produce better designs than data-driven approaches in terms of number of classes, cohesion, and coupling. The benefits of CRC cards are widely documented, known, and appreciated within the object community.

It is critical to identify the main public responsibilities of something (e.g., class, cluster, external) before worrying about such implementation details as the properties and operations which are required to support the responsibilities.

5.1 Object CRC Cards

The front and back of the object CRC card are shown below in Figures 5.1 and 5.2, respectively.

---

[1]No Instance Responsibility Collaborator Card is required because all instances of the same class share the same responsibilities. If the collaborators are different because of the use of different constructors, this can still be captured on the CRC card.

5.2   Cluster CRC Cards

The front and back of the cluster class responsibility collaborator card are shown below in Figures 5.3 and 5.4, respectively.

5.3   Role Responsibility Collaborator Cards

The front and back of the role responsibility collaborator card are shown below in Figures 5.5 and 5.6, respectively.

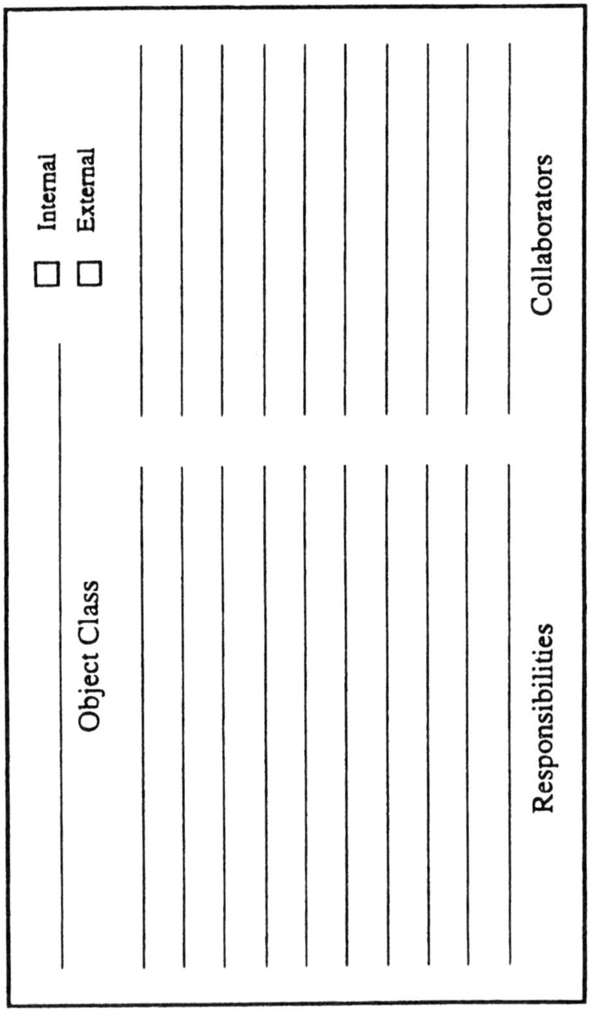

Figure 5.1. Front of the object CRC card.

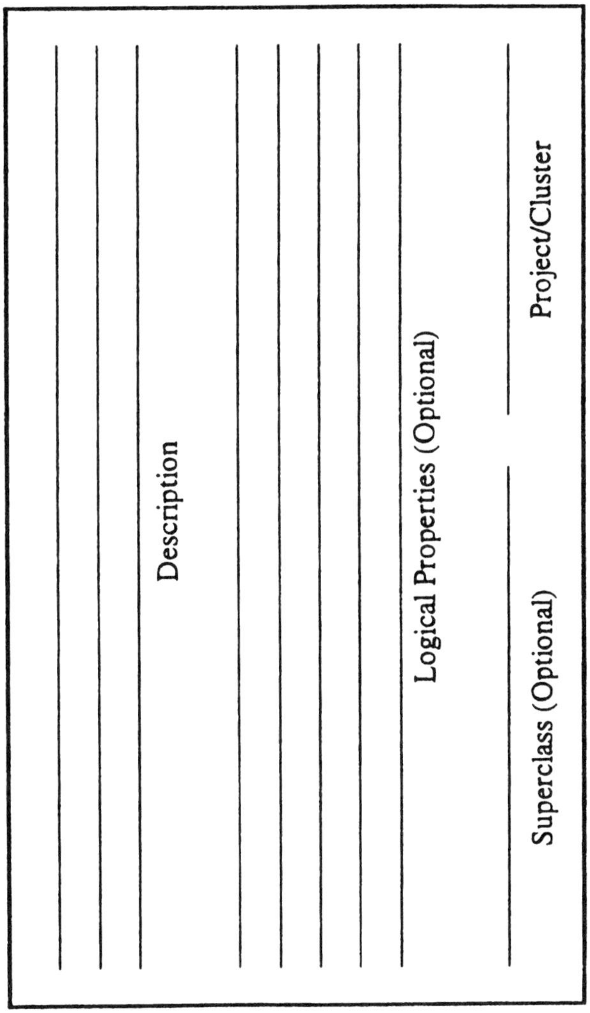

Figure 5.2. Back of the object CRC card.

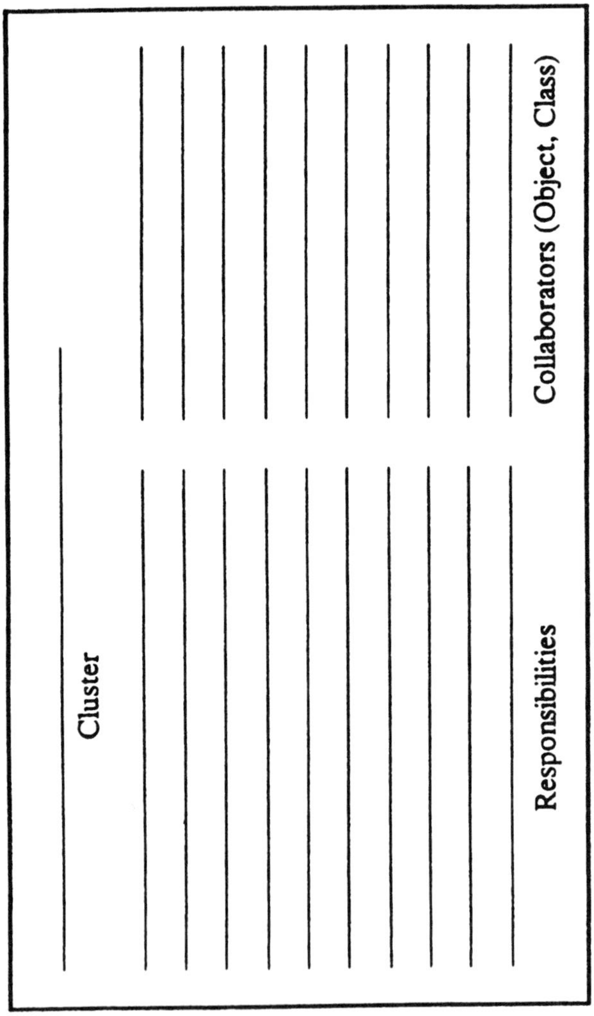

Figure 5.3. Front of the cluster class responsibility collaborator card.

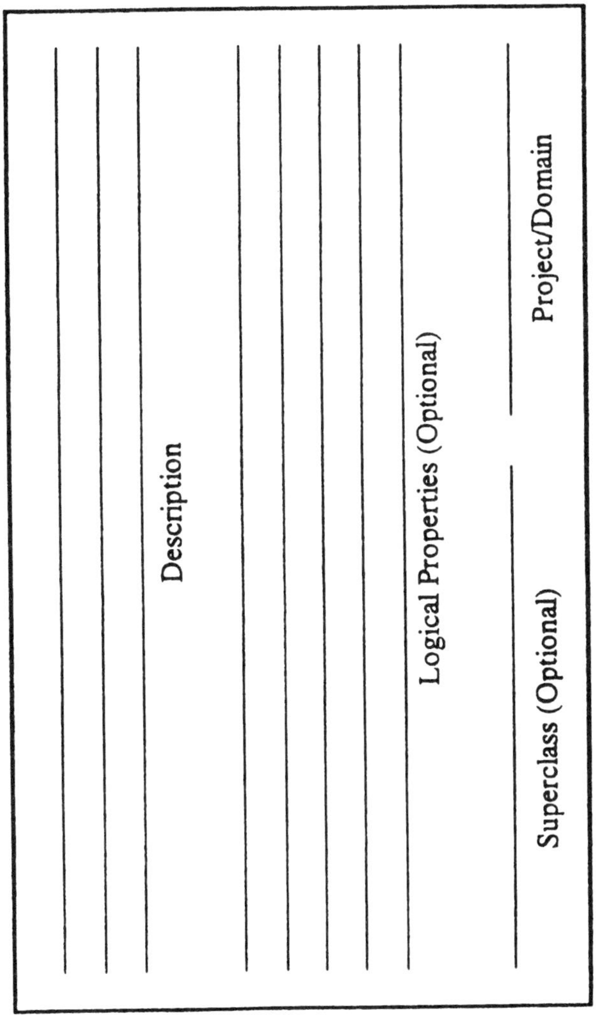

Figure 5.4. Back of the cluster class collaborator card.

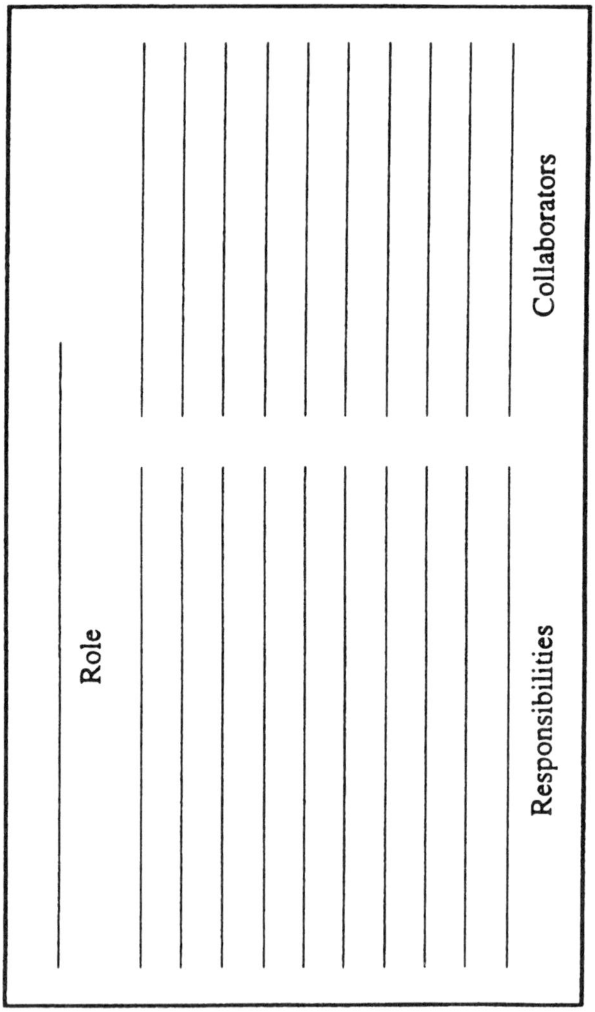

Role

Responsibilities

Collaborators

Figure 5.5. Front of the role responsibility collaborator card.

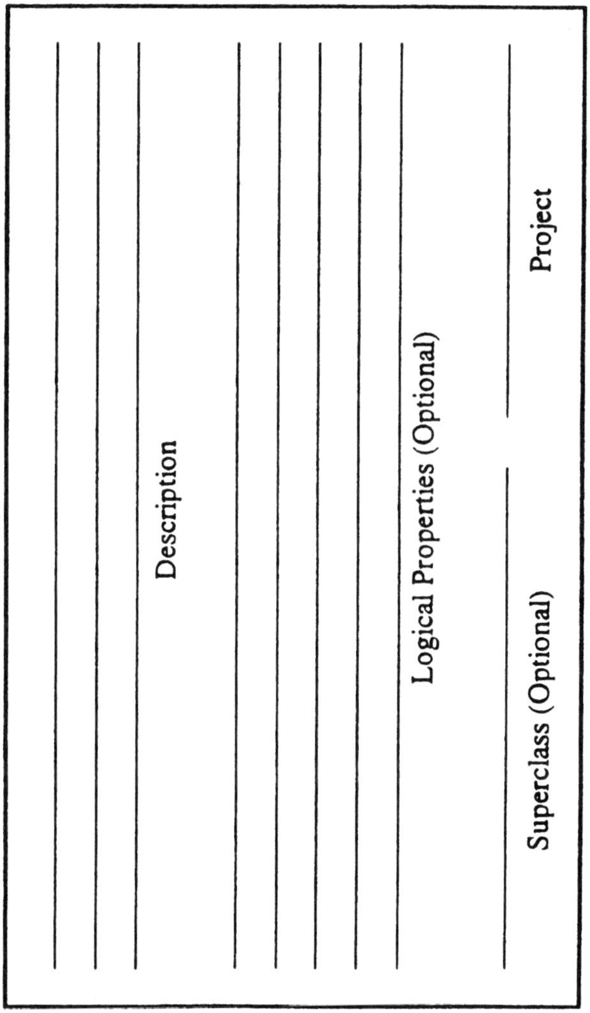

Figure 5.6. Back of the role collaborator card.

6 Appendices

6.1 Charts of Icons to Diagrams

The tables begin on the following page.

6.1.1 Icons on Semantic Nets

The following table documents the valid *nodes* on semantic nets:

Nodes on Semantic Nets	Context Diagram	Layer Diagram	Configuration Diagram	Cluster Diagram	Inheritance Diagram	Deployment Diagram
Object (Instance)	No	No	No	Primary	No	No
Object Class	No	No	No	Primary	Primary	No
Object Type	No	No	No	Primary	Primary	No
Object Class Imp.	No	No	No	Secondary	Secondary	No
Human Actor	Primary	No	No	Secondary	No	No
HW External	Primary	No	No	Secondary	No	Primary
SW External	Primary	No	No	Secondary	No	No
Persist. Memory	Primary	No	No	Secondary	No	Primary
Other External	Secondary	No	No	Secondary	No	No
Cluster Instance	Primary	Primary	Primary	Primary	Secondary	No
Cluster (Class)	Primary	Primary	Primary	Secondary	Secondary	No
Cluster Type	No	No	No	Secondary	No	No
Cluster Class Imp.	No	No	No	Secondary	No	No
Role	No	No	No	Secondary	No	No
Scenario	No	No	No	Secondary	No	No
Scenario Class	No	No	No	Secondary	No	No
Operation	No	No	No	No	No	No
Property	No	No	No	No	No	No
C.G. Data[1]	No	No	No	Secondary	No	No
C.G. Operation	No	No	No	Secondary	No	No
State	No	No	No	No	No	No
Guard	No	No	No	No	No	No
Drop-Down Box	Secondary	Secondary	Secondary	Secondary	Secondary	Secondary
Note	Secondary	Secondary	Secondary	Secondary	Secondary	Secondary

---

[1]C.G. = Common Global.

The following table documents the valid *arcs* on semantic nets:

Arcs on Semantic Nets	Context Diagram	Layer Diagram	Configuration Diagram	Cluster Diagram	Inheritance Diagram	Deployment Diagram
Linkage	Primary	Primary	Primary	Primary	Secondary	Primary
Association	Secondary	Secondary	Primary	Primary	Secondary	Primary
Aggregation	Secondary	No	Secondary	Primary	Secondary	No
Containment	Secondary	No	Secondary	Primary	Secondary	No
Message Flow	No	No	No	No	No	No
Exception Flow	No	No	No	No	No	No
Object Flow	No	No	No	No	No	No
Specialization Inheritance	Secondary	Secondary	No	Secondary	Primary	No
Interface Inheritance	Secondary	Secondary	No	Secondary	Secondary	No
Implementation Inheritance	Secondary	Secondary	No	Secondary	Secondary	No
Conforms To	No	No	No	Secondary	No	No
Instance Of	No	No	No	Secondary	No	No
Plays the Role of	Secondary	No	No	Primary	No	No
Implements	No	No	No	Secondary	Secondary	No
Is Implemented By	No	No	No	Secondary	Secondary	No
Uses	No	No	No	No	No	No
Precedes	No	No	No	No	No	No
Invokes	No	No	No	No	No	No
Transition	No	No	No	No	No	No

6.1.2 Icons on Interaction Diagrams

The following table documents the valid *nodes* on interaction diagrams:

Interaction Diagrams	Cluster Collaboration Diagram	Scenario Collaboration Diagram	Internal Collaboration Diagram	Blackbox Sequence Diagram	Whitebox Sequence Diagram
Object (Instance)	Primary	Primary	Primary	No	Primary[2]
Object Class	Primary	Primary	Primary	No	Primary[2]
Object Type	No	No	No	No	Primary[2]
Object Class Imp.	No	No	No	No	No
Human Role Actor	Secondary	Secondary	Secondary	Primary[2]	No
Hardware External	Secondary	Secondary	Secondary	Primary[2]	No
Software External	Secondary	Secondary	Secondary	Primary[2]	No
Persistent Memory	Secondary	Secondary	Secondary	Primary[2]	No
Other External	Secondary	Secondary	Secondary	Primary[2]	No
Cluster (Instance)	Secondary	Secondary	Secondary	No	No
Cluster Class	Secondary	Secondary	Secondary	No	No
Cluster Type	No	No	No	No	No
Cluster Class Imp.	No	No	No	No	No
Role	Secondary	Secondary	No	No	Secondary
Scenario	No	No	No	Secondary	Secondary
Scenario Class	No	No	No	Secondary	Secondary
Operation	No	No	Primary	No	No
Property	No	No	Primary	No	No
C. G. Data	Secondary	Secondary	Secondary	No	Secondary
C. G. Operations	Secondary	Secondary	Secondary	No	Secondary
State	No	No	No	No	No
Guard	No	No	No	No	No
Drop-Down Box	Secondary	Secondary	Secondary	No	No
Note	Secondary	Secondary	Secondary	Secondary	Secondary

---

[2]Timeline icon.

The following table documents the valid *arcs* on interaction diagrams:

Arcs on Interaction Diagrams	Cluster Collaboration Diagram	Scenario Collaboration Diagram	Internal Collaboration Diagram	Blackbox Sequence Diagram	Whitebox Sequence Diagram
Association	Primary	Primary	Primary	Primary	Primary
Linkage	Primary	Primary	Primary	Primary	Primary
Aggregation	Primary	Primary	Primary	Primary	Primary
Containment	Primary	Primary	Primary	Primary	Primary
Message	Primary	Primary	Primary	Primary	Primary
Exception Flow	Primary	Primary	Primary	Primary	Primary
Object Flow	No	No	Primary	No	No
Specialization Inheritance	Secondary	Secondary	Secondary	No	No
Interface Inheritance	Secondary	Secondary	Secondary	No	No
Implementation Inheritance	Secondary	Secondary	Secondary	No	No
Instance Of	No	No	No	No	No
Conforms To	No	No	No	No	No
Plays the Role of	No	No	No	No	No
Implements	No	No	No	No	No
Is Implemented By	No	No	No	No	No
Uses	No	No	No	No	No
Precedes	No	No	No	No	No
Invokes	No	No	No	No	No
Transition	No	No	No	No	No

6.1.3 Icons on Scenario Class Diagrams and State Transition Diagrams

The following table documents the valid *nodes* on use case diagrams and state transition diagrams:

Valid Nodes vs. Diagrams	Mechanism Diagram	Task Script Diagram	Use Case Diagram	State Transition Diagram
Object (Instance)	No	No	No	No
Object Class	No	No	No	No
Object Type	No	No	No	No
Object Class Implementation	No	No	No	No
Human Role Actor	No	No	Primary	No
Hardware External	No	No	Primary	No
Software External	No	No	Primary	No
Persistent Memory External	No	No	Primary	No
Other External	No	No	Secondary	No
Cluster (Instance)	Primary	No	Primary	No
Cluster Class	Primary	No	Primary	No
Cluster Type	No	No	No	No
Cluster Class Implementation	No	No	No	No
Role	No	No	Primary	No
Scenario	Primary	Primary	Primary	No
Scenario Class	Primary	Primary	Primary	No
Operation	No	No	No	No
Attribute	No	No	No	No
C.G. Data	No	No	No	No
C.G. Operation	No	No	No	No
State	No	No	No	Primary
Guard	No	No	No	Secondary
Drop-Down Box	Secondary	Secondary	Secondary	Secondary
Note	Secondary	Secondary	Secondary	Secondary

The following table documents the valid *arcs* on use case diagrams and state transition diagrams:

Valid Arcs vs. Diagrams	Scenario Class Diagram	State Transition Diagram
Association	Secondary	No
Linkage	Secondary	No
Aggregation	No	No
Containment	Secondary	No
Specialization Inheritance	Secondary	No
Interface Inheritance	No	No
Implementation Inheritance	No	No
Instance Of (is a)	No	No
Conforms To (is a)	No	No
Plays the Role of (is a)	No	No
Sequential Message	No	No
Synchronous Message	No	No
Asynchronous Message	No	No
Exception Flow	No	No
Implements	No	No
Is Implemented By	No	No
Object Flow	No	No
Uses	Primary	No
Precedes	Secondary	No
Invokes	Primary	No
Normal Leaving Transition	No	Primary
Normal Remaining Transition	No	Secondary
Exceptional Leaving Transition	No	Secondary
Exceptional Remaining Transition	No	Secondary

6.2   OML Light vs. Full OML

In order to make OML easier for the beginner to learn and use, the most commonly used icons have been collected into a subset called OML 'Light.'

6.2.1   OML Light Icons for Nodes

The following table documents the node icons that are a part of OML Light:

Node Icons	OML Light
Object (Instance)	Primary
Multiobject	No
Object Class	Primary
Object Type	Primary
Object Class Implementation	No
Human Role Actor	Primary
Hardware External	Primary
Software External	Primary
Persistent Memory External	Primary
Other External	No
Cluster (Instance)	Primary
Cluster Class	Primary
Cluster Type	No
Cluster Class Implementation	No
Role	No
Scenario	Primary
Scenario Class	Primary
Operation	No
Property	No
Common Global Data	No
Common Global Operation	No
State	Primary
Guard	Secondary
Drop-Down Box	Secondary
Note	Secondary

6.2.2 OML Light Icons for Arcs

The following table documents those relationship arc icons that are a part of
OML Light:

Icons for Relationship Arcs	OML Light
Unidirectional Association and Linkage	Primary
Bi-directional Association and Linkage	Secondary
Observer Association and Linkage	No
TBD Association and Linkage	Secondary
Aggregation Symbol	Primary
Containment Symbol	Primary
Specialization Inheritance (a kind of)	Primary
Interface Inheritance	No
Implementation Inheritance	No
Instance Of (is a)	Secondary
Conforms To (is a)	Secondary
Plays the Role Of (is a)	Secondary
Sequential Message	Primary
Synchronous Message	No
Asynchronous Message	No
Exception Flow	Secondary
Implements	Secondary
Is Implemented By	Secondary
Object Flow	No
Uses	Primary
Precedes	No
Invokes	Primary
Normal Leaving Transition	Primary
Normal Remaining Transition	No
Exceptional Leaving Transition	No
Exceptional Remaining Transition	No

6.3 Comparing OML COMN and the UML Notation

It is our professional opinion that OML COMN is currently the best available notation for object-oriented modeling. It is superior to the UML because it is more consistent with the object paradigm, better suited to the object-oriented development cycle, and easier to learn and use.

The choice between OPEN's COMN and Rational's UML is important because the language you use influences, both subtly and not so subtly, the way that you think and the results you produce. COMN and Rational's UML notation are two graphical languages that are to object-oriented modeling what a programming language is to coding. Although almost all models can be captured in either of these two languages, the choice of modeling language will have a significant influence on how that model is viewed and ultimately on the kinds of models that are created. Assuming reasonable infrastructure (e.g., documentation, CASE tool support), the choice should be made on technical grounds rather than as a result of a massive marketing campaign.

At the highest level of abstraction and based on the latest available information (version 0.91) on Rational's UML, the following table captures what we feel to be the fundamental differences in philosophy and mindset between OPEN's OML COMN and Rational's UML Notation.

OPEN'S OML COMN	Rational's UML Notation
Revolutionary	Evolutionary (primarily from OMT)
State of the Art	Traditional Notations Extended
Pure	Hybrid
Promotes Object-Oriented Mindset	Promotes Extended Relational Mindset
Responsibility Driven	Data Driven
Emphasizes High-Level of Abstraction	Emphasizes Low-Level of Abstraction
Emphasizes Analysis & Logical Design	Emphasizes Physical Design & Code Generation
Intuitive and Easy to Learn	Requires excessive Rote Memorization
Scaleable across Life-Cycle Activities	Too Inflexible

Specifically, the methodologists of the OPEN Consortium actively looked for the best currently available notations, regardless of the consequences to their own aging notations, and produced a state of the art notation that is far more revolutionary than evolutionary. The UML Notation, however, clearly shows its evolutionary nature by being an extension of the traditional OMT notations, which themselves are roughly a decade old.

COMN has been strongly influenced by the mindsets of Smalltalk, Eiffel, and object databases. COMN only supports non-OO concepts as extensions to its pure OO core due to the need to document the physical design of hybrid software (e.g., C++, Ada95). However, UML can be categorized as a hybrid modeling language due to the strong influences that relational technology and C++ have had on it.

The OPEN methodologists have thus actively tried to promote an object-oriented mindset by rejecting many of the traditional influences found in UML. COMN is therefore strongly responsibility driven via its use of drop-down boxes and CRC cards, whereas UML is strongly data driven (e.g., because of its emphasis on attributes, its choice of aggregation notation).

COMN has historically emphasized an initially high-level of abstraction, treating objects, classes, and types as blackboxes characterized by their descriptions and responsibilities, whereas UML has historically emphasized early on a low-level of abstraction, requiring the modeler to document attributes and operations, often at the C++ level. Thus, COMN emphasizes requirements analysis and logical design, whereas UML emphasizes physical design and the ability to automatically generate C++ code.

Because COMN is primarily intended for use by and communication with humans (e.g., domain experts, customers, modelers) rather than for forward and reverse engineering, one of the primary goals of COMN has been to be intuitive and easy to learn and use. However, UML has tended to use an unnecessary number of arbitrary or counter intuitive icons because of its traditional nature and emphasis on relational modeling and C++.

COMN's emphasis on simple icons and the use of drop-down boxes has allowed it to be flexible and scaleable across the activities of an iterative, incremental development cycle. On the other hand, UML's use of standard compartments in class icons has tended to restrict flexibility and force the developer to consider physical design details too early.

In conclusion, COMN has taken the best from existing notations (including UML). Where UML notation was found to be as good or better than COMN and we could not identify any way to improve UML, we adopted the UML notation. However, when COMN was determined to be better than UML in our professional opinion, we did not sacrifice quality to adopt UML notation just to make the two languages more consistent.

This appendix compares OML COMN and the UML Notation, identifying where they are the same and where they are different. This appendix also provides our rationale as to why we believe OML COMN to be better than UML.

6.3.1 Nodes and Arcs

Objects and Multiobjects

Modeling Concept	OPEN's OML	Rational's UML
Object	house (solid pentagon with vertical parallel sides)	solid rectangle
Object label	character string	character string underlined
Stereotypes	text enclosed in curly braces, either below label or in optional drop-down box	text enclosed in guillemets "<< >>" above label
Visible Object	object icon attached to boundary of encapsulating node	N/A
Hidden Object	object icon nested inside boundary of encapsulating node	N/A
Concurrent Object	Two slashes "//" preceding the label	stereotype "active"
Multiobject	two object icons stacked to upper right	two object icons stacked to upper right or multiplicity indicator
Human Role Actor	stick figure labeled with the name of the actor	stick figure labeled with the name of the actor
Device External	solid three-dimensional box labeled with the name of the external	either a stick figure or a solid three-dimensional box labeled with the name of the external
Software External	dashed rounded rectangle labeled with the name of the external	N/A
Persistent Storage External	solid cylinder labeled with the name of the external	N/A
Other External	solid cloud labeled with the name of the external	N/A
Object property values	Optionally listed in relevant drop-down box	Optionally listed in icon below label

UML use a single icon to represent both objects and classes of objects. Although classes are a kind of object, OML COMN considers them different enough to deserve different objects.

OML COMN chose the house icon to represent internal objects because:

- It is easy to draw.
- It is similar to the class icon (i.e., the tablet).
- The class icon can contain the object icon inside it, implying that it is more than just a class and has extra contents (which define the instance).
- One can cut one's self with a knife, but not with a knife class. The object icon is sharp and the class icon is smooth.

COMN's use of the letters 'C' and 'M' to denote classes and metaclasses for characteristics was chosen over UML's use of underlining the labels of objects because:

- The same annotation can be used in drop-down boxes and internal collaboration diagrams to represent the less common class-level and meta-class-level characteristics.
- The letters 'C' and 'M' are easier to remember than the relatively arbitrary or programming language-specific symbols of other notations (e.g., $ for static or class-level).
- Underlining makes the icons look cluttered and ugly.

UML does not provide a good way to graphically document the visibility of an object within another object or cluster.

UML can produce cluttered icons (e.g., by listing numerous stereotypes or the property values of an object below the label of the object.

The COMN annotation of two slashes "//" to signify parallel processing is intuitive and cuts down on the number of stereotypes.

UML uses the term "actor" for human roles and "node" for hardware devices, and does not clearly offer a unifying concept. OML uses the term "external" for all external things, reserving the term "actor" for human role externals.

UML Version 0.9 considers externals to be a kind of class, whereas OML includes both external instances and external classes.

UML represents an actor using either a stick figure or their class icon with the stereotype <<actor>> on use case diagrams. UML Version 0.9 uses the 3-D box for nodes on deployment diagrams.

UML does not cleanly distinguish between the models of external things and the corresponding internal models of the same things, which is unfortunate because they are different models with different responsibilities.

COMN uses standard, relatively intuitive, icons for different kinds of externals.

Object Classes, Types, and Class Implementations

Modeling Concept	OPEN's OML	Rational's UML
Class	tablet (i.e., rectangle with rounded top corners)	solid rectangle, optionally divided into three compartments for name, attributes, and operations
Class Label	character string	character string
Stereotypes	text enclosed in curly braces, either below label or in optional drop-down box	text enclosed in guillemets "<< >>" above class name or in operations or attributes area
Parameterized Class	stereotype "generic" with parameters in the relevant drop-down box	class rectangle impacted by small dashed rectangle containing list of parameters in attribute form
Concurrent Class	Two slashes "//" preceding the label	stereotype "active"
Visible Class	class icon attached to boundary of encapsulating node	N/A
Hidden Class	class icon nested inside boundary of encapsulating node	N/A
Type	tablet (i.e., rectangle with rounded top corners) with zigzag bottom	small unfilled circle on implementation stick or reified as class
Class Implementation	rectangle with zigzag top	N/A

The distinctive COMN tablet was chosen over the UML rectangle in order to:

- Avoid ambiguity because the traditional shape (rectangle) is heavily overloaded
- Clearly differentiate COMN as a pure OO modeling language UML which is more data driven due to its strong OMT roots in traditional data modeling and entity relationship (ER) attribute diagrams.

The UML class icon, with its 3 compartments, forces the developer to think in implementation terms too early, does not have a place to capture exceptions and business rules, does not scale well for real classes which may have numerous operations and attributes, and uses arbitrary characters to differentiate the different kinds of operations and attributes.

UML's notation for types makes it difficult to show inheritance relationships among types, inheritance relationships among class implementations, and the implements relationships from class implementations to types. OML provides separate icons for classes, types, and class implementations, making it easier to show the inheritance and implementation relations.

By allowing the modeler to select the appropriate drop-down boxes to provide the information when needed, OML provides the flexibility needed to show the correct amount of information at the correct level of abstraction at the correct time and avoids the restrictions of the UML notation.

Clusters

Modeling Concept	OPEN's OML	Rational's UML
Cluster (instance)	dashed rounded rectangle labeled with the name of the cluster	file folder (rectangle with rectangular tab on top left)
Cluster Class	dashed rounded rectangle labeled with the name of the cluster class preceded by a capital C	N/A
Cluster Type	dashed tablet (i.e., rectangle with rounded top corners) with zigzag bottom	N/A
Cluster Class Implementation	dashed rectangle with zigzag top	N/A
Visible Cluster	cluster icon attached to the boundary of encapsulating node	N/A
Hidden Cluster	cluster icon nested inside the boundary of encapsulating node	N/A

Instead of OML's term 'cluster' which is widely used in the object community, UML version 0.8 used the terms 'category' and 'subsystem', both of which have been replaced by the term 'package' in version 0.9. UML uses a tabbed folder icon.

UML does not support cluster encapsulation because it does not support the documenting of the cluster interface vs. implementation.

UML does not support the concept of cluster instantiation.

Drop-Down Boxes

UML does not offer the flexibility of drop-down boxes. Only some icons (e.g., those for classes and objects) exist in multiple forms.

Association and Linkage

Modeling Concept	OPEN's OML	Rational's UML
Unidirectional Association or Linkage	solid line with arrowhead on server end labeled with its name and multiplicity	solid line with arrowhead on server end
Bi-directional Association or Linkage	solid line with arrowheads on both ends labeled with the names of the two unidirectional associations or links and multiplicity	solid line
Observer Association or Linkage	solid line with two facing arrowhead on the server end labeled with the name of the primary association or link and the multiplicity	N/A
TBD Association or Linkage	solid line labeled with the name of the association	N/A
Associative Properties	Rejected. Reified as a class.	anonymous degenerate class with only attributes attached to association line by dashed line
Associative Class	Reified as class and object	class attached to association/link line by dashed line
N-ary Association or Linkage	Rejected. Instead reify as class and object with association/linkage arcs to each participating class/object	diamond with lines to each participating class
Role	Rejected. Not needed.	name next to end of association near class, far end
Or Association or Linkage	Rejected. Instead use combination of association or linkage and inheritance	dashed (dependency / constraint) line across all associations with constraint "or"

Associations and linkages can be drawn between more than just object classes and objects respectively. OPEN supports TBD directionality and has a more intuitive use of arrow heads for bi-directionality.

As illustrated in Figure 3.59, OPEN does not recognize properties of associations or linkages; any such relationships (e.g., Stock with property quantity) should be reified to become classes and objects respectively in their own right. Compare with Figure 10, page 15 in UML Notation Summary version 0.8.

As illustrated in Figure 3.60, OPEN also reifies all ternary and higher-level associations and links. Compare with Figure 9, page 14 and Figure 14, page 16 in UML Notation Summary version 0.8.

As illustrated in Figure 3.61, OPEN does not recognize "Or-associations"; a case where an or-association might be desired is typically a sign that a missing abstract superclass is needed. Compare with Figure 15, page 30 in UML Notation Summary version 1.0.

As illustrated in Figure 3.62, OPEN recommends using role classes rather than subclassing person. Compare with Figure 7, page 14 in UML Notation Summary version 0.8.

Aggregation

Modeling Concept	OPEN's OML	Rational's UML
Aggregation	Aggregation symbol (circle with plus sign) attached outside the bottom of the aggregate and connected by the appropriate association/link arc to each part. Fork structure used with multiple parts	diamond at aggregate end of association/linkage line

UML uses a diamond at the aggregation end of the association/link arc to represent aggregation and the Rational Rose tool draws the aggregation arc from the part to the aggregate, thus making it look like an arrow with diamond arrowhead pointing at the aggregate. The UML notation makes sense from the standpoint of relational databases, in which the part tables have foreign keys to the aggregate table. However, the opposite is true for objects!

COMN uses a more intuitive approach and is drawn in the direction of visibility and dependency. The COMN notation for aggregation is therefore more appropriate for objects, whereas the UML notation for aggregation is more appropriate for relational database design.

Compare Figure 3.66 with Fig. 16, p. 41 in UML Notation Summary version 1.0.

Compare Figure 3.67 with Fig. 12, p. 15 in UML Notation Summary version 0.8.

Containment

Modeling Concept	OPEN's OML	Rational's UML
Containment	Containment symbol (circle with union sign) attached outside the bottom of the container and connected by the appropriate association/link arc to each element. Fork structure used with multiple elements	diamond at aggregate end of association or linkage line

Unlike COMN, UML does not differentiate aggregation which produces structures and containment which produces containers.

Inheritance

Modeling Concept	OPEN's OML	Rational's UML
Specialization Inheritance	solid double-lined arrow drawn from the child to the parent	directed line with a closed, unfilled triangular arrowhead at the parent end
Interface (Blackbox) Inheritance	small filled in solid square on child end of the inheritance arc	N/A
Implementation (Whitebox) Inheritance	small empty solid square on child end of the inheritance arc	N/A
Partition	all inheritance arcs from children in the partition join at connector before continuing on to parent	dashed line across all inheritance arcs
Discriminator	inheritance arc from connector to parent labeled with discriminator name	label on every arrow between parent and children
Complete vs. Incomplete children	stereotype on joined inheritance arc	stereotype on each inheritance arc
Disjoint vs. Overlapping children	stereotype on inheritance arc	stereotype on each inheritance arc
Ordering of Superclasses	optionally listed on inheritance arcs	rejected as unnecessary

UML version 0.9 does not differentiate specialization, interface inheritance, and implementation inheritance. UML represents inheritance by a directed line with a closed, unfilled triangular arrowhead at the superclass end. Because UML does not funnel all inheritance arcs from a partition through a connector, the discriminant needs to be repeated on each arc and there is no way to denote the kind of partition (e.g., complete vs. incomplete[3], disjoint vs. overlapping). Because UML provides no way to distinguish among specialization, interface inheritance, and implementation inheritance, common misuses of inheritance resulting from interface or implementation inheritance are not flagged for evaluation and justification.

---

[3]UML version 0.9 suggests the optional use of the ellipsis symbol to denote missing children.

Compare Figure 3.52 with Figure 23, page 55 in UML Notation Summary version 1.0.

Classification

Modeling Concept	OPEN's OML	Rational's UML
Is an Instance Of	solid double-lined arrow drawn from an instance to one of its classes and labeled.	dashed arrow from instance (object or class) to class
Conforms To	solid double-lined arrow drawn from an instance to one of its types and labeled.	N/A
Plays the Role Of	solid double-lined arrow drawn from an instance to one of its classes and labeled.	N/A

UML uses a dashed arrow (special case of dependency) from the object to the class or type to represent classification. UML does not differentiate *conforms to* from *is an instance of* or *plays the role of.*

Implementation

Modeling Concept	OPEN's OML	Rational's UML
Implements	solid double-lined arrow drawn from a class implementation to one of its types and labeled.	solid line
Is Implemented By	solid double-lined arrow starting with an aggregation symbol and drawn from a class to one of its types or class implementations.	N/A

Messages and Exceptions

UML does not support exception handling on diagrams. OML uses the same numbering scheme as UML for optionally numbering interactions of collaboration diagrams.

Multiplicity

Modeling Concept	OPEN's OML	Rational's UML
Multiplicity	1 0-1 0-* 1-* 3-5,7,15 3-*	1 0..1 * 1..* 3..5,7,15 3..*

The OML for multiplicity is logically identical with that of UML, except that UML's use of the two dots (e.g., '3..5') was replaced by a hyphen (e.g., '3-5') because the hyphen notation is more standard and less arbitrary (e.g., the number of dots).

6.3.2 Diagrams

OPEN's OML	Rational's UML
1. Semantic Net	Class Diagram
1.1 Context Diagram	Use Case Model
1.2 Configuration Diagram	Class Diagram
1.3 Cluster Diagram	Class Diagram
1.4 Inheritance Diagram	Class Diagram
1.5 Deployment Diagram	Platform Diagram (V0.8) Deployment Diagram (V0.9)
2. Scenario Class Diagram	Use Case Model
2.1 Mechanism Diagram	N/A
2.2 Task Script Diagram	N/A
2.3 Use Case Diagram	Use Case Model
3. Interaction Diagram	Interaction Diagram (V0.9)
3.1 Collaboration Diagram	Object Message Diagram (V0.8) Collaboration Diagram (V0.9)
3.1.1 Cluster Collaboration Diagram	N/A
3.1.2 Scenario Collaboration Diagram	Object Message Diagram (V0.8) Collaboration Diagram (V0.9)
3.1.3 Internal Collaboration Diagram	N/A
3.2 Sequence Diagram	Message Trace Diagram (V0.8) Sequence Diagram (V0.9)
3.2.1 Blackbox Sequence Diagram	N/A
3.2.2 Whitebox Sequence Diagram	N/A
4. N/A	Module Diagram (V0.8) Component Diagram (V0.9)

Semantic Nets

UML uses the term Class Diagram, which is somewhat restrictive. UML also uses a modified entity relationship diagram that emphasizes data modeling over object and class modeling.

- **Context Diagrams.**

  UML uses either a use case diagram or an object (a.k.a., collaboration) diagram as its context diagrams. Use case diagrams capture the dynamic view of the context and object diagrams are at too low of a level of abstraction.

- **Configuration Diagrams.**

  UML does not have a convenient way of showing the visibility of packages (a.k.a., clusters).

  UML version 0.9 only shows dependency relationships among packages, but does not label them, making them more difficult to understand.

- **Cluster Diagrams.**

  OML allows externals as well as object, classes, and clusters on cluster diagrams. OML documents the visibility of objects, classes, and clusters within clusters.

  OML does not support roles on associations/linkages. OML emphasizes unidirectional associations/ linkages over bi-directional associations/ linkages.

- **Inheritance Diagrams.**

  UML does not differentiate specialization from inheritance nor interface inheritance from implementation inheritance. Because UML does not capture invariants and exceptions, it does not completely capture the inheritance of characteristics as OML can when using drop-down boxes.

- **Deployment Diagrams.**

  UML uses a single node icon whereas OML uses its hardware external icon. UML does not label the arcs between nodes (except perhaps with the type of network), whereas OML labels the linkage/association arcs with verb phrases that capture the relationship between the nodes. UML uses role labels to label the nodes, whereas OML uses names for the same purpose. UML version 0.8 lists software below the associated node, whereas OML uses drop-down boxes to capture the allocation of software and major processes to the hardware.

Scenario Class Diagrams

The authors of the UML notation advocate an (unspecified) process which is use case driven. Because use cases are inherently functional in nature, OML (which is responsibility driven) primarily uses use cases to verify and validate the other models.

Interaction Diagrams

OML uses the same terms for interaction diagrams, collaboration diagrams, and sequence diagrams.

- **Collaboration Diagrams**

  — **Cluster Collaboration Diagrams**
    UML collaboration diagrams do not document:
    - cluster boundaries and the visibility of cluster components.
    - external nodes that internal nodes interact with.
    - classes as objects.
    - exceptions.

  — **Scenario Collaboration Diagrams**

    UML tends to use collaboration diagrams to show the same information that is on sequence diagrams, and the Rational Rose™ CASE tool allows the developer to toggle between collaboration diagrams and sequence diagrams. OPEN collaboration diagrams and sequence diagrams tend to have different scopes and purposes.

  — **Internal Collaboration Diagrams**
    UML does not provide a way to document the internal structure of complex classes.

- **Sequence Diagrams**

  UML 0.8 refers to these diagrams as interaction diagrams, whereas UML 0.9 also refers to them as sequence diagrams. OMT referred to them as Message Trace Diagrams.

  UML does not support the capturing on sequence diagrams branching, looping, and concurrency. OML uses the same notation (i.e., logic boxes) to capture branching, looping, concurrency, and temporal requirements.

— **Blackbox Sequence Diagrams**

UML documents the length of execution of the operation, whereas OML considers this to be unnecessary. Unlike UML, OML allows one to explicitly identify the object, class, external, or application to which the time line belongs, which is important when the same label may apply to multiple things (e.g., a external and its associated internal object). Unlike UML, OML provides a way to clearly document logic (e.g., branching, looping). OML documents concurrency and timing in a consistent manner with other logic.

— **Whitebox Sequence Diagrams**

UML documents the length of execution of the operation, whereas OML considers this to be unnecessary. Unlike UML, OML allows one to explicitly identify the object, class, external, or application to which the time line belongs, which is important when the same label may apply to multiple things (e.g., a external and its associated internal object). Unlike UML, OML provides a way to clearly document logic (e.g., branching, looping). OML documents concurrency and timing in a consistent manner with other logic.

State Transition Diagrams

Whereas UML essentially uses traditional Harel State Charts with little discussion of how they relate to objects and to the other models, OML uses Embly, Kurtz, and Woodfield state modeling as extended by Firesmith.

Unlike UML, OML defines its state modeling concepts in object-oriented terms:

- state = equivalence classes of property values
- trigger = message, operation, exception, or exception handler
- guard = expression of property values of enumeration type
- action = operation[4]
- activity = operation.

---

[4]Because actions and activities are defined as operations that may cause relatively instantaneous state transitions by changing property values into another equivalence class, there is no need to make the distinction between instantaneous actions and activities that have significant duration.

Unlike UML, OML does not restrict triggers to asynchronous transmissions of information.

In UML, concurrency is due to an object having multiple parts, each with its own state. In OML, concurrency is due to an object having multiple state properties.

UML restricts guard conditions to Boolean expressions, whereas OML allows any expression of enumeration type. Whereas UML lists guard conditions on transition arcs, OML explicitly shows the resulting branching by making guards branch nodes on transitions.

UML does not differentiate normal from exceptional transitions.

OML places operations on drop-down boxes so as not to clutter up the state and transition icons.

Unless different kinds of "events" are reified as classes related by inheritance, OML does not recognize hierarchies of triggers (e.g., messages, exceptions).

CRC Cards

UML is relatively data-driven, whereas OML is relatively responsibility driven. UML does not recognize CRC cards, and the notation summary only refers to responsibilities at the operation level.[5] OML handles responsibilities at the correct level and extends the concept to clusters and externals. OML documents responsibilities via:

1. Drop-down boxes attached to the bottom of class, cluster, and external icons on diagrams.
2. CRC Cards for classes of objects, clusters, and externals.

---

[5]This does not make sense because a single class responsibility is typically implemented by one or more operations. A single operation does not have its own responsibilities, but rather implements a functional abstraction.

6.3.3 Notation for State Modeling

Modeling Concept	OPEN's OML	Rational's UML
State	rounded rectangle labeled with the name of the state	rounded rectangle labeled with the name of the state
Start State	solid rounded rectangle with stereotype {start}	filled dot pointing at start state
Normal State	solid rounded rectangle	solid rounded rectangle
End State	thick solid rounded rectangle	filled dot in circle at end of transition arc
Substate	substate icon is a part of the superstate icon	state icon nested in icon of composite state
Visible Substate	substate icon attached to boundary of encapsulating state	N/A
Hidden Substate	substate icon nested inside boundary of encapsulating state	N/A
Transition (normal)	transition arc has solid line	transition arc has solid line
Transition (exceptional)	transition arc has dashed line	N/A
Transition (leaving)	transition arc touches pre-state	transition arc touches pre-state
Transition (remaining)	transition arc does not touch pre-state and has bar on pre-state end	N/A
Transition (sequential)	single transition arc between states	single transition arc between states
Transition (synchronous)	multiple transition arcs join or single transition arc diverges	heavy vertical bar with multiple input and or output transitions
Transition (group)	transition arc from or to superstate	transition arc from superstate
Concurrency	concurrency of states is shown by the use of remaining transitions, synchronous transitions, and multiple state machines	concurrency of substates is shown by dashed lines

Notation for State Modeling (*continued*)

Guard	diamond labeled with guard condition	listed in square brackets on transitions
State properties	Listed in appropriate drop-down box	listed in optional middle section of state icon
Operation	Listed in appropriate state and transition drop-down boxes	listed in optional bottom section of state icon or on transition arc
State Machine	dash-dotted rectangle labeled with the name of the state machine	N/A

6.4 Glossary

The following terms are organized alphabetically within a specialization hierarchy:

aggregate *n.* any modeling element that has other modeling elements of the same metatype as collaborating parts that form a structure.

> For example, a car engine consists of pistons, cylinders, spark plugs, etc. and these component parts have specific interpart relationships.

> Contrast the term "aggregate" with the term "container" (car trunk) which contains relatively independent entries.

assertion *n.* any business rule that is a constraint on the property values of an object.

- **invariant** *n.* any assertion that must hold both before and after the execution of all operations.
- **precondition** *n.* any assertion that must hold before the execution of the associated operation(s).
- **postcondition** *n.* any assertion that must hold after the execution of the associated operation(s).

binary unidirectional dependency relationship *n.* any relationship between two model elements that is directed in the direction of dependency from client to server (i.e., dependent).

- **definitional relationship** *n.* any binary unidirectional dependency relationship that either defines one modeling element in terms of another modeling element of the same metatype or indicates that one modeling element conforms to or was instantiated from the definition of another modeling element of different metatype.

  — **classification** *n.* any "is a" definitional relationship(s) from an object (instance) to its class(es) or type(s).

    – **instance of** *n.* the classification relationship from an instance to its class(es).
    – **conforms to** *n.* the classification relationship from an instance to its type(s).

  — **specialization** *n.* (1) the definitional relationship from a more specialized node (child) to a more general node (parent), whereby the child is *a kind of* its parent(s). (2) any specialized node at the child end of a specialization arc.

  — **inheritance** *n.* the definitional relationship from a child to its parent(s), whereby the child is formed as a possibly extended and modified union of its parent(s).

    Inheritance is a way of creating new definitions (e.g., subtype, subclass or derived class) in terms of one or more existing definitions (e.g., supertype, superclass or base class).

    – **interface inheritance** *n.* the blackbox inheritance that implies only interface conformance (subtyping), but not specialization.
    – **implementation inheritance** *n.* the whitebox inheritance that is used for the purpose of reusing implementation.
      Polymorphic substitutability is not guaranteed.

- **referential relationship** *n.* any binary unidirectional dependency relationship whereby one modeling element refers to another.

  — **association** *n.* any referential relationship that represents a general structural dependency relationship between kinds of things (e.g., class, type) that can be considered to be a class or type of corresponding linkages between instances.

Association partitioned by directionality include:

- **unidirectional association** *n.* any class or type of unidirectional linkages.
- **bi-directional association** *n.* any class or type of bi-directional linkages.
- **observer association** *n.* any class or type of observer linkages.
- **TBD association** *n.* any class or type of TBD linkages.

Association partitioned by kind include:

- **aggregation** *n.* the special form of association and linkage that captures the logical relationship that exists from an aggregate (whole) to its component parts.

  Because the aggregate is [partially] defined in terms of its component parts in the object paradigm, the parts are visible to the aggregate and the aggregate can therefore delegate some of its responsibilities to its parts (i.e., one can navigate from the aggregate to its parts).

  Aggregations provide an example of the practical use of abstraction. Initially, the modeler can work at a higher, blackbox level of abstraction, deferring consideration of the encapsulated, lower level parts until later.

  ⇒ **bi-directional aggregation** *n.* the shorthand convention representing the rare case in which a unidirectional aggregation relationship and a semi-strong inverse association/linkage exists, allowing the part to know about and navigate to the aggregate.

  Bi-directional aggregation is used in the Mediator pattern. Note that bi-directional aggregation does not mean that the part contains the aggregate, but merely that there is a reason to model a semi-strong inverse relationship (i.e., is a part of) back to the aggregate.

- **containment** *n.* the special form of association and linkage that captures the logical relationship that exists from container to its component entries.

  Because the container holds its entries in the object paradigm, the entries are visible to the container.

— **linkage** *n.* any referential relationship that represents a general structural dependency relationship between individual things (e.g., object, external, cluster).

- **unidirectional linkage** *n.* any one-way linkage from a client on a server[6] and is implemented as a link property of the client that is maintained by operations of the client.
- **bi-directional linkage** *n.* any short hand way of expressing the combination of two one-way linkages between peers, whereby each of the corresponding one-way links is the semi-strong inverse of the other and the corresponding operations in the peers ensure referential integrity.
- **observer linkage** *n.* the specialized kind of bi-directional linkage which captures the observer pattern from the patterns book by the Gang of Four (Gamma et al., 1995).
- **TBD linkage** *n.* any linkage, the directionality of which is yet To Be Determined (TBD).

- **transitional relationship** *n.* denotes any relationship in which one modeling element transitions or transforms into another.

- **invokes relationship** *n.* the binary dependency relationship between two scenario classes whereby the server scenario class is invoked at a specific point in the execution of the client scenario class.

- **precedes relationship** *n.* the binary dependency relationship between two scenario class whereby the server scenario class must complete execution before the server scenario class is permitted to begin execution.

- **uses relationship** *n.* the binary dependency relationship between a external and a scenario class.

characteristic *n.* any resource or feature that characterizes something.

Characteristics partitioned by parent include:

- **cluster characteristic** *n.* any characteristic of a cluster (i.e., any object, multiobject, object class, cluster, common global data, common global operation).

- **cluster class characteristic** *n.* any characteristic of a cluster class (i.e., any object class, object type, or role).

- **external characteristic** *n.* any characteristic of an external (i.e., any property, operation, or assertion).

- **object characteristic** *n.* any characteristic of an object (e.g., property, operation, or assertion).

---

[6]The client and the server may be the same.

Characteristics partitioned by level include:

- **class-level characteristic** *n.* any characteristic of a class as a whole rather than its instances.

  For example, constructor operations (e.g., new in Smalltalk) are class-level operations.

- **instance-level characteristic** *n.* any characteristic of an instance of a class rather than the class as a whole.

  For example, initialization operations that set the values of the properties of an instantiated object are instance-level operations.

Characteristics partitioned by inheritance include:

- **deferred characteristic** *n.* any characteristic that has a current declaration but does not have a complete current implementation.

- **effective characteristic** *n.* any characteristic that has a current declaration and also has a complete current implementation.

- **overridden characteristic** *n.* any characteristic, the current implementation of which hides a previous implementation.

  — **replaced characteristic** *n.* any overridden characteristic, the current implementation of which replaces its previous implementation.

  — **refined characteristic** *n.* any overridden characteristic, the current implementation of which delegates to its previous implementation (e.g., using the pseudo-variable super).

class *n.* any definition of a single kind of instance. Optionally, a class can be used to instantiate instances that capture the same abstraction and have the same or similar characteristics. A class consists of an interface of one or more types[7] that are implemented by one or more implementations.

Classes partitioned by kind of instance include:

- **cluster class** *n.* any class, the instances of which are clusters.
- **external class** *n.* any class, the instances of which are externals.
- **object class** *n.* any object that is also a class, the instances of which are objects.

---

[7]Note that the terms type and class are not synonymous. A type is not an instance and does not provide an implementation. A class is an instance of a metaclass, contains one or more types, and does provide an implementation.

- **object metaclass** *n.* any class, the instances of which are object classes.
- **scenario class** *n.* any class, the instances of which are scenarios.
  - — **mechanism** *n.* any scenario class consisting of a mid-sized pattern of collaborating roles, the cooperative behavior of which provides a desired functional abstraction.
  - — **task script** *n.* any scenario class that defines a business process, possibly independent of any application.
  - — **use case** *n.* any scenario class that defines a general, requirements-level way of using a application described in terms of interactions between the blackbox application and its externals. A class of usage scenarios.

Classes partitioned by instantiability include:

- **abstract class** *n.* any incomplete class that therefore cannot be used to instantiate semantically meaningful instances.
  - — **deferred class** *n.* any abstract class that declares the existence of one or more characteristics that must be implemented by its descendants prior to instantiation.
- **concrete class** *n.* any complete class that therefore can be used to instantiate semantically meaningful instances.

class implementation *n.* any declaration of hidden characteristics that [partially] implements the associated class by implementing one or more of the types of a class.

- **cluster class implementation** *n.* any class implementation that [partially] implements a cluster class.
- **external class implementation** *n.* any class implementation that [partially] implements an external class.
- **object class implementation** *n.* any class implementation that [partially] implements an object class.

class responsibility collaborator card (CRC)[8] *n.* any kind of index card used as a simple, manual upperCASE tool, the purpose of which is to document the responsibilities and associated collaborators for a class of objects, clusters, or externals.

---

[8]No Instance Responsibility Collaborator Card is required because all instances of the same class share the same responsibilities. If the collaborators are different because of the use of different constructors, this can still be captured on the CRC card.

- **object CRC card** *n.* any CRC card, the purpose of which is to document the responsibilities of a class of objects.
- **cluster CRC card** *n.* any CRC card, the purpose of which is to document the responsibilities of a class of clusters.
- **role responsibility collaborator card** *n.* any CRC card, the purpose of which is to document the responsibilities of a role.

collaborator *n.* any server on which the thing documented by the responsibility collaborator card depends in order to fulfill its associated responsibility.

common global data *n.* any application-internal data that is not stored as a property of some object.

common global operation *n.* any application-internal operation that is not stored as an operation of some object.

common global operations *n.* any logically or physically cohesive collection of common global operations.

container *n.* any modeling element that contains other modeling element of the same metatype that do not form a structure.

For example, a car trunk (boot) can contain many items and these items do not have relationships.

- **homogeneous container** *n.* any container that contains entries of a single type.
- **heterogeneous container** *n.* any container that contains entries of multiple types.

controller *n.* the stereotype of an object, class, type, or role, the primary responsibilities of which involve the detailed controlling of its servers.

coordinator *n.* the stereotype of an object, class, type, or role, the primary responsibilities of which involve the coordination of its collaborating servers.

diagram *n.* any directed graph of nodes connected by arcs representing binary unidirectional dependency relationships.

- **interaction diagram** *n.* any diagram, the purpose of which is to document the interactions either among externals and the application or among objects and classes within [part of] the application. The nodes of an interaction diagram represent either things or their time lines, and the arcs of the graph represent the interactions between nodes.

  — **collaboration diagram** *n.* any interaction diagram in the form of a graph, the purpose of which is to document the potential collaboration of a cluster of classes and objects in terms of the messages and exceptions they may send and raise.

  If the associations, linkages, aggregation arcs, and containment arcs on cluster diagrams are viewed as roads connecting the classes and objects, then the messages and exceptions on the collaboration diagrams can be viewed as the traffic on those roads. Collaboration diagrams typically have the same nodes and topology as the corresponding cluster diagrams, but the arcs are labeled with messages and exceptions rather than with static relationships.

  In many cases, especially in concurrent situations, the ordering of this message and exception "traffic" is important. Thus, the arcs on collaboration diagrams can be optionally labeled with sequence numbers.[9]

  - **cluster collaboration diagram** *n.* any specialized collaboration diagram, the purpose of which is to document the potential collaboration of a cluster of blackbox classes and objects in terms of the messages and exceptions they may send and raise.
  - **scenario collaboration diagram** *n.* any specialized collaboration diagram, the purpose of which is to document the collaboration of blackbox classes and objects in involved in a scenario in terms of the messages and exceptions they may send and raise.
  - **internal collaboration diagram** *n.* any collaboration diagram, the purpose of which is to document the potential collaboration of operations within an individual class or object, in terms of control flow (i.e., message passing, exception raising) and object flow (the reading and writing of properties within the class or object).

---

[9]If the sequence of interactions is important, sequence diagrams are often used instead of collaboration diagrams.

— **sequence diagram** *n.* any interaction diagram in the form of a "fence" diagram, the purpose of which is to document the sequence of interactions among either externals and the application or among objects within [part of] the application.

   – **blackbox sequence diagram** *n.* any sequence diagram, the purpose of which is to document the sequence of interactions between externals and the blackbox system or software application involved in a single path of a use case.
   A blackbox sequence diagram treats the application as a blackbox and is used to capture user-oriented requirements, verify the context diagram, and document an acceptance test case.

   – **whitebox sequence diagram** *n.* any sequence diagram, the purpose of which is to document the sequence of interactions among objects and classes involved in a single mechanism, design pattern, or [partial] path of a use case.
   A whitebox sequence diagram treats the application as a whitebox, showing the interactions among its internal objects. It is used to capture user-oriented requirements, verify the context diagram, and document an acceptance test case.

• **scenario class diagram** *n.* any diagram, the purpose of which is to document a set of collaborating scenario classes and the invocation and precedes relationships between them.

   — **mechanism diagram** *n.* any scenario class diagram, the purpose of which is to document one or more mechanisms, any associated objects or classes, and the semantically important relationships between them.

   — **task script diagram** *n.* any scenario class diagram, the purpose of which is to document one or more task scripts, any associated externals, and the semantically important relationships between them.

   — **use case diagram** *n.* any scenario class diagram, the purpose of which is to document one or more use cases, any associated externals that either use or are used by them, and the semantically important relationships between them.

• **semantic net (SN)** *n.* any diagram, the purpose of which is to document the static structure of a cohesive collection of related things (e.g., externals, classes, objects, clusters) connected by the semantically-meaningful relationships (e.g., associations, aggregation, inheritance) between them.

The semantic net is the most important and most widely-used diagram type in the OPEN method.

— **configuration diagram** *n.* any semantic net, the purpose of which is to document the configuration of an application, layer, or subdomain in terms of its component layers, subdomains, and clusters respectively, their visibility (i.e., encapsulation), and the dependency relationships among the component parts.

Aggregation is documented by nesting if the number of components is small and by using aggregation arcs if the number of components is large. Although this is typically one of the first diagrams to be started when using the OPEN method, it is also one of the last to be completed because of the iterative and incremental nature of the object-oriented development cycle. This diagram is used to communicate with domain experts, business analysts, customers, managers, and architects.

- **system configuration diagram** *n.* any configuration diagram, the purpose of which is used to document the configuration of an entire system consisting of hardware, software, wetware (people), and paperware (documentation)
- **software configuration diagram** *n.* any configuration diagram, the purpose of which is to document a software application.

— **cluster diagram** *n.* any semantic net, the purpose of which is to document the static structure of a cluster or mechanism of collaborating objects or roles respectively in terms of the semantically meaningful relationships between them.

— **context diagram** *n.* any specialized semantic net, the purpose of which is to document the context of a blackbox application, layer, or subdomain in terms of its externals and the semantically-meaningful relationships between them (e.g., associations, aggregation, inheritance).

A context diagram is typically one of the first diagrams developed using the OPEN method. This diagram is used to communicate with domain experts, business analysts, customers, managers, and architects.

- **system context diagram** *n.* any context diagram, the purpose of which is to document the context of an entire system consisting of hardware, software, wetware (people), and paperware (documentation).
- **software context diagram** *n.* any context diagram, the purpose of which is to document the context of a cohesive collection of software

> (e.g., an entire software application, a layer, or a subdomain within the application).
>
> — **deployment diagram** *n.* any semantic net, the purpose of which is to document the structure of hardware on which an application runs and the [static] allocation of the software to the hardware.
> — **inheritance diagram** *n.* any semantic net, the purpose of which is to document the static structure of all or part (e.g., branch) of an inheritance graph.
> — **layer diagram** *n.* any semantic net, the purpose of which is to document the software architecture of an application or the software allocated to a processor.
>
> A layer diagram is typically one of the first diagrams developed using the OPEN method. This diagram is used to communicate with domain experts, business analysts, customers, managers, and architects.

- **state transition diagram (STD)** *n.* any diagram consisting of a directed graph of states (nodes[10]) connected by transitions (directed arcs), the purpose of which is to specify the common *qualitative*[11] behavior of the instances of a class. An STD describes the potential life history of objects of a given class, in terms of the ways they respond to interactions (messages from, exceptions raised by) other objects.

discriminant *n.* any value of a property of the parent class that is used to differentiate the members of a partition of child classes.

drop-down box *n.* any optional rectangular node attached to the bottom outside of its parent node, used to display a subset of the information stored about its parent node based on a selection of traits.

entry *n.* any modeling element contained in a container.

generalization *n.* any generalized node at the parent end of a specialization arc.

---

[10]Although guard conditions are also graphed as nodes, they are better considered a part of the transition they control.

[11]By qualitative behavior, we mean whether or not an operation executes or which path of a logic branch is taken.

guard condition *n.* any condition (either Boolean or of enumeration type) that must evaluate properly in order for the trigger to cause the corresponding transition to fire.

information holder *n.* the stereotype of an object, class, type, or role, the primary responsibilities of which involve the storing of information.

instance *n.* any uniquely-identified model of a single thing, whereby the model is defined by one or more classes and conforms to one or more types.

- **cluster** *n.* any instance of a cluster class, consisting of a cohesive collection of collaborating objects, classes, clusters, and optionally non-object-oriented software such as common global data and common global operations. Any instance of a cluster class. Clustering is also used to control size and complexity by providing a unit of modularity larger than a class. A cluster is usually used to encapsulate the software that is typically developed as a unit by a small team layer, but it is also used to capture the implementation of a pattern, a layer, a subdomain, or a distribution unit.

  — **logical cluster** *n.* any requirements analysis-level or logical design-level cluster used for documenting.

  — **physical cluster** *n.* any physical design-level or coding-level cluster used for allocating actual software to hardware.

  — **layer** *n.* any large, horizontal cluster used as a strategic architectural unit of design.

  — **distribution unit** *n.* any cluster, the members of which are guaranteed to be allocated to a processor or process as a group. Distribution units have the stereotype 'location'. Members of the same distribution unit communicate locally, whereas members of different distribution units may communicate remotely if distributed to different processors or processes.

- **object** *n.* any uniquely-identified abstraction that uses its *characteristics* to model a single thing that is important in the current application. In order to be a complete abstraction, an object captures all of the essential characteristics (i.e., *properties, behavior,* and *rules*) of the thing being modeled while ignoring the thing's non-essential, diversionary details.

  — **concurrent object**[12] *n.* Any object that is *inherently* capable of running

---

[12]OML does not use the terms active and passive as synonyms for concurrent and sequential because concurrent objects (e.g., some objects containing tasks in Ada95) can be passive, only using their thread to protect themselves from corruption due to simultaneous access.

concurrently (i.e., simultaneously) with other objects because it contains, either directly or indirectly, one or more of its *own* threads of execution. An object may be concurrent because:

1. it directly has its own thread of execution (e.g., an object in the Actor language),
2. one or more of its properties are concurrent, or
3. one or more of its operations are directly concurrent (i.e. have their own inherent thread of execution).

— **sequential object** *n.* any object that is not *inherently* capable of running concurrently (i.e., simultaneously) with other objects because it does not contain, either directly or indirectly, one or more of its *own* threads of execution.

— **external** *n.* any instance of an external class that uses its characteristics to model a single thing that is *external* to the current application and is important to document during modeling (e.g., because it interacts with the application or implies the existence of a corresponding object inside the application).

Externals partitioned by degree removed include:

– **direct external** *n.* any external that interacts directly with the current application.
– **indirect external** *n.* any external that interacts indirectly with the current application via other externals.

Externals partitioned by direction of dependency include:

– **client external** *n.* any external that depends on the current application.
– **peer external** *n.* any external that is both a client external and a server external.
– **server external** *n.* any external on which the current application depends.

Externals partitioned by kind of thing modeled include:

– **actor** *n.* any external that models a role played by a human.
– **hardware external** *n.* any external that models a hardware device, either with or without significant processing power.
– **other external** *n.* any external that is not an actor, hardware external, persistent memory external, or software external.
– **persistent memory external** *n.* any external that models some persistent memory (e.g., a file, a database, a relational database table, a tape, a disk).

- **software external** *n.* any external that models some software (e.g., a legacy application).

interaction *n.* any form of communication sent by one instance to another.

- **exception** *n.* any abnormal interaction consisting of an object which models an exceptional or error condition that is raised by an operation in order to notify a client that the exception has occurred.
- **message** *n.* any normal interaction.
  - **sequential message** *n.* any message (e.g., Smalltalk, C++) involving only one thread of control that is temporarily passed from the sender to the receiver, thereby blocking the sender until the server's operation(s) area completed.
  - **synchronous message** *n.* any message (e.g., Ada rendezvous) that synchronizes two threads of control, thereby potentially blocking either the sender or the receiver until both are ready to communicate.
  - **asynchronous message** *n.* any message involving two threads of control that do not synchronize during message passing so that neither the sender nor the receiver is blocked by having to wait for the other.

interfacer *n.* the stereotype of an object, class, type, or role, the primary responsibilities of which involve communicating with one or more externals.

internal non-OO database *n.* any application-internal non-object-oriented (e.g., relational, network, hierarchical) database, database table, file, etc.

multiobject *n.* any homogeneous collection of objects that are instances of the same class or type.

multiplicity *n.* the potential number of things.[13]

- **multiplicity of an aggregate** *n.* the potential number of the aggregate's component parts.
- **multiplicity of a class** *n.* the potential number of the class's instances.
- **multiplicity of a container** *n.* the potential number of entries in the associated container.

---

[13]Multiplicity is often confused with cardinality, which is defined as the *actual* number of things.

- **multiplicity of a multiobject** *n.* the potential number of objects in the associated collection.

- **multiplicity of a cluster** *n.* the potential total number of cluster characteristics (e.g., objects, classes, clusters) in the cluster.

- **multiplicity of a cluster class** *n.* the potential total number of cluster class characteristics (e.g., object classes, types, cluster classes, roles) in the cluster class.

- **multiplicity of an association** *n.* the potential number of objects that are involved at each end of the association.

notifier *n.* the stereotype of an object, class, type, or role, the primary responsibilities of which involve the forwarding of messages to one or more servers. A notifier may either pass on the notification without change or may translate the notification so that it makes sense to the server.

object flow *n.* the shorthand way of representing on a class-internal collaboration diagram the sending of read or write accessor messages (typically to self) referencing the associated property, thereby resulting in the flow of object represented by that property. Analogous to the term 'data flow' on a traditional data flow diagram.

object interface *n.* the externally visible characteristics of an object.

object implementation *n.* the encapsulated hidden characteristics of an object.

object operation *n.* any functional abstraction that models a discrete activity, action, or behavior that is performed by an object, typically in response to a message. An operation consists of a *signature* (i.e., interface) and a *method* (i.e., implementation).

part *n.* any modeling element that is a component of another modeling element of the same metatype.

The aggregate usually, but not always, hides its component parts. For example, the switch on a motor as a visible, public part of the motor.

The life of a part is usually, but not always, confined to that of its aggregate.

As a counterexample, a car engine may be reused meaning that it may exist after the first car exists but before the second car exists.

path *n.* any contiguous list of instances or classes that are involved in a single scenario. A scenario class may have multiple paths, each of which may be traversed by multiple scenarios of the scenario class.

- **primary path** *n.* any path through a given scenario class that is more important and commonly traversed.

- **secondary path** *n.* any path through a given scenario class that is less important and less commonly traversed. Secondary paths are often variants of a primary path that provide exception handling.

property *n.* any kind of characteristic capturing a static aspect of its encapsulating object or external.

All properties are either logical or physical. Logical properties are used during requirements analysis and logical design, whereas physical properties are used during physical design, forward engineering to code, and reverse engineering from code. A property is assumed to be logical unless explicitly annotated as physical.

Properties partitioned by kind include:

- **attribute** *n.* any descriptive property. An attribute is usually hidden, but may be visible. An attribute provides the only reference to an internal hidden object, the life span of which matches that of the object of which it is an attribute. An attribute may reference only a single object.

- **entry** *n.* any property of a container that references an object contained by the container. An entry is usually hidden, but may be visible. An object is typically an entry of only one container at a time. The life span of an entry is usually not that of its container, but could be. The entries of a container do not reference each other and any organization is provided by the container (e.g., a car trunk).

- **exception** *n.* any object modeling an exceptional or error condition that is raised by an operation in order to notify a client that the condition (e.g., an assertion has been violated) has occurred.

- **link** *n.* any property that references an external object. Although the link is usually hidden, the object it references is not. Multiple links in multiple objects may reference the same object. The life span of the object referenced by a link is independent of the object encapsulating the link.

- **part** *n.* any property of an aggregate that references a component of the aggregate. A part is usually hidden, but may be visible. An object is typically a part of only one aggregate at a time. The life span of a part is usually that of its aggregate, but need not be. At least some of the parts of an aggregate reference each other, thus creating a structure (e.g., a car engine) that depends on the correct interaction of its parts.

Properties partitioned by level of abstraction include:

- **logical property** *n.* any property that implements a responsibility for knowing by representing a query that can be made of its object or class.

  A logical property it typically implemented by an operation that returns a copy or reference to an object that results from either referencing one or more physical properties, calculating the returned value, or sending messages to servers.

- **physical property** *n.* any property consisting of a named reference[14] to an object.

responsibility *n.* any purpose, obligation, or required capability of the instances of a class of objects or clusters. A responsibility is typically implemented by a cohesive collection of one or more characteristics. A responsibility can be a responsibility for doing, a responsibility for knowing, or a responsibility for enforcing.

role *n.* any partial declaration of a kind of object, the declared characteristics of which are required to fulfill a cohesive set of responsibilities. Such an object is said to play the role.

scenario *n.* any specific, contiguous set of interactions that is not completely implemented as a single operation within an instance or class. Any instance of a scenario class.

- **usage scenario** *n.* any scenario that captures a complete functional abstraction that provides something of value to the users of the application.

service provider *n.* the stereotype of an object, class, type, or role, the primary responsibilities of which involve providing one or more services to its clients.

---

[14]A property is different from the object it references. A property that does not reference an object is called a dangling property and represents either an error in the model or a reference that is temporarily uninitialized.

state *n.* any equivalence class of property values[15] used to represent a status, situation, condition, mode, or life-cycle phase of an instance during which certain rules of qualitative behavior apply. A state typically lasts for a significant period of time. OML recognizes the following kinds of state:

States partitioned by level of aggregation include:

- **aggregate state.** any general state that has specialized substates.
- **atomic state** *n.* any state that is not decomposed into substates.

States partitioned by level of transitions include:

- **start state** *n.* any atomic state of an object or class upon instantiation and initialization.
- **stop state** *n.* any terminal state from which the object or class cannot transition.

States roles are partitioned as follows:

- **substate** *n.* the role played by any state that specializes another state (its superstate). Note that the equivalence classes of property values of substates partition (i.e., form a disjoint cover of) the equivalence class of their superstates. A substate therefore inherits the outgoing group transitions of its superstate.
- **superstate** *n.* the role played by any aggregate state that is specialized by its substates. A superstate has a default starting substate to which incoming group transitions point.

stereotype *n.* any character string of enumeration type that is used to conceptually classify a modeling element independently from inheritance or provide some other important information about the modeling element.

structurer *n.* the stereotype of an object, class, type, or role, the primary responsibilities of which involve maintaining referential relationships with one or more servers.

trait *n.* Any specific information about a particular modeling element, typically documented in the element's drop-down box (e.g., its description, its responsibilities, its public protocol, its assertions, its characteristics of a class).

---

[15]Note that all properties need not influence the qualitative behavior of objects. In fact, many objects do not exhibit any significant state behavior at all and therefore do not need a state transition diagram.

trait kind *n.* any general kind of information about a modeling element (e.g., "description," "responsibilities," "public protocol," "assertions," "characteristics," "stereotypes"); a class of traits.

transition *n.* any change in state. Because states are defined in terms of property values, a change in state is typically of such short duration compared to a state as to be instantaneous. OML recognizes the following kinds of state transitions:

Transitions partitioned by cause type include:

- **exceptional transition** *n.* any transition caused by an exception or exception handler.

- **normal transition** *n.* any transition caused by a message or operation.

Transition partitioned by impact on pre-transition state include:

- **leaving transition** *n.* any transition that causes the object to leave its pre-transition state and transition to its post-transition state.

- **remaining transition** *n.* any transition that causes the object to remain in its pre-transition state while also transitioning to its post-transition state. This changes the situation from a single pre-transition state to multiple post-transition states.

Transitions partitioned by level of aggregation include:

- **group transition** *n.* any transition to or from a superstate.

Transitions partitioned by concurrency include:

- **sequential transition** *n.* any single transition from and to a single [sub]-state. A sequential transition does not increase or decrease the number of concurrent states.

- **synchronous transition** *n.* any single transition from or to multiple [sub]states. A synchronous transition increases or decreases the number of concurrent states.

trigger *n.* anything that causes a state transition by changing the associated state property values. Most state modeling techniques refer to triggers as events, without specifying what they are in terms of object-oriented concepts.

type *n.* any declaration of visible characteristics that form all or part of the interface of a single kind of instance that conforms to the type:

- **cluster type** *n.* any type of cluster. A cluster conforms to a cluster type if and only if its interface is consistent with the type (i.e., the set of visible characteristics in the interface of the cluster is a superset of the set of characteristics declared by the type).

- **object type** *n.* any type of object. An object conforms to an object type if and only if its interface is consistent with the type (i.e., the set of characteristics in the interface of the object is a superset of the set of characteristics declared by the type).

- **scenario type** *n.* any type of object that declares the externally visible aspects of a scenario class, typically including name, parameters (if any), preconditions, and postconditions.

Index

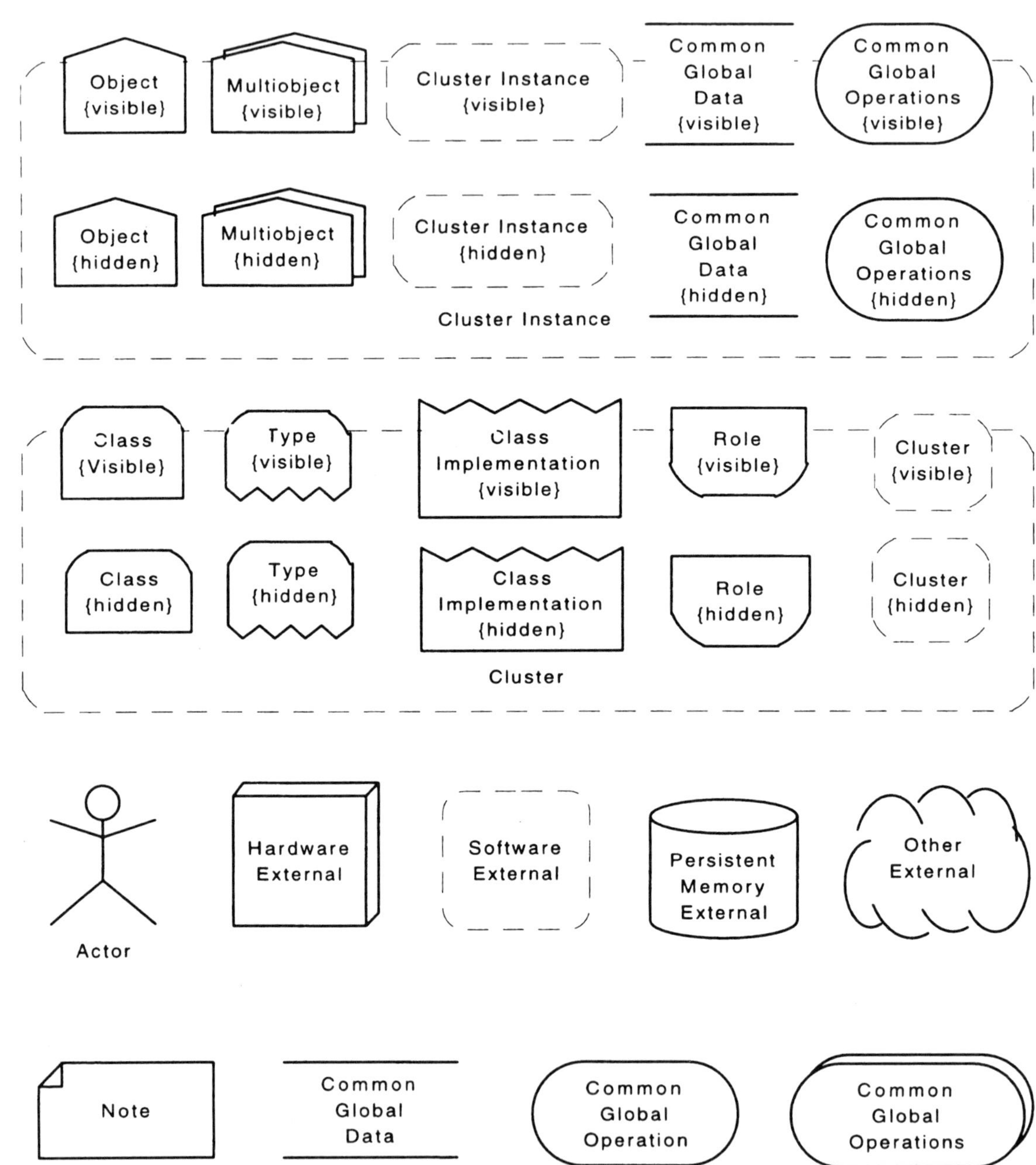

Icons for Nodes